"Financial disagreements often erode the goodwill between a couple and drive them into a psychotherapist's office. If you're having financial problems, *The Couple's Guide to Love and Money* will provide you with sensible solutions. If you're doing okay, this book will bring you and your partner to a new level of joy and prosperity. Every couple needs this book!"

—Sharron Williams, Psy.D., Psychologist, Newport Beach, CA.

The Couple's Guide to

Jonathan Rich, Ph.D.

New Harbinger Publications, Inc.

Distributed in the U.S.A. by Publishers Group West; in Canada by Raincoast Books; in Great Britain by Hi Marketing, Ltd.; in South Africa by Real Books, Ltd.; in Australia by Boobook; and in New Zealand by Tandem Press.

Copyright © 2003 by Jonathan Rich
New Harbinger Publications, Inc.
5674 Shattuck Avenue
Oakland, CA 94609

Cover design by Lightbourne Images
Edited by Kayla Sussell
Text design by Tracy Marie Carlson

ISBN 1-57224-311-2 Paperback

New Harbinger Publications' Web site address: www.newharbinger.com

05   04   03

10   9   8   7   6   5   4   3   2   1

First printing

To Jodi, the love of my life

Contents

Acknowledgments. vii

Introduction. 1

PART I
The Psychology of Money

CHAPTER 1   *Initial Investment*. 6

CHAPTER 2   *Money Self-Talk* 15

CHAPTER 3   *Men, Women, and Money*. 25

CHAPTER 4   *Your Financial Personality* 33

CHAPTER 5   *Risk: The Gambler/Banker Dimension* 39

CHAPTER 6   *Lifestyle: The Monarch/Spartan Dimension* 45

CHAPTER 7   *Dependence: The Homesteader/Pioneer Dimension*. 58

CHAPTER 8   *Where Does the Money Come From?*. 68

CHAPTER 9   *Where Does the Money Go?*. 76

CHAPTER 10   *Your Money Circle* 81

CHAPTER 11   *Your Financial Life Path*. 92

PART II
Money-Growing Strategies

CHAPTER 12   *Shared Dreams*. 102

CHAPTER 13   *Spending and Debt* 110

CHAPTER 14   *Work I: Time for a Change?* 116

CHAPTER 15   *Work II: Creating Your Ideal Work Situation* 130

CHAPTER 16   *Investments* 139

CHAPTER 17   *Savings and Insurance: Your Financial Fortress* 146

CHAPTER 18   *Your Financial Set Point*. 153

CHAPTER 19   *Financial Planning for the Lifestyle You Want* 162

CHAPTER 20   *Money-Saving Strategies*. 171

PART III
Final Accounting

CHAPTER 21   *When Self-Help Is Not Enough* 178

CHAPTER 22   *Summing It All Up* 186

APPENDIX A   *The Money Personality Scale* 191

APPENDIX B   *Multiplying Your Money*. 198

              References 199

              Bibliography 201

I am grateful to the people at New Harbinger for their help and support in creating this book. I have long admired psychologist, publisher, and author Dr. Matthew McKay and have used his books since graduate school. I am indebted to him for his encouragement and willingness to give a new author a break. I am grateful to Acquisitions Editor Tesilya Hanauer for helping to guide me from proposal to manuscript, and to Senior Editor Kayla Sussell for her expert copyediting.

Jodi, my wife and closest friend, has contributed immeasurably to my understanding of love, money, and everything else that has value. And my children, Steve, Stacey, and Sean, have given me a wild ride that I wouldn't trade for anything, and they have taught me more about life and love than I ever learned in school.

Introduction

Sharing Finances: The Number One Relationship Challenge

It's hard enough to deal with money when you're single. First figuring out how to get it, and then what to do with it, can become an all-consuming fixation. When you add another person to the mix, you have an almost certain formula for disagreement and conflict.

It seems straightforward enough. Money is, after all, quite tangible. You can reach into your pocket and probably find some. On paper, it's all very clear-cut: money is represented by numbers, fractions, and decimal points. You might think there wouldn't be too many surprises when it comes to money. But that's precisely what makes money so tricky. It looks as if it should be neat, obvious, and predictable. After all, business is business and love is love. But try as you may to keep them apart, when you are a couple, they are inseparable.

Money: It's More Than Just Numbers

Money is not just numbers and decimal points. It's one of the most fluid and mysterious resources on earth. It is exchanged for an investment of time, labor, and personal sacrifice. Money can represent control and power. It can represent freedom. To some it symbolizes love; to others it is an aspect of self-image and self-esteem. It's fair to say that for all of us it's a mix of these and other powerful symbols.

There's nothing that money "should" represent to you. It's different for everyone. How you think of it and deal with it, as an individual, will affect your personal happiness. How you think of it and deal with it with your spouse or partner will affect the happiness you find in your relationship.

How This Book Can Help You

The purpose of this book is to help you maximize your personal and relationship happiness. It will help you to discover your own and your partner's conscious and unconscious assumptions about money. In that way, it will help you and your partner with the process of self-discovery. Moreover, this book will take you through the steps you need to take to merge your attitudes and habits about money—your style—so that as a couple you can create a joyful and prosperous life together.

Here are some of the concrete benefits you can expect to receive from working with this book:

- You will stop arguing about money, and learn to negotiate effectively with your partner about finances and shared responsibilities.

- You will learn how to change the way you think about money and how to help your partner change his or her thinking, so that financial gains can be maximized.

- You will discover money management techniques that can put you on firmer financial ground.

- You will go to the next financial level, and discover creative ways to move toward wealth and financial freedom, for yourself and your family.

The goal is not necessarily for you and your partner to agree and hold identical attitudes or to have the same style. On some dimensions you might be closely aligned; in other areas, the two of you might be at opposite poles. Different styles can enhance your partnership and even can increase your financial success. Each chapter will discuss how you can best work with your style and your partner's.

As a couple, your financial solution might include a shift in thinking for one or both of you. It might include a change in how you manage your day-to-day expenditures and your long-term goals. It might involve changes in how you structure your work, investments, shopping, and savings. It might involve a shift in roles between the two of you. Whatever it might involve, remember, your long-term goals are self-discovery, prosperity, and personal happiness. Save this workbook. In the future, you may want to return to specific chapters to see how you've changed and to better map your future direction.

How to Use This Book

This is a workbook. It is a guide to self-discovery, if you carefully do the exercises in each chapter. As you do the exercises, you'll discover something about your own attitudes about money and those of your partner. Note that in each chapter, you'll find things that you want to discuss with your partner.

You can complete the workbook chapter by chapter, or you can start with the areas that are of greatest importance to you. When you come across an exciting new idea, remember that your partner may or may not share your enthusiasm. You probably know your partner's personal style better than anyone; some partners will want to share every detail with you, others would rather just hear about the bottom line.

Here are some of the benefits you can get from this book. Check the short-term goal that is most important to you. Then ask your partner what his other goals are. Being aware of your partner's goals will help you to engage him or her. That knowledge will provide you with the key about the viewpoint to emphasize when the two of you discuss some of the issues.

My Short-Term Goals

_____ To argue less about money.   _____ To worry less about money.

_____ To reduce work stress.   _____ To have more free time.

_____ To increase personal wealth.

My Partner's Short-Term Goals

_____ To argue less about money.   _____ To worry less about money.

_____ To reduce work stress.   _____ To have more free time.

_____ To increase personal wealth.

How Not to Use This Book

A psychologist's office is often a battleground. Couples come to see me when they are furious with each other. Frequently, the first session is more like a courtroom battle than a psychotherapy session. Each partner struggles to demonstrate how foolish, wrong, and intolerable the other is.

For this book to work, there needs to be one goal above all others. That goal is to maximize your happiness and success as a couple. If you find yourself using this book as a tool to demonstrate that you're smarter, more sensitive, or more "right" than your partner, it won't help much, and may even be harmful.

Any self-help book has its limits. It's important to understand these limits, and to realize when professional intervention is needed. Most of the chapters in this book assume that you and your partner enjoy reasonably good emotional health. I'm also assuming that you are in a loving relationship; meaning that although you have disagreements with each other, you also have mutual caring about each other's welfare, and you are willing to work through problems.

Problems like mental illness, domestic violence, and addictions to drugs, alcohol, or gambling require professional intervention before the techniques in this book can be applied. However, some of these problems are discussed in Part III, in chapter 21, "When Self-Help Is Not Enough."

Involving Your Partner

Doing the exercises in this book by yourself can help you achieve greater personal and financial success. Since you're the one reading the book, you're also the one who's most motivated to make changes. Your spouse or significant other might share your enthusiasm—but, then again, he or she might not. Here's how I'd suggest you might get your partner interested:

1. Approach him or her as you would any valued friend and confidant: with respect and love.

2. Let your partner know that you are thinking of changing some of the ways you deal with money, and that you'd like feedback and ideas from him or her.

3. Let your partner decide how much involvement he or she wants to have. Here are the high, medium, and low options for such involvement:

   • High: You and your partner can read each chapter and participate in the exercises. After both of you have finished a chapter, you can schedule a fifteen-minute meeting to review what you both learned and wrote.

   • Medium: You can read each chapter, and then schedule a fifteen-minute meeting with your partner. Then, you can talk about what you learned, what you intend to do differently, and get your partner's thoughts and responses to what you've said.

   • Low: You can do the exercises in the workbook by yourself. Then, occasionally and casually, you can share your new thoughts and insights with your partner and ask for some responses. It's possible that your partner will want to shift from one option to another. For instance, after you share some of your new insights, your partner might just grab the book from you and say, "Let me try that!"

4. Here are some rules for discussing important issues. Remember, you can apply these rules not only for talking about the topics in this book, but also for discussing other issues with your partner:

   • Stay on the topic. It's a good idea to set a fixed time (like the fifteen minutes suggested above) so you remain focused.

   • Avoid competition. Trying to prove you're right, smarter, or more sensitive might work in a political debate. It is almost never a good strategy in an intimate relationship. If you disagree with your partner, try to understand his or her point of view, get feedback, and then re-express your own view of the matter.

   • Avoid destructive criticism. When you're close to someone, you know each other's weak spots and sensitive areas. It may be tempting to use this knowledge as a weapon, particularly when you're feeling wronged or vulnerable. Insulting, destructive remarks to a partner can be much more subtle than the insults strangers would use. Be aware not only of your words but also of your intentions. When you feel as if your partner has "zinged" you with a hurtful statement, don't argue with the content, rather inform him or her that you were hurt.

   • Remember that you are a partnership. Remember, too, that you are working toward common goals; so if one of you loses, you both lose. Stay on the same team and you will both reap the rewards.

PART I

The Psychology of Money

There are lots of books around to tell you what to do with your money. I've read many of them and you may have too. They'll tell you to: "Buy stocks and hold onto them a long time"; "Pay yourself first"; "Work hard and be clever"; "Pay off the debt you have, and cut up all your credit cards."

Okay, so I'm oversimplifying. But this is my point : While you sit in your easy chair, reading financial guides and dreaming about how you're going to get rich, your partner may be yelling at you about paying the overdue bills or needing a new car. Or maybe you opened the credit card statement, and now you're the one doing the yelling?

When you were a teenager, it was pretty easy to fall in love. So easy, that most of us did it several times a month. In adulthood, love takes on a whole new, more serious flavor. Your partner is still the same, wonderful person who first attracted you. That person still has the same wonderful qualities that fascinated you, and brought you joy. But, somehow, life itself has gotten a lot more serious.

Money is no longer just the extra spending cash that you pick up at summer jobs; it's the stuff that you both need—to eat, to keep a roof over your heads, and to keep your lifestyle going. And unless your partner is your identical clone, he or she has different ideas about such questions as, "How much money do we need?" "Where should it come from?" and "Where should it go?"

Part I of this book will help you and your partner figure out how getting and spending money is interwoven with your emotions and, of course, with your relationship. Moreover, this workbook can help you sort out how money has come between you.

CHAPTER 1

Initial Investment

CHAPTER GOALS: To discover why money is causing problems in your relationship, and to find out where in this book to find solutions.

Michael sat in front of the stack of bills. He looked at Denise and declared, "We're broke."

Denise had heard this declaration hundreds of times before and it always gave her a sinking feeling in her stomach. She knew that Michael wasn't giving her a financial update; he was provoking a fight. She was exhausted by these battles over money. She knew she'd need to pick her next words carefully, or they'd both be simmering with rage for the whole day. She sighed, and said, "I get paid at the end of the week. That should help a little."

Michael's response was measured and deliberate, as though he were struggling with himself to be civil. "I appreciate that you want to help, but I don't think you understand. We're going under. Your check is hardly enough to make a difference, and by the time it comes, we'll have more bills. I'm sick and tired of all the responsibility. I just can't keep up with it. You just never learned how to deal with money responsibly."

His words stabbed Denise. Michael was always so damn smug, and these arguments made her feel so inadequate.

So, she let him have it. "I spend a lot less money than any of my friends. I don't buy new clothes, I shop in secondhand stores, and I skimp on food. Let me tell you something that might help you. If you were more of a leader and had a better personality, you'd be better liked, and you would have been promoted by now. Y'know, it's a shame we have to live like this, just because your boss doesn't respect you." The moment her stinging words stopped, Denise knew she had scored a direct hit. Michael looked stunned. Denise knew she was "winning" at that moment. But she also knew that the day was ruined for the two of them, and that they were both chipping away at the foundation of their relationship.

Money: The Number One Relationship Problem

Denise and Michael are wrestling with the relationship problem that ranks as number one in terms of causing difficulties for couples: money. When you read their dialogue, did you feel like taking sides? Did you think that one of them was being unreasonable? Did it remind you of an argument that you've had? Or did it remind you of the way your parents argued?

Nothing is more personal than money. That sentence might sound strange to you. Usually, when we think about money, we think about it abstractly. We think about it in relation to accounting practices, business models, and economic theory, and other cut-and-dried financial matters such as mortgages and income taxes.

We don't think about money as a personal issue in the way that we think love is a personal issue. For example, when you think about being in love and being close to someone, what do you think about? Stop for a moment and come up with some images before you read any further.

Did your images look like something from a Hallmark card? Did you think of a cozy fireplace, hugs, walks along the beach, looking deep into each others eyes over a candlelit dinner? You probably didn't come up with images about balancing a checkbook, writing a budget, planning careers, and making financial decisions together. So when we find that love is about money, too, it blindsides us. This new insight can produce gut-wrenching emotions and frustrations.

Have you ever had any of the following thoughts or experiences? Put a checkmark next to any of the statements below that sound familiar. (Don't be afraid to write in this book—remember, this is a workbook. You'll be doing lots of writing.):

_____ I've had nasty arguments about money with my partner.

_____ I've kept quiet about our money problems, but I feel resentful.

_____ I feel as if the work I do is not appreciated.

_____ My partner sometimes makes bad decisions about money.

_____ Sometimes, I make bad decisions about money.

_____ Sometimes, I feel hopeless about ever having enough money.

_____ I worry a lot about our finances.

_____ Money problems are damaging my good relationship with my partner.

_____ Other couples don't have the kind of money problems that we do.

How many checkmarks did you make? When I've given this quiz to clients they usually hand it back with lots of checkmarks (often every statement) and a comment like, "I'm really bad off, aren't I?" And I tell them, "No, you're normal."

The thoughts and problems in the checklist above are experienced by almost all couples at some point. You're not alone, not by any means. And guess what? Every one of these problems can be solved with the doable, concrete steps in this book. People just like you—no smarter, no more capable, and with partners no more stubborn than yours—have overcome these problems.

EXERCISE: WHY ARE YOU FIGHTING?

The following exercise lists the main reasons that cause couples to fight about money. After you read each item, give it a rating from 1 to 5, to determine how much each item contributes to the arguments or to negative feelings about money in your relationship with your spouse or significant other.

Doing this exercise will help you in two ways. You'll discover that the underlying issues that cause resentments or arguments between you and your partner are not unique to you, that many other people experience the same difficulties. You'll also become clearer about what's causing you to struggle with your partner. By rating each area from 1 to 5, you'll be able to see which are your biggest problems. Then you can decide which problem area you want to tackle first. These are the problem areas:

- How to Spend Money

- Where Should Money Come From?

- Security versus Taking Risks

- Careers: Their Meaning and Importance

- Family Roles

- Trust

How to Spend Money

Anne announced, "I have to have a new car with airbags—that's my bottom line. I don't want to be stranded somewhere because my old car's engine fails, and I don't want to be hurt in an accident."

Tom looked at Anne with a concerned expression. "I understand that, but we can get a nice, solid used car that'll work fine. You're talking about safety. Hanging onto that extra $10,000 will keep us a lot more secure than airbags will. It'll help me expand my business, and we need some money for a cushion. People have been driving cars without airbags for almost 100 years. That's really not a priority."

Clearly, "security" means two different things to Tom and Anne. For Anne, physical protection is important to her security. Tom saw money itself as a form of security. Both were using money to protect against their worst fears, fears that they had learned from past experiences and from the experiences of friends and family.

No doubt you have your own "bottom lines" about how money should be spent. You also have ideas about the kind of lifestyle you should have, and about how decisions should be made in your family. Every couple has disagreements about these issues. You can learn how to settle these disagreements without damaging your relationship.

How much of a problem are your disagreements over how to spend money? (Circle a number below.)

1. No Problem

2. Small Problem

3. Some Problem

4. Big Problem

5. Huge Problem

Where Should Money Come From?

"It's just temporary," Kim pleaded. "We can move in with my parents until we can get on our feet. It'll give us a chance to save some money, and we'll have the whole upstairs to ourselves."

Fred was tired of their tiny apartment too. But he wasn't ready to move. "I know your parents mean well. But we're adults. We have to stand on our own feet. I couldn't respect myself—I'm not a moocher."

All of his life, Fred had heard the saying, "There's no such thing as a free lunch," and he knew that living with Kim's parents would have many hidden costs. They might save some money, but they would lose privacy, he'd feel embarrassed about not completely supporting his family, and he would worry about being a burden. Kim felt that her parents should help her out when she needed it, and if everyone sacrificed a little, she and Fred could have a better future.

There are several different ways that people can disagree about where money should come from. Kim and Fred have different philosophies about accepting support from parents. Other couples may disagree about which of them should earn most of the money. There also can be disagreements about accepting other kinds of financial support, such as government assistance.

Now think about how much your partner and you differ about where your money should come from. How much of a problem has this difference created for the two of you? (Circle a number below.)

1. No Problem

2. Small Problem

3. Some Problem

4. Big Problem

5. Huge Problem

Security versus Taking Risks

Pedro had worked as an attorney for the county for five years. He received a small raise each year, vacation and sick time, health benefits, and a retirement plan. But he was becoming restless. His future was limited, he had gone as far as he was going to go with the county, and he was tired of the politics. He felt that he could do better on his own. His wife, Maria, was nervous about making a change. If Pedro opened his own practice, it would mean long hours and lower pay for a few years. There was the potential for more money in the future, but their baby was due in two months. Maria thought that this just wasn't the right time to take such a risk.

A lot of life's most important decisions involve weighing risks. "Should I stay home tonight or go to the party and try to meet new people?" "Should I quit my day job and pursue my dreams?" "Should I keep my money in the bank or invest in real estate?" "Should I get more education or work with what I have?" These are the kinds of questions about security and risk that most people deal with at various times in their lives.

Life is full of uncertainties. Risk adds more stress and more uncertainty. But avoiding risk has its costs too. If you are too cautious, you are unlikely to achieve great financial success. Moreover, if you always make cautious decisions—doing secure but unexciting work and never venturing outside your comfort zone in your personal and business relationships—then you could not only end up with less money, but also miss out on a sense of meaning and excitement in your life.

If you and your partner have a different tolerance for risk, you can expect some disagreements. If you take risks that your partner is uncomfortable with, and matters don't work out the way you hoped they would, it may be hard for your partner not to blame you and feel resentful.

Do you disagree with your partner about how much risk you're willing to take with money? How much of a problem is this? (Circle a number below.)

1. No Problem

2. Small Problem

3. Some Problem

4. Big Problem

5. Huge Problem

The Meaning and Importance of Careers

Sally had worked as a real estate agent since she and Tom were married, ten years ago. She made a good living at this, but she couldn't see herself doing it for the rest of her life. She brought up the issue cautiously.

"Tom, how would you feel if I did another kind of work? I've always wanted to do something to help kids. Like teaching or social work."

Tom's first response was to feel panic. He really wanted Sally to be happy in her work, but he also knew that the bills had to be paid. He answered her this way, "We've got our own kids to look after. This just isn't the time to switch careers."

Career satisfaction is very important. If you like your work, you feel happier about your life, and your good feelings about the work you do can enrich your family relationships. But what if your job satisfaction places a burden on your family by requiring them to make financial sacrifices, or by taking too much of your time and emotional energy?

Have you felt frustration or conflict about your partner's career and job choices? Do you feel that your partner doesn't understand how important your work is to you? Or has your partner even mentioned these kinds of frustration to you? How big a problem have these issues been? (Circle a number below.)

1. No Problem

2. Small Problem

3. Some Problem

4. Big Problem

5. Huge Problem

Family Roles

It had been a long, tiring day at work. Ralph came home to true chaos. The baby was screaming and the house looked as if a hurricane had passed through it. He slumped down into his favorite chair and turned on the TV. He turned up the volume to drown out the noise around him. Anita was exhausted and infuriated. She stood in front of the TV screen and shouted at him, "I could use a little help around here!"

Ralph replied, "I don't know what you do all day, but this place is an unholy mess. I've already done my work today—taking care of the house is your responsibility."

When you were growing up, you got certain ideas about what the roles of men and women in a committed relationship should be, and how responsibilities should be divided up by what you saw in your own family. Early experiences gave you a blueprint about how family roles should function, and it takes a conscious effort to change such early ideas.

We all have certain notions about what we are responsible for and what our partner is responsible for. You may feel that these assumptions are so obvious that you don't even need to talk about them. Here are some of the ideas my clients have expressed to me about the way roles and responsibilities in a relationship should be divided.

- I'm a man, so I shouldn't have to do any housework.

- I'm a woman, so I shouldn't have to concern myself with money issues.

- I bring home more money, so I should have less responsibility at home.

- I'm better looking than my partner, so I should be pampered and protected from life's hard knocks.

- I'm better educated than my partner, so I should be the one to make the important decisions.

This list could go on for several pages. Some assumptions may seem reasonable to you, others may seem ridiculous. The trouble comes when you and your partner disagree about the roles you should play, or when being too rigid about your roles keeps you from trying out arrangements that might work better for you both.

To what extent do you feel that ideas about roles have caused problems for you and your partner? (Circle a number below.)

1. No Problem

2. Small Problem

3. Some Problem

4. Big Problem

5. Huge Problem

Trust

Vanessa couldn't wait for Dane to get home. She had saved for months to get this new dress and she felt gorgeous wearing it. When Dane came through the door, Vanessa twirled around with a broad smile. "Like it?" Dane rushed past her. "Yeah, love it. How much did that set us back?" Vanessa stood still, and her smile evaporated. She was crushed and felt too hurt to argue. "I'll change into something else. Don't worry, I'll take it back to the store."

Dane remembered the bitter arguments his parents used to have over money. The same argument over and over: his mother bought expensive clothes at Bloomingdale's, his father told her that her selfishness was driving him "to the poorhouse." Now it seemed like it was happening all over again. Dane had been married for just a few months, and already his new wife was going wild at the store (and he was sounding just like his father).

Dane's experience growing up and the newness of his marriage both contributed to his discomfort and distrust of Vanessa's ability to handle money. Vanessa saw the dress as a wonderful way to celebrate her happiness and to make herself lovelier for her new husband. She believed that she had been very careful with money, and she felt that Dane's comments had been cruel and unfair.

Trust, or rather the lack of it, is at the root of almost all marital and relationship disagreements. When you feel that your partner has your best interests at heart, and you believe that your partner can make good decisions, then deciding things together is a much more comfortable process. If you feel that your partner is looking out only for himself or herself, at your expense, or you believe that your partner makes bad decisions, then the process of deciding things together leads to disagreements that are bound to become a struggle.

Your lack of trust may be based on experiences with your partner. For instance, if your partner has spent the grocery money at bars, or has invested and lost money in one harebrained scheme after another. But the lack of trust may also be your own issue, based on experiences that have nothing to do with your current relationship.

How much have problems related to trust caused problems in your relationship? (Circle a number below.)

1. No Problem

2. Small Problem

3. Some Problem

4. Big Problem

5. Huge Problem

Your Priorities

Now, use the chart below to summarize what you marked above. Put an "X" to the right of each type of problem to show what you marked above. For instance, if you indicated above "How should money be spent," that it is "Some Problem," then put an "X" to the right of "How should money be spent" under the heading "Some Problem." When you finish, the chart will show which areas have created the biggest problems for you:

	No Problem	Small Problem	Some Problem	Big Problem	Huge Problem
How should money be spent	_____	_____	_____	_____	_____
Where should money come from	_____	_____	_____	_____	_____
Security versus taking risks	_____	_____	_____	_____	_____
The importance of careers	_____	_____	_____	_____	_____
Family roles	_____	_____	_____	_____	_____
Trust	_____	_____	_____	_____	_____

Look at your chart above, and find the issues that have been the biggest problems for you (those that you marked with X's furthest to the right). You might want to address these problems first, or you might go through the book chapter by chapter, or a combination of these approaches: It's up to you and your partner. If you want to address the most pressing problems first, the guide below will show you where to go in this book.

Spending Problems

Chapter 6: Find out how a Monarch Personality can cause spending havoc, and what to do about it.

Chapter 9: You and your partner have the power to choose a lifestyle. Making conscious choices can prevent your lifestyle from taking over your lives.

Chapter 13: Get control of debt before it drowns you.

Problems with Where Money Comes From

Chapter 8: There are three places to find money. Find out where, and how to tap into these sources in a way that works for both you and your partner.

Security versus Risk Problems

Chapter 5: Whether you and your partner are Gamblers or Bankers reflects your tolerance for risk. Here you find how to get a workable balance with your finances and with your partner.

Chapter 16: When you consider investments, you need to consider your risk tolerance.

Career Problems

Chapters 14 and 15: In chapter 14, you'll weigh whether a career change makes sense for you or your partner. In chapter 15, you'll look at ways to maximize the career and talents that you have now.

Family Role Problems

Chapter 3: Some problems are rooted in our male and female brains and upbringing. In this chapter, you'll learn to see things through the eyes of the other gender.

Chapter 10: When it comes to money, where do you draw the line? Figure where your own and your partner's financial boundaries lie.

Trust Problems

Chapter 2: The way you think can cause money and relationship problems. Find out how to think your way to a better life.

Chapter 11: Understanding your own and your partner's financial history can give clues to the problems you're having now.

Chapter 19: Sometimes the problems are too big to solve alone. This chapter will help you to figure out if that's the case, and where to go for help.

You've started on an exciting journey. We're going to look at how you and your partner deal with money, and why money causes problems between you. Parts of this trip will be fun, and other parts will take some soul searching. As you move through this book, you'll get a better handle on your money problems, and begin to see how to move beyond them. Then, you'll see the goal post: prosperity and joy, and a joyful, sharing relationship with the partner who enhances your path through life.

CHAPTER 2

Money Self-Talk

CHAPTER GOAL: To learn how to change money-related thoughts that cause problems in your relationships and your life, and that limit your financial potential.

The Rules You Live By

Your mood, your actions, your relationships, and even your finances are controlled by your thoughts. You're aware of some of your thoughts, but some are so much a part of you that they've faded into the background, and you may not even know they are there.

Think of someone you know whose life has gone fairly smoothly. Sure, this person has had ups and downs, but he or she is able to maintain happy, long-term relationships, find enjoyable work and, when problems come along, deal with them. You probably also know someone whose life has been a series of disasters. Maybe that person has been through a divorce or two, lost jobs, and had money and job-related problems.

What makes these two people so different from each other? If it were just "luck," you wouldn't see such consistency in their lives, year after year. You can also rule out looks, intelligence, inheriting money, and connections. It's easy to think of people with all of these gifts who manage to make a shambles of their lives (some movie stars come to mind).

Have you ever been to a high school reunion? You may have been shocked to discover that some of the most popular kids in high school had adult lives that were mundane or worse. Clearly, being good-looking, getting good grades, or being charming and having lots of friends in high school did not guarantee success as an adult.

The key element, the one that makes all the difference, is your thoughts.

That statement may come as a surprise to you. Perhaps you're thinking, "Maybe that's some other person's problem, but it's not mine. My problems aren't just in my head—my problems are *real!*"

Yes, there are real problems. People get sick and die, cars break down, people get laid off, stocks crash, businesses fail, and so on. These real events can be upsetting, even devastating. But by changing your thoughts, you can greatly reduce the odds that difficult problems will happen to you, and if they do happen, you can learn to deal with them in more effective, realistic ways. Changing you thoughts can change your life. This is great news! Because, unlike many of the things that you think are holding you back, your thoughts are under your control.

How Did You Get This Way?

As you grew up, you absorbed information from your family and the world around you. You were affected by the way your parents thought about things and by the events that took place in your school, neighborhood, or community. Some of your thoughts served you well—that's why you held onto them. But some of the thoughts that served you well in the past may not be useful any longer.

The most common dysfunctional thoughts about money are listed below. After you read the list, see if you can come up with some other thoughts that you or your partner may have about money.

Common Errors About Money That Hold You Back

1. **Using feelings rather than reality as the basis for spending decisions.**

   Related thoughts:

   "I deserve a certain lifestyle and I will spend money accordingly to achieve and maintain that lifestyle."

   "I can never spend money on myself until everything else is taken care of."

2. **Viewing finances as controlled by forces outside yourself.**

   Related thoughts:

   "I will never have enough money, no matter what I do."

   "Enough money will always show up; the Universe (or God, my spouse, society, or my neighbors) will always take care of me."

3. **Giving one factor in a career more importance than all the others.**

   That one factor might be one of the following:

   - security
   - salary
   - flexibility
   - prestige

- following your dreams
- autonomy

4. **Using money (or the lack of it) as the main way to affect others' opinions about you.**

Related thoughts:

"If I look pitiful, people will help me."

"People won't respect me unless I look well-off."

5. **Believing that your money is a measure of your worth as a person.**

Related thoughts:

"I couldn't respect myself if I drove an old car."

"To feel that I've achieved something, I have to earn more money than my neighbor (or father, sister, spouse, or the average person my age) earns. Or, I need to earn more than I earned last year."

6. **Having unrealistic expectations of others.**

Related thought:

"Everyone is always trying to take advantage of me."

"If I'm open and trust people, I'll never be disappointed."

7. **Viewing the future unrealistically.**

Related thoughts:

"We might as well enjoy today; the future's too uncertain to make any plans."

"We can't afford any enjoyment now: but hard work and self-denial will make our future bright."

What Do These Thoughts Cost?

Believing in the truth of any one of the thoughts listed above might be reasonable under a limited set of circumstances. But such thoughts become problems when they become inflexible and rigid and/or you keep thinking them, even when they do not help you.

Some of these thoughts can bring you certain things that you want, and they might even make you feel good for a while. But they can also be very costly. Taken to the extreme, the price of hanging onto any of these thoughts could be relationship problems, money problems, anxiety, and, finally, depression. Now, let's look at some examples of the power that these thoughts wield over the lives of the people who think them.

The Scale for Rating Emotional Costs and Benefits

The two characters below, Stella in the first account, and then Keith, rate the emotional costs and emotional benefits of their beliefs on a 0 to 100 scale. Rating feelings and experiences in this way is a technique often used by psychotherapists (particularly those with a cognitive behavioral orientation) to help their clients to view events more realistically in their lives.

If holding onto a belief causes you tremendous emotional distress you would give the emotional cost a rating of "100." On the other hand, if a belief never causes any problems for you, it would have an emotional cost rating of "0." The same is true for emotional benefits: If holding onto the belief brings you great emotional rewards and pleasure, you'd rate the emotional benefit at "100." If it never brings you any good feeling, you'd rate it at "0." Most beliefs have emotional costs and benefits that would be rated as more than zero but less than 100. It is common for people to hang onto beliefs because they provide good feelings in the short run, even though they have a high emotional cost in the long run.

Stella: Thinking Her Way to a Better Life

Stella had been raised in a large family, with eight brothers and sisters. Her parents had never had enough time to "head off" trouble or to talk over her day with her. She got her parents' attention only when there was a problem.

Stella's dysfunctional belief: "If I look pitiful, and I have problems, people will help me."

Stella's behavior as an adult: Stella was always complaining. She looked sad all the time. When anyone casually asked, "How are you doing?" Stella would immediately start describing her many woes. She went on and on about her aches, pains, and financial problems. Whenever Stella went out to eat with friends, when the bill came, she would meekly announce that she was "a little short."

Stella's husband, Bob, enjoyed taking charge. She always deferred all important decisions to him.

The effect on her life: Like most dysfunctional beliefs, Stella's behavior worked to some extent. People did help her, but they grew more and more resentful and angry. She lost some friends. Others (including her husband Bob) played the role of social worker, constantly advising her on how to improve her life and expressing their disappointment if she didn't follow their advice. Stella resigned herself to laying low. She believed that if she ever earned any more money or took on any more responsibilities, then more would be expected of her, and she would lose the support of those people she depended on.

Changing her beliefs: Stella listed the advantages and disadvantages of her belief as follows:

Advantages: "When I seem pitiful, people pick up the check, give me extra time to pay the rent, and express their sympathy. I get about $50 extra every month in this way, and about twice a week people tell me they feel sorry for me. Bob handles the hard decisions."

Monetary Benefits: $50 per month

Emotional Benefits: 20 (on a 0–100 scale)

Disadvantages: "I've had the same position at work for ten years because I'm not seen as capable of handling more responsibility (and when I was offered the chance, I did not accept any). I lost some good friends, and the friends I've kept try to control my life. I've lost my self-respect, and I've started believing that I'm actually as pitiful as I act."

Monetary Costs: $500 a month (how much extra other people are making who started at my job and got promoted)

Emotional Costs (on the 0–100 scale): 50.

As with almost all dysfunctional thoughts, the short-term benefits had blinded Stella to the long-term problems that her thoughts were causing. Once she did this cost-benefit analysis, she saw that her thoughts could not benefit her in the long run. Here are some of the new thoughts she adopted:

Stella's Functional Thoughts:

"If I start to act competently, people will treat me with more respect."

"If I rely on others, I'm limited to what they're willing to give. If I rely on myself, the sky's the limit."

"I'm more competent than I've been acting."

"I have a lot to offer others; there's no reason why I should always be taking."

"It feels good to be in control of situations rather than always allowing others to take charge."

Changing New Thoughts into Actions

Once Stella made the decision to change her thinking, she came up with small, definite actions that she could do from day to day to begin making larger changes. She offered to pick up the check when she went out with friends. She volunteered for additional responsibility at work, and she began actively exploring other job and career possibilities. Whenever she felt strongly about an issue at home and at work, she began to express her viewpoint, even if it meant disagreeing with someone.

Of course, all of these changes did not go smoothly. Change makes people uncomfortable. Stella's friends and her husband began asking her, "What's got into you?" They were afraid of losing their positions as "helpers," positions they cherished because helping Stella provided them with someone they could always feel superior to.

Some of her coworkers felt threatened by Stella's newfound ambition, afraid that she might be vying for their positions. Stella had to review her list of costs and benefits frequently to stick with the changes she was trying to effect. She made a point of noting any improvements she experienced in her life or in her feelings about herself. She talked to Bob about the changes she was making, and pointed out to him how her efforts to change could have advantages for both of them.

Keith: Thinking His Way to a Better Life

Keith was the only child of two physicians. He had been born when both of his parents were established professionals, in their late thirties. Before he was born both of his parents had worked long hours and maintained a modest lifestyle, but as a child, Keith had never lacked for anything he wanted. His parents had put a big premium on "quality" and appearance. His father had often instructed him, "Don't be cheap. You get what you pay for." Although his parents sometimes talked about their earlier, less well-off years to Keith, their stories sounded like one of those parental myths, like, "We walked five miles in sub-zero temperatures, through six-foot piles of snow, just to get to school. . . ."

Keith's dysfunctional belief: "I deserve a certain lifestyle and I will spend money accordingly to maintain that lifestyle."

Keith's behavior as an adult: At twenty-five, Keith had just finished law school and was studying for the bar. He had friends who drove old cars and lived in small apartments. But he felt that such a modest lifestyle wasn't for him. He said he "wouldn't be caught dead" in anything but the best clothes or the nicest car, and he "needed" to live in a penthouse that overlooked the city. Darlene, a stunningly attractive woman, had been Keith's girlfriend for the past three years. Keith boasted to his friends about having "good taste in women," a phrase that Darlene found particularly annoying and demeaning.

The effect on his life: Keith looked the part of the model "yuppie" and lived the life he felt he deserved. His parents boasted about their successful son to their friends. His friends told him, "You've got it made."

But Keith spent money based on what he felt he *should* have, rather than on what was realistic (in terms of his true income). Before long, his credit cards were maxed out, and he was having sleepless nights over making his apartment rent and car payment. When he didn't pass the bar on the first try, he began feel desperate. He could see his life-style and his image fading.

Darlene had put $10,000 away to finish college. Keith saw that money—along with a hot stock tip—as the key to his future. He poured on the charm and argued his case relentlessly. Finally, he convinced Darlene that he could turn her $10,000 into at least $100,000 within weeks. Against her better judgment, Darlene loaned Keith the money.

Keith bought the "hot stock." They opened their newspaper to read the stock prices every day. Within a few days, the $10,000 had turned into $12,000. Keith was ecstatic. Darlene wanted him to sell, but Keith exclaimed, "You ain't seen nothing yet." He was right. The stock started moving down. When it was worth $9,000, Darlene became insistent about selling it; Keith was adamant that selling at that point would be absurd. You can guess the rest of the story: the stock tanked, and Darlene, feeling badly used and extremely frustrated, split up with Keith. He was devastated. He had no money left, no prospects, and no girlfriend. But he did have strong motivation to change.

Changing his belief: Keith listed the advantages and disadvantages of believing this thought: "I deserve a certain lifestyle and I will spend money accordingly."

Advantages: "When I look good and appear successful, people like being around me. They tell me I'm doing great. This gives me more confidence. I might even make more money, because clients and employers think I 'have it together.'"

Monetary Benefits: None yet

Emotional Benefits: 75 (on a 0–100 scale)

Disadvantages: "It's very expensive to keep this up. My lifestyle costs an extra $4000 a month more than the lifestyle of some of my friends. The kind of people who are attracted to my successful image don't always value me as a person. Sometimes I feel like a fraud.

Monetary Costs: $4000 a month

Emotional Costs (on a scale of 1–100): 20 ("When I have money"); 90 ("When I run out of money")

Keith's cost-benefit analysis was quite different from Stella's. He found that his thoughts were causing him severe financial problems. He knew that his successful appearance had yet to put any money in his pocket. Nevertheless, he struggled with the idea of adopting a simpler, less expensive lifestyle. He had been to "success" seminars and had heard people say that, "If you want to be successful, you need to 'look the part.'"

But when he really thought about it, his flashy appearance and luxurious lifestyle were not a good financial strategy. They really were a way to buy good feelings and protection from criticism.

Keith's Functional Thoughts

"I'm not a prince. I don't 'deserve' to live a princely lifestyle until I earn it."

"Appearances are helpful in business, but I won't get a better job because my apartment has a beautiful view. I can look professional for much less than I've been spending."

"It's the same with relationships. I can look attractive without going broke. Anyway, I want to attract someone who will share the struggle with me, like Mom did with Dad. I don't want to date golddiggers."

"Trying to buy a good self-image is a bad use of money. I'm intelligent, attractive, and a good friend no matter what car I drive or what brand I wear."

Changing New Thoughts into Actions

Keith knew he was a capable person. He had gone through college and law school with good grades, so he knew he would be able to get through these financial difficulties eventually. (You can think of things you've done, too, that prove you're capable. Maybe it was educational achievement. Maybe you've survived abuse, or successfully dealt with a difficult job or a difficult family situation. In any case, it never hurts to remind yourself that you have personal resources.)

Keith began to think of success differently. He reminded himself that it wasn't just about outward appearance, it was also about building a future and being able to handle financial responsibilities. He found a roommate to share the rent, and traded in his car for a less expensive model.

One day, he asked Darlene to go out with him again, and she reluctantly agreed. He told her about the lifestyle changes he was making. She was still furious with him for losing her tuition money on the stock market. Keith heard her out and said that he had wanted to see her again to make arrangements to pay her back over time. He promised to pay her back in full, and he made good on his promise. After having been "burned" once, she was quite fearful about becoming involved with him again. But she had always enjoyed being with Keith, and the changes she saw in him were very attractive to her. They began dating again, and six months later they were engaged.

Your Turn

Now, you will go through the same steps as the people you've just been reading about. By doing this exercise, you'll be able to evaluate one of your beliefs about money and determine whether it truly serves you.

EXERCISE: CHANGING YOUR DYSFUNCTIONAL THOUGHTS ABOUT MONEY

Note: You might want to copy this and other exercises in the book so that you can reuse them, or so you can invite your partner to try them. For this exercise, you'll need one copy for each belief you want to test.

Step 1: Write one of your thoughts or beliefs about money in the space provided in this workbook or in a separate journal. The first time you do this, it may be easiest to pick from the list above (under "Common Errors About Money That Hold You Back"). After you try this exercise a few times, you'll be able to come up with some of your own beliefs without help. Remember, you keep your beliefs because they seem right to you, so it's okay if the belief seems reasonable to keep, or if you're not sure that you want to change it:

"I believe: _____ "

Step 2: Advantages: What are the advantages of keeping this belief? How does it help you? Think about how it improves your relationships, your feelings about yourself, and any financial benefits:

This belief helps me because:

_____

_____

_____

_____

Personal advantages: Look at what you wrote above and think about how this belief helps you personally. Express this as a number from 0 (no help at all) to 100 (tremendously helpful). You might have two numbers, one for long-term and one for short-term advantages.

Rating (0–100): _____

Financial advantages: Look at what you wrote above and think about how this belief helps you financially. Express this as a dollar amount, showing the average amount of extra money you have or get, every month, because of this belief. You might have two amounts, one for long-term and one for short-term finances.

Rating: $ _____ per month

Step 3: Disadvantages What are the personal and financial disadvantages of keeping this belief?

Personal disadvantages: Look at what you wrote above and think about how this belief hurts you *personally*. Express this as a number from 0 (no problem at all) to 100 (tremendous problems). You might have two numbers, one for long-term and one for short-term disadvantages.

Rating (0–100): _____

Financial disadvantages: Look at what you wrote above and think about how this belief hurts you *financially*. Express this as a dollar amount, showing the average amount of money you lose, every month, because of this belief. You might have two amounts, one for long-term and one for short-term finances.

Rating: $ _____ per month

Step 4: Cost-Benefit Analysis: Now look at the net gain or loss from your belief. Write in the numbers from above.

_____ minus _____ = ____

Personal advantage – Personal disadvantage = Net personal gain/loss

_____ minus _____ = _____

Financial advantage – Financial disadvantage = Net financial gain/loss

Step 5: Deciding Whether You Should Change. If your belief brings you both personal and financial gain, then there's no reason to change it; it's working for you. If there's a loss in both areas, then the decision to change is a slam dunk: This belief just isn't working for you.

If there's a personal gain and a financial loss, then you have some thinking to do. This means you are paying to feel good or for personal satisfaction. There's nothing wrong with that; after all, that's what people do when they go to Disneyland. But you'll want to think about whether you are getting a good deal for your money, and whether you could get the same positive feelings with less financial cost.

If there's a personal cost but a financial gain, then you're making a personal sacrifice in exchange for more money. You'll need to think about this carefully. Think about both short-term and long-term goals. Think about how the money will affect your personal and relationship happiness, and think about whether you will feel happy or regretful when you look back on this sacrifice.

After careful thought, check one of the choices below. By checking "Yes" you're making a commitment to change your belief—and to improve your life.

Check one:

_____ YES, my belief is causing problems and I've decided to change.

_____ NO, my belief isn't causing problems (or not enough problems so that I'm ready to change it yet).

Step 6: Functional Thoughts. If you checked "Yes," you've made the decision to challenge, or argue with, your belief. This belief has been your friend for a long time, but now it has overstayed its welcome and is causing you problems. Reread how Keith and Stella argued with their beliefs, and then write down your arguments and new beliefs below:

_____

_____

_____

Step 7: Changing Thoughts into Action. Now think about how your new beliefs will change your day-to-day behavior. You might decide to change your spending or saving habits. Maybe you'll decide to make changes in your work or in the way you deal with money with your partner or in other relationships. Make a promise to yourself to do something different, consistent with your new thoughts. Make sure it's something that you can actually do and that you can make a commitment to honor your new thought. It's fine to start small. You can always step up the pace later. You'll find that doing even small things consistent with your new beliefs will have a snowball effect. Your new behavior will strengthen your new beliefs; the new beliefs will lead to further changes in your behavior.

Consistent with my new beliefs, I am going to:

_____

_____

_____

$ $ $ $ $

You've just examined how your thoughts can wreak havoc in your relationship with your partner and in your financial life. Changing your thoughts is a powerful way to improve your life. Shifting your thoughts can improve your mood, your finances, and your relationships.

CHAPTER 3

Men, Women, and Money

CHAPTER GOAL: To discover the differences in the way that men and women communicate with the aim of improving communication skills.

Differences between male and female communication styles can lead to frustration and anger. In this chapter, you will learn how men and women communicate differently, and begin to understand how those differences can help you to work with and enjoy your partner more deeply.

Disclaimer: It's very hard to talk about differences between groups of people without offending someone. We all know that there are differences between men and women, but when we get down to particulars, especially the differences in the ways we act, talk, and think, it's bound to rub someone the wrong way. Keep in mind that when I discuss male and female characteristics, I'm speaking in broad, sweeping generalities that may or may not apply to you and your partner. Just take the parts that you find useful and leave the rest. And lest I be labeled a sexist, I should mention that my closest and dearest friend is a woman, and is married to me.

Gender Differences: They Really Do Exist

Lately, I've been watching a lot of Andy Griffith reruns with my family. It's very comforting to escape to a friendly, one-sheriff town every evening. Andy, Opie, and Aunt Bee deal with simple problems in a simpler time. This time around, though, I noticed that every few shows, Aunt Bee tries to venture boldly into the men's world, and fails. In one episode, she defiantly runs for town counsel, while Andy supports an opposing candidate. By the end of the show, she realizes that her opponent, a man, of course, is much better qualified than she is, and she humbly advises the town to vote for him. In another episode, she invests in a Chinese restaurant. Again, she ventures out—into the man's world—against Andy's better judgment. In this show, Aunt Bee finally realizes that she doesn't have the temperament to weather the uncertainties of the business world, and she returns to her kitchen with a great sense of relief.

There probably never will be a new television show created in which a woman sheepishly retreats from the larger world back to her domestic chores. A lot has happened since the days of the Andy Griffith show. The civil rights and black power movements of the Sixties led to the women's liberation movement of the Seventies, and to the basic ideas of feminism.

These ideas make a lot of sense. They begin with the premise that we are all equal and that men and women can function well in the same roles. As feminist Wilma Scott Heide declared, "The only jobs for which no man is qualified are human incubators and wet nurse. Likewise, the only job for which no woman is or can be qualified is sperm donor" (Heide, no date).

As with any new movement, some of its spokespersons went to extremes. "Equality" somehow got translated into "exactly alike." In some circles, it became heresy to suggest that there were any characteristics typical of males and females. In the Seventies, some psychological literature began to promote "androgyny" as the pinnacle of psychological health (Kaplan and Bean 1976). By the eighties and nineties, the pendulum started to swing back. First in whispers and then in shouts, we became aware once again of what has been obvious for most of human history: men and women *are* different.

John Gray's "Venus and Mars" books caught on because they came at the right time, and reminded us of something that we couldn't admit for fear of being seen as backward and politically incorrect. Men and women see the world differently, they act differently, and think differently. And these differences affect the way the two sexes deal with their finances.

You're Not Hearing Me!

Sam and Alice had been seeing each other for two years before they started living together in Sam's small apartment in Boston. When Alice moved in, it was a freezing cold day in February. They had both had hard days. At his job, Sam had just been passed over for a promotion, and Alice, who was just starting her nursing career, was finding her job very stressful and too fast-paced. On top of everything else, she was coming down with a cold. She sneezed violently and said, "I can't stand these cold winters. I just want us to move to Florida, or somewhere where we don't have to battle the elements."

Sam couldn't believe what he heard. "That's crazy! We're just getting started, and you want to uproot everything and move? So we're both supposed to start from scratch, right? It costs money to move, you know! You'll need to get your nursing license in another state, we'll need to find a place to live, and on top of it all, I'll need to find a new job! That's just great—why can't you be more practical?"

Alice tried to hold back her tears. After a long pause, she said quietly, "I *know* it's not practical, and I know we're just getting started. But I'm feeling discouraged and blue, and the thought of Florida made me feel better. You don't have to do anything—just sympathize with how I feel." Sam and Alice were speaking two different languages: feelings and practicalities.

From the time they are small children, boys are trained to think about practicalities. The necessity to compete and the virtue of "standing on your own two feet" are common themes in boys' socialization. For women, their emotions, the need to cooperate rather than to compete, and the need to nurture others reign supreme.

Psychologists are still arguing about whether such gender differences are biological or whether they are caused by the way children are socialized. Today, most researchers would probably agree that both "nature" and "nurture" are involved in creating gender differences. Testosterone does make the human male more aggressive, and even some enlightened parents get a little nervous when their son plays with Barbie and Ken dolls, or their daughter prefers to play with army tanks and GI Joe action figures.

Hey! You're Different, Aren't You?

In spite of the changes that feminism has made in our society, men and women still have different career courses. Most men expect to start working when they finish their education and to keep on working, without a break, until they retire. Women, on the other hand, are more likely to have their work lives interrupted by the need to stay at home and raise the kids. So, here's an oversimplified picture of the current situation between the sexes:

Boys and young men have male hormones coursing through their veins, causing them to want to get out there to hunt, fight, and compete. Their dads, and all the messages society sends, tell them to "act like a man" and "stand on your own two feet." When they become fathers, if they choose to stay home and raise their kids, to be "house-husbands," as it were, their neighbors gossip about them and put them down. Meanwhile, their sisters and wives find their allegiances are split between having children and staying home to rear them, and the big world of work out there.

Gender Differences in the Brain

Men have been socialized to think and work in a linear fashion. Their brains may even be organized to work that way. In linear thinking, fact A leads to fact B, and so that must mean fact C. Some research has shown that men experience less integration between and across the two hemispheres of the brain than women do (Hales 1999).

It is known that the left hemisphere governs language use and the right hemisphere governs images and emotions. This may mean that men have less ability to link words together with pictures and emotions. These physiological differences, combined with everything else that is different in the experience of men and women, mean that the two sexes communicate differently and they solve problems differently. This isn't a good or a bad thing, but it does explain some of the problems that crop up when men and women wish to communicate with each other.

As every therapist knows, the vast majority of adults who come voluntarily to counseling and psychotherapy are women. I've heard many of my female colleagues complain about men being "resistant" in counseling. In fact, it might be more accurate to say that "men just don't talk the way counselors expect clients to talk." Instead of talking, exploring, and examining their feelings, men want *definitions, diagnoses, and solutions.*

Pease and Pease (2000) give a pretty clear breakdown of how men and women differ in their communication styles. They argue that these differences are based in biological brain differences and in our primordial history: For men, problem-solving and dealing with emotions are two separate brain functions; in women they are integrated.

Men define themselves and their value by their work; women define their self-worth by the quality of their relationships. For men, expressions of love are concrete acts—doing things and giving things. For women, expressions of love are emotional support, romance, and intimate conversation. Pease and Pease (2000) theorize that under stress, the logical, problem-solving, space-oriented parts of a man's brain are activated, and that, under stress, a woman's speech function is activated.

So, stressed men clam up; they size up what's going on around them, and they try to figure out solutions; stressed women start talking. In stressful circumstances, men tend to shut down the emotional part of their brain, while when women are stressed, the part of the brain that deals with emotions is activated. When a woman offers or receives advice, it's seen as a relationship builder. Men view advice as a form a criticism, as a way of saying, "You're not good enough," or "Here's something you couldn't figure out for yourself."

Money: Two Different Views of Its Value

How do these differences between men and women play out when it comes to money? Here's what researchers have found:

- Men value money more than women do, and, in general, they have more positive feelings about it (Lynn 1993; Newcomb and Rabow 1999).

- Women are less likely to take financial risks. They are less likely to be speculators, more likely to seek stable, long-term investments (Powell and Ansic 1997).

- Women *think* they know less about money, but they actually know just as much as men do, and, overall, they tend to be just as good as men at investing (Eisenberg 1996).

- In spite of the push for equality, there's still a lot of social pressure for the man to be the main breadwinner. One study conducted in the late 1990s (Riggs 1997) found that college students of both genders approved of mothers who sacrificed financial security to stay home with their children, and they expected fathers to be the main financial providers. Another study done by the Queen Mary's School of Medicine in London (United Press International 2001) surveyed more than 10,000 middle-aged men. The researchers found that the men were more likely to become depressed when their wives were working full-time outside the home.

- Women tend to think about their careers differently than men. It is still more common for men to be the main breadwinner in a family, with the woman providing supplementary income. This gives women more room to think about career satisfaction, and to be less concerned with the "bottom line." For example, several female broadcasters who work with National Public Radio have stated that they willingly sacrificed higher salaries for job satisfaction, preferring to keep their NPR jobs while many of their male colleagues moved to the commercial market for more pay (Eisenberg 1996).

For a number of years I taught future marriage therapists at a state college. I found that I needed to drive home the point that a successful counselor is not a missionary; that the practitioner must understand that his or her practice is a business, and that counselors must be paid by their clients for their work. This point was not always popular among my female students. One student even commented that she thought it created a "conflict of interest" to counsel someone and to collect money for the counseling from that person!

All of these factors join together to give men and women very different ideas about the world of finances. That's why talking to your partner about money issues can sometimes feel like talking to a visitor from the planet Jupiter.

Translations: Andro and Gyno Idioms

"We're having money problems."

Men: To a man, this sentence presents a problem to be solved. It also can mean "I'm not a good enough provider." Depending on the man and the relationship, he might respond in one of two ways. The statement might be heard as a call for action, an imperative to get out and work harder and longer. However, because it can also be heard as personal criticism, some men will respond in kind, by noting their partners' smaller contribution to family finances, or out-of-control spending habits.

Women: For women, this statement expresses or evokes financial insecurity. Money problems affect the ability to care for the family (i.e., paying the monthly mortgage or rent, buying food, and so forth); the quality of the relationship; and the amount of time the couple has to spend with each other. Although a woman knows that a solution must be found, her first priority is to deal with the feelings of fear and insecurity that come up for her after hearing such a statement.

"I need a better job."

Men: Earning capacity is an important gauge of success for most men, and good work is work that pays well. The ability to "bring home the bacon" is a measure of their success as a provider at home, and as "go-getters" in the workplace. You're unlikely to hear many men say, "I'm looking for more satisfying work, even if it pays less." That's because, for a man, pay is closely interwoven with work satisfaction.

Men tend to be more aggressive and competitive than women are. In the workplace, they are inclined toward jobs that allow them to stand out, demonstrate that they excel in certain areas, and exercise authority.

Bad work for men is work with no opportunity to advance and rise above others. Because men are more likely than women to have uninterrupted careers, lasting forty or more years, progressive career growth is more important to them than career flexibility.

Women: For women, work that involves helping other people in personal ways is apt to be defined as good. Not that power and money are unimportant to women, but they're not given as much emphasis by most women as by most men.

The elements that make for a bad job for women are lack of support, and job expectations that force the job to take precedence over family.

"Let's put some money in the stock market."

Men: To men, a stock market investment is a way to show they can outsmart other people and is also a shortcut up the financial ladder. Men are more likely to be day traders, buying and selling quickly (which, according to most financial advisors, is not the best investment strategy).

Women: Women tend to see the stock market or other unsecured investments as fairly dangerous. "Don't risk the baby's college fund!" When women do invest, they're more likely to buy and hold onto stocks than to trade them frequently.

EXERCISE: PART 1
BRIDGING THE GENDER GAP

Think about an argument you've had with your partner over money. The first step in this exercise is to write a summary of what your partner did or said during your argument, and then the essence of what you did or said. You can write your summary in the space below, or you can write in your journal.

Now, here's an example of an argument plus an example of how to rephrase words that are sure to create conflict:

What We Said and Did

My partner keeps working late at the office. He's never home to help out at night. When I said to him, "I feel neglected and I'm tired of you working so long," he got mad at me. So then I told him, "I wish you had a better job, so you wouldn't be away so long." Then he really blew! He yelled at me that I "should go to work, so he doesn't have to do everything. "

Now, keep in mind that even though both partners are speaking English, they're speaking very different dialects. Here's a translation of what the woman's partner heard:

"You're not a very good provider. Other men could do better than you. Even though you're busting your tail twelve hours a day, trying to provide for your family, it's not good enough for me."

Yikes! No wonder that particular "discussion" didn't end well. Here's a dialog for these two people that might work better. Remember that you want what you write to reach the other side of the gender universe—intact. You want it to be immune from the horrible mutations that gender rays can cause.

What the woman might have said:

"Honey, I really miss you when you're not home in the evening. I really enjoy being with you. I want us to figure out a way that we can spend more time together."

If said that way, the implied insult is gone, and there's no suggestion that the man is a deficient provider. Furthermore, if the woman says she wants "us to figure out a way" she's giving the male brain something it responds well to, like a problem to be solved.

Now try this yourself. The second step in this exercise is to think back to the argument you summarized in the first step. Or, if you prefer, if there are problems you'd like to discuss with your partner right now, you can use this worksheet to rephrase how you'll present your side of an issue.

EXERCISE: PART 2
COMMUNICATING ACROSS THE GENDER GAP

What We Said and Did

My partner said: _____

_____

_____

I said: _____

_____

_____

Now try to translate what you said into the way your partner heard it, through your partner's "opposite-sex ears." Remember that for men, competition and achievement are primary motives. Women prefer to work cooperatively. Men think in terms of practicalities while women give more emphasize to relationships and feelings.

What my partner may have heard: _____

_____

_____

Next, write something that might work better, keeping in mind that it has to cross the gender gap intact.

What I might have said instead: _____

_____

_____

$ $ $ $ $

Yes, men and women *are* different. Most people have outgrown the need to prove that one gender is better, smarter, stronger than the other. But you cannot deny that men and women often see and hear things differently. The more you practice this exercise, the more often you'll be able to bridge the gender gap with your partner. Moreover, you can breathe a sigh of relief: the two of you are not alone. Men and women have disagreed about since money ever since it was invented.

CHAPTER 4

Your Financial Personality

CHAPTER GOALS: To determine your own and your partner's financial personality, to help you better understand the causes of conflict and to help you reduce it; and to increase your potential for financial success.

Everyone has certain unique ways of dealing with the world and other people. Even babies and toddlers exhibit uniquely different behaviors: some babies are timid, quiet, shy, and cautious, and others are energetic, loud, restless, and excitable. You were born with a certain temperament: bold or shy, active or calm, focused or scattered. You took your temperament into the world. Your parents, teachers, friends, and the rest of the world reacted to you, and you reacted to them. All of these experiences formed your personality, the way you think and act today.

Your *financial personality* was also formed by a lot of different influences as you grew up, and it shapes all of your financial decisions today. It affects your decisions about your education, the type and amount of work you do, where you live, what you drive, and what you wear. Decisions about when to buy and sell investments, whether to buy or rent a house, how much of your income to spend when you go out for entertainment, and how much to save for the future—all of these decisions reflect your financial personality. In chapter 3, you learned to identify male and female attitudes about money, and to start to change some of your customary habits and thoughts and dialogues about money. These are all a big part of your financial personality.

You and Your Partner

Chances are, you and your partner don't agree on all of your financial decisions. You might disagree about the kind of lifestyle you want, now or in the future. You might have different ideas about how hard to work or how responsibilities should be divided between the two of you. There's nothing wrong with these kinds of disagreements; it's what makes relationships interesting. The important thing is learning to make the best use of these differences.

Instead of struggling, you want to learn from each other, so that you can make the best possible life together for yourselves. In this chapter, you'll find out what type of financial personalities you and your partner have. In the next few chapters, you'll learn how you and your partner can work together to make the best use of your different personality styles.

The Dimensions of Your Financial Personalities

Everyone's financial personality has three dimensions. Most people's financial personalities fall somewhere in the middle between the extremes of each dimension, but they probably lean more in one direction than the other:

1. **Lifestyle: Spartan versus Monarch.** This dimension reflects your ideas about lifestyle. If you picture yourself living in luxury and feel uncomfortable in humble surroundings, you're a Monarch. If you shun elegance and luxury and think that simplicity is a virtue, you're a Spartan.

   This personality dimension is the valve that controls your spending. The lifestyle that you experienced growing up sets up your basic point of comparison, and strongly influences whether you are a Spartan or Monarch. Just like a prince or princess, if you grew up in lavish surroundings, you may feel you are entitled to this lifestyle, regardless of your actual financial capabilities. If you grew up in humble surroundings, you're better able to tolerate financial scarcity, but you may also feel that you don't deserve anything better than scarcity.

2. **Risk Tolerance: Gambler versus Banker.** This characteristic reflects your tolerance for risk. Does the thought of investing in the stock market make you feel slightly queasy? Does a steady paycheck sound better than working for commissions, even if that means earning less money in the long run? Then you're a Banker. Gamblers don't mind taking risks. Almost all self-made billionaires have Gambler personalities; but, then again, a lot of Gamblers end up filing for bankruptcy.

   Whether you're a Gambler or a Banker can change depending on your circumstances. This dimension has a lot to do with your feelings about security. Your feelings of security or insecurity may be completely realistic, based on how things are actually going in your life, or they may be completely unrealistic, based on ghosts from your past.

   If things are going well, for example, you're in a secure relationship, have an evolving career, and economic times are good, you have more room to gamble. When times are tough, you tend to pull in the reins. So you might basically be a Gambler, but one who can pull back and become a Banker when you're feeling less secure.

   It has been found that men tend to take bigger financial risks than women (Powell and Ansic 1997). But it's also been found that men don't necessarily make financial decisions that end up being any better or worse than women make (Eisenberg 1997).

3. **Financial Dependency: Pioneer versus Homesteader.** Who's responsible for bringing home the bacon? If you feel that you're the "captain of your own ship," and you need

to always pull your own financial weight, then you're a Pioneer. If you expect or will accept financial help and support from your partner or from other people, then you're a Homesteader.

This dimension is related to feelings about financial dependency. Traditionally, women have been the Homesteaders and men the Pioneers. Even though people are freer today than ever before to try out new roles, men are still more likely to feel responsible for their family's financial support, and women are still more likely to feel responsible for taking care of all the activities that take place in the home. There's still a lot of social pressure for both sexes to keep their traditional roles.

In a study by Riggs (1997) college students of both genders tended to view a woman as doing something positive when she risked financial security to stay home with her child, but they had negative feelings about men who did the same thing.

A secure, happy relationship can provide more leeway with these roles. For instance, a Pioneer might think that the Homesteader she or he lives with has an easier life and is taking advantage. Or a Homesteader might think that his/her Pioneer partner has all the control. But if, as a couple, you trust each other, you will be less worried about your partner taking advantage of you, and you are both freer to take on the roles and responsibilities that work best for each of you.

EXERCISE: DISCOVERING YOUR FINANCIAL PERSONALITY

This exercise will help you and your partner discover your financial personalities. Then, in the next three chapters, you'll find various problems and their solutions that accompany your particular styles.

Circle the T (for True) or the F (for False) in the following statements:

Spartan versus Monarch

I need luxury to feel comfortable.	T	**F**
I insist on buying high quality things.	T	**F**
It's important to look successful.	T	**F**
I enjoy having people wait on me.	T	**F**

Now, count the number of times you circled **F**, and then circle your Lifestyle type below:

> **Scoring:** 2 or fewer: **Monarch**
> 3 or more: **Spartan**

Gambler versus Banker

I'd rather run my own business than work for somebody else.	**T**	F
You can't be successful unless you take some chances.	**T**	F
I feel restless and bored if I'm not trying new ventures.	**T**	F
Being too conservative with money can cause financial problems.	**T**	F

I feel too nervous unless I have a job with a steady paycheck.   T **F**

I won't invest a lot of money if there's a chance I could lose some.   T **F**

I prefer a life with no surprises.   T **F**

"Slow and steady" really does win the race.   T **F**

Now, count the number of your responses that appear in **Boldface** type, and then circle your Risk-Taking style below:

> **Scoring:** 4 or fewer: **Banker**
>   5 or more: **Gambler**

Homesteader versus Pioneer

My partner tends to be more responsible than I am.   **T** F

I've never been very good at handling responsibility.   **T** F

I expect my partner to take care of me.   **T** F

I know my partner has more responsibility, so I try not to "rock the boat."   **T** F

I don't mind sacrificing, so my partner and/or family can live well.   **T** F

I'm willing to work as long and as hard as necessary to make ends meet.   **T** F

Seeing that bills are paid is more important to me than it is to my partner. **T** F

If we're having financial problems, I'm the one to solve them.   **T** F

Now, count the number of your responses in **Boldface** type, and then circle your Dependency type below:

> **Scoring:** 3 or fewer: **Pioneer**
>   4 or more: **Homesteader**

Now, do the same exercise to determine the parameters of your partner's financial personality. This will be more accurate and helpful if your partner answers the questions himself or herself. If your partner chooses not to answer these questions, you can fill it out for him or her. (Note that your responses for your partner may not always be the same as those that your partner might choose.)

EXERCISE: DISCOVERING YOUR PARTNER'S FINANCIAL PERSONALITY

Circle the T (for True) or the F (for False) in the following statements:

Spartan versus Monarch

I need luxury to feel comfortable.   T **F**

I insist on buying high quality things.   T **F**

It's important to look successful.   T **F**

I enjoy having people wait on me.   T **F**

Now, count the number of times your partner (or you answering for your partner) circled **F**, and then circle your partner's Lifestyle type below:

Scoring: 2 or fewer: **Monarch**
3 or more: Spartan

Gambler versus Banker

I'd rather run my own business than work for somebody else.	**T**	F
You can't be successful unless you take some chances.	**T**	F
I feel restless and bored If I'm not trying new ventures.	**T**	F
Being too conservative with money can cause financial problems.	**T**	F
I feel too nervous unless I have a job with a steady paycheck.	T	**F**
I won't invest a lot of money if there's a chance I could lose some.	T	**F**
I prefer a life with no surprises.	T	**F**
"Slow and steady" really does win the race.	T	**F**

Now, count the number of your partner's responses that appear in **Boldface** type, and then circle your partner's Risk Taking style below:

Scoring: 4 or fewer: **Banker**
5 or more: **Gambler**

Homesteader versus Pioneer

My partner tends to be more responsible than I am.	**T**	F
I've never been very good at handling responsibility.	**T**	F
I expect my partner to take care of me.	**T**	F
I know my partner has more responsibility, so I try not to "rock the boat."	**T**	F
I don't mind sacrificing so my partner and/or family can live well.	T	**F**
I'm willing to work as long and hard as necessary to make ends meet.	T	**F**
Seeing that bills are paid is more important to me than it is to my partner.	T	**F**
If we're having financial problems, I'm the one to solve them.	T	**F**

Now, count the number of your partner's responses in **Boldface** type, and then circle your partner's Dependency type below:

Scoring: 3 or fewer: **Pioneer**
4 or more: **Homesteader**

Now, summarize your own and your partner's financial personalities by circling the appropriate labels below:

You	**Your Partner**
Spartan/Monarch	Spartan/Monarch
Gambler/Banker	Gambler/Banker
Homesteader/Pioneer	Homesteader/Pioneer

When you complete this exercise, you will have gained useful information about your own and your partner's financial personality styles. This information can be a powerful tool. If and when you have an argument about money, understanding your different financial personality styles will help you to find and name the source of your conflict. You can also learn how to turn things around, so that the personality differences that cause problems actually can become an asset on your road to financial prosperity.

Here's a quick example to illustrate the value of understanding these personality parameters:

Suppose you're a Homesteader, and your partner is a Pioneer. In the worst-case situation, you may feel as if you're stuck with the all the "dirty work": staying at home taking care of the children, and doing the same old boring chores every day, while your partner goes out into the exciting world of business and commerce. Not only do you resent your partner for enjoying the prestige and status of a career, but you also resent the financial control that comes with this. Your partner, on the other hand, may feel as if he or she is shouldering the entire financial burden and all the responsibility, and that you are a dependent "hanger-on."

Now let's look at the same styles from a different perspective. I will take it as a given that you are both bright, competent people who respect and love each other. Let's also suppose that you've just had you're first child.

For many reasons, having someone stay home with the baby is a priority for both of you. If you're in a secure relationship, it makes great sense for the Homesteader to be the one primarily responsible for taking care of the baby and for the Pioneer to bring home the money. Both are difficult, valuable roles. The Pioneer will feel good about the baby's safety and development; the Homesteader can concentrate on child rearing and worry less about financial security.

The tradition in most societies has been for the man to be the Pioneer and the woman the Homesteader. But when two people are particularly secure about their relationship and themselves, they can reverse these roles, or can move back and forth between roles at different times.

In the next few chapters, you'll see how to best work together with your partner, in light of your different personality styles. You'll learn what problems to expect, and how to view your roles in ways that will improve your relationship and increase your potential for financial success.

One more comment about your test results. These simple tests were designed scientifically, and they are good measures of the way you deal with money. (See Appendix A for information about how the tests were developed.) But no test is perfect. Your test results can change over time. Also, extreme scores mean more than scores that are near the cut-off points. For example, if you score 0 on the Gambler-Banker scale, then you are more clearly a Banker than if you score 3.

Clearly, these tests can't possibly capture everything about your personality, life situation, and relationship. After reading the descriptions of the financial personality types, you might feel that you or your partner is somewhat different than the tests say you are. That's fine. If you score as a Gambler but feel that you're basically a Banker, then feel free to try some of the Banker exercises in the chapters that follow.

CHAPTER 5

Risk: The Gambler/Banker Dimension

CHAPTER GOAL: To make better financial decisions, given your own and your partner's tolerance for risk.

Risk and Caution: When to Hold and When to Fold

In the last chapter, you learned whether you and your partner were Gamblers or Bankers. That is, do you crave risk, or do you shun it? It's important to know that when I talk about gambling, I'm talking about taking reasonable, informed risks. Roulette tables and slot machines don't give you reasonable risks. The laws of chance tell you that the longer you play games like these, the less money you'll have. That's why casinos are so lavish and why their habitual visitors often look so sad and worn-out.

A *reasonable* gamble is one with the odds on your side. Investments in the stock market, education, real estate, and starting your own business can be, but aren't always, reasonable risks. One or two reasonable risks can catapult you to financial security, even wealth. But they can also mean disaster if the risks weren't as reasonable as you thought they were. That's why a Gambler personality and a Banker personality are sure to have some disagreements.

A Gambler and a Banker: Battle or Balance?

Carl was excited, if a bit impatient, as he went over the plan with Annette, his wife of three years. "Here's the idea. We take out a second mortgage on our house. That'll give us some seed money and show investors that we have something at stake in our new business. I'll hire a programmer to create the Web site. My old friend from college, Jim, can do the marketing. This could really be big. I think we're talking about the next Amazon.com or Yahoo."

Annette frowned and said, "Carl, I don't know. We don't have any experience with stuff like this. And if it doesn't work out, we lose our house. It would be great to have a lot of money, but I don't need to be rich. Can't we just go to work every day like everybody else and get our checks at the end of the week?"

"Annie, I saw my dad do that, year after year. It's like a slow death. The raises we get can barely keep up with inflation. I'm begging you, we've got to do this thing."

Clearly, Carl and Annette have different ideas about success, failure, and risk. Annette is perfectly comfortable going to work, saving a little, maintaining their current lifestyle, and moving ahead at a slow, steady pace. But, to her partner, this is like a "slow death," and is nearly intolerable.

If Carl does manage to convince Annette, he could pull her into an exciting, much more prosperous lifestyle. But there's also the chance that they might face a lot of hardship if their start-up business fails. Then Annette will feel angry and resentful, and wonder why she ever agreed to his dumb idea of taking out a second mortgage.

On the other hand, Annette could insist that Carl not go through with his plans. So they would keep their jobs and their slow, steady pace. But Carl might feel more and more resentment as the years go by. He may even hear about a friend who pursued a similar idea, and "hit it big." Then he will blame Annette for the missed opportunity.

How can Annette and Carl make a reasonable decision that both of them will be happy with? Doing the exercise below can help a Gambler and a Banker come to a decision together:

EXERCISE: FOR A GAMBLER AND A BANKER

Your partner, the Gambler, has an earthshaking idea, but you're not so sure about it. Or, perhaps you may be ready to plunge forward, but your partner, the Banker, is holding you back. By completing the exercise below, you can get a better notion about how realistic the Gambler's idea is. You might decide, at that point, to go along with your partner. If not, you'll have a better way to present your objections to your partner.

In the first step of this exercise, you must write down what the idea is. Try to be brief, and describe it in no more than a few sentences. You can write in the space provided below, or in a separate notebook.

The Idea

_____

_____

_____

What's your estimate of this idea's chances for success?

_____ Almost Certain (98% or more)

_____ Likely (Over 81–97%)

_____ Probably (51–80%)

_____ Maybe Not (21–50%)

_____ Probably Not (3%–20%)

_____ Almost None (2% or less)

If it is successful, how big will our gain be?

_____ Large (radical improvement in our lives, i.e., financial independence, reduced stress, greatly increased life satisfaction)

_____ Medium (some improvement in our lives, i.e., noticeably decreased work hours, increased income, or increased life satisfaction)

_____ Small (barely noticeable improvements)

If it fails, how big will our loss be?

_____ Large (financial problems, resulting in noticeable changes in lifestyle, increased work hours, reduced life satisfaction, stressful levels of debt)

_____ Medium (some problems, such as manageable and temporary debts, small and temporary increases in work hours)

_____ Small (barely noticeable changes)

After you complete this exercise, it is quite likely that there will be a number of areas where you disagree. For example, you may size up the risk differently. Gamblers tend to underestimate risk and Bankers tend to overestimate it. If this is the main point of contention, it would be helpful to gather some hard evidence. Do some research or find out about the experience of those who have tried to do what you want to try, or, if you can't find information precisely about what you want to try, try to gather information from those who have tried something similar.

You might have different ideas about what your life will look like if the idea succeeds, or fails. Again, you need to do careful research. If you're investing money, you cannot rely on what a salesperson or someone else with a vested interest will promise you about the proposed investment.

Even if you agree about the risks and benefits of the idea, you may still disagree about your final decision. A true Banker wants to eliminate almost all risk. So, even if the Banker agrees that the idea will (1) probably succeed, (2) success will bring modest gains, and (3) failure will bring barely noticeable problems, a Gambler and a Banker might still disagree about the wisdom of moving ahead with the idea.

Here are some of the issues to consider when weighing these decisions. What will be the eventual effect of many decisions like this over time? What are the chances that your life together will become very unpleasant or arrive at a point from which you couldn't recover? What are the chances your life together could greatly improve? Remember that reasonable risk is an important element of success, but that foolish risk can produce permanent problems.

A successful Banker/Gambler union takes work, but it can also be very stimulating and successful. They balance each other. The Gambler can prevent stagnation, and the Banker can guard against disasters that might be caused by being too impulsive.

Christina and Gary

Christina is fifty-six years old. She has a "Banker" financial personality. After thirty-five years of marriage, she has learned to work well with her "Gambler" husband, Gary. She describes their experiences this way:

"Money represents security and comfort to me. To my husband, it represents status and freedom. We argue about the debt we are carrying frequently. To me, all debt is an encumbrance and should be paid off as quickly as possible. To my husband, certain types of debt are good financial decisions.

"My family always took care of the bills first. Holidays and luxuries were saved for from the money that was left over, *after* bills were paid. We always lived within our means. My husband's family always put fun, luxury, vacations, new possessions way above the importance of paying bills. They always lived beyond their means, and were always trying to 'catch up.'

"Gary and I have overcome our differences by talking, arguing, making budgets, throwing them out, and then starting all over again. If I had not held my husband back at times, we would probably be financially ruined today. If I had not followed his lead in money matters at times, we would have missed out on many wonderful opportunities and life experiences."

Two Bankers: Playing It Close to the Vest

Two Bankers can get along quite well. The problem here is not in finding a point of agreement. The problem is that they wind up agreeing on very low-risk strategies, and, eventually, they may see many of their peers passing them by financially. This is a hard pattern to break out of, because it never seems to be a problem to them. They go to work every day, save a little money in the bank at fairly low interest, and have enough to cover their bills. But as they go through life, they see big differences between the people they went to school with and themselves. They discover that some of the people they used to know have moved so far up the economic ladder that they are no longer in the same class. The two Bankers might think that those people got "lucky breaks" or inherited money. This transition happens so gradually, and they are so hard working and conscientious, that it never occurs to them that there's something they could be doing differently.

If you and your partner are both Bankers, it's important to sit down together and analyze your financial strategies. If you're renting a home, talk about buying one. If your savings are all in fixed-interest investments, consider buying some stocks or other investments that offer a better return. If you've always worked for a salary, consider starting a business. Look at "Part II: Money Growing Strategies" to explore more fully how to introduce a *reasonable* amount of risk into your financial life.

EXERCISE: FOR TWO BANKERS

The following activities involve some financial risk but they have the potential for increasing your net worth over the long run. Next to each activity, rate your level of comfort. Then consider which activity you could actually put into action.

How willing would you be to do the following? (Rate the choices on a scale from 1 (Absolutely Not!) to 10 (Sounds Like a Great Idea!):

_____ Take some money out of savings (or start setting money aside), and make a long-term investment in carefully picked stocks, or some other reasonable investment that is not guaranteed to return a profit.

_____ Ask for a raise, or find another way to make your time worth more money.

_____ Start your own business, with the goal of eventually reducing or eliminating your salaried employment.

_____ Buy a home (if you don't yet own your own home).

_____ Other: _____

Now, look at the activity you ranked the highest. Get some input from your partner. Then complete the lines below:

I've decided to increase my financial risk for the prospect of long-term benefits. This is what I'll do: _____

_____

_____

This is what I'll do *this week* to begin working toward this goal: _____

_____

_____

The Perils of Two Gamblers

When two Gamblers work side by side or live together, it's always "life in the fast lane." Gamblers are always looking for a new challenge, and when two live and/or work together they often play off of each other, looking for higher mountains to climb, and taking bigger risks. Careful, calculated risks are one thing, but financial risks for the sake of excitement can lead to financial disasters. The key in this case is for both people to slow down and consider together each financial decision in terms risks, benefits, and long-term consequences.

If both you and your partner are Gamblers, the chances are good that there are some holes in your financial strategy. A financial hole is a risk that could end up causing you great financial hardship. Think about the way your financial life is arranged, and look carefully to see whether you have any holes.

If you or your partner were to have an injury or illness would there be serious financial problems because of lost work or medical bills? Could you get through a recession? Are you so dependent on a certain type of work or industry that things could quickly sour for you (remember the World Wide Web mania of the late nineties)?

EXERCISE: FOR TWO GAMBLERS

Financial holes, like a deep, long recession, or a lengthy illness, could swallow you up financially. To find out how secure your really are, put a check mark next to any potential problem areas or any that you're unsure of and need to look into:

_____ Not enough medical insurance to cover a severe illness or injury

_____ Not enough disability insurance to cover an extended time off work

_____ Not enough savings to cover emergencies

_____ Large amount of money in risky investments

_____ Unstable work situation

_____ Activities that are likely to result in lawsuits

_____ Other: _____

Look at the activities you checked. Get some input or further information from your partner. Then complete the following:

This is what I'll do *this week* to plug up my financial holes: _____

_____

"Calculated risks" can move you ahead financially. The devil is in making the right calculations. If you're too careful, you lose out on opportunities. Not just financial opportunities, but the opportunity to grow personally, learn new things, and meet new people. But if you stick your neck out too far, or take too many poorly thought-out risks, and you can end up losing the farm.

$ $ $ $ $

When you work these issues out with your partner, remember that usually there is no wrong or right approach when it comes to risk-taking. What's important is that both of you share your ideas and visions for the future. If there's risk involved, you both need to understand this. You both need to go into it with your eyes wide open, and you need to agree on what will happen if things don't work out as planned.

CHAPTER 6

Lifestyle: The Monarch/Spartan Dimension

CHAPTER GOAL: To learn how to develop a lifestyle that works for both of you, and to identify issues that underlie your arguments about money and spending.

Within Your Means ... or Just Plain Mean?

In chapter 3 you learned whether you and your partner were Spartans or Monarchs. For Spartans, the watchwords are "Live simply," but Monarchs crave luxury. As with any personality trait, it's all a matter of balance. Staying in balance instead of living in the extreme is always a good idea.

You may remember from Greek history that the people of Sparta emphasized discipline, self-denial, and simplicity. They shunned luxuries and leisure. Certainly, there's something to be said for this idea. If everyone worked hard and denied themselves luxuries, there would almost always be enough to go around. If credit cards had existed in ancient Greek, the Spartans probably would have scissored them all up. Or, at the very least, they would have paid off their balances at the end of every month.

But although thrift is considered a virtue, stinginess is not. At a certain point, self-denial and/or denying your family comfort or enjoyment stops making sense. Taken to the extreme, a Spartan lifestyle makes people irritable and diminishes their joy in living.

If a lifestyle based on scarcity causes chronic tension in your home, making all family members feel as though they are struggling over scant resources, then that lifestyle has crossed the line from "simple" to absurd. In fact, being too Spartan can actually cost money! You don't need to dine on steak and lobster every night, but being fanatical about cheap food can cause health problems and doctor bills. You don't have to drive a Rolls Royce, but driving an old, broken-down car can cause safety problems, unexpected repair bills, and time missed from work. The key is to find a point of balance, and make reasonable financial decisions that can work both in the short and long term.

Monarch Style

A Monarch craves luxury, and feels entitled to it. Of course, there's nothing wrong with treating yourself well. There might be a lot of things that you buy for yourself, your partner, or your family that aren't necessary but that enrich your lives. You might buy a cappuccino when your go to work every morning, and a massage at the end of every work week. You might subscribe to several magazines or to extra channels on cable TV. You might get extra features when you buy a car. None of these are necessities, but they all add pleasure to your life. However, when a Monarch's love for luxury begins causing problems for himself or herself, or for others, they can become tyrants.

Of course, lifestyle has a lot to do with income. But when personality styles are extreme, they don't change when the circumstances demand change. You can be practicing a Monarch lifestyle, even though you have very limited means, buying luxuries in preference to paying your rent, and begging, borrowing, and maybe even stealing to get the lifestyle you feel you deserve. Needless to say, a poor Monarch does not make a good friend or life partner.

Note that you can also be a wealthy Spartan. This is not a contradiction in terms. Wealthy Spartans are fanatical and live way below their means. They hoard old appliances, save soap chips, buy only secondhand clothing, and deny their families and themselves all conveniences and luxuries. As you can imagine, a wealthy Spartan is no joy to live with either.

Two Spartans: Live Simply

Two Spartans can have a peaceful life together. If you both agree to live simply and you're content with this lifestyle, it can be a relatively low-stress existence. Even two Spartans, however, can have problems and arguments about money. Either of the following two situations can set the stage for such an argument:

1. **The Church of Frugality:** Being a member of this church means being a world-class pennypincher. Frugality is raised to the status of a religion. Two true believers in one household may criticize each other constantly for spending too much money on nonnecessities. Statements like the following can fly back and forth:

   "I would never have spent that much money on something like that."

   "I don't know why you buy your lunch every day, when I make do with a peanut butter sandwich on day-old bread."

   "You bought that? Now I see where all the money goes."

2. **Living in Siberia:** In this situation, you both spend so little money that your lives have become oppressive. Even though you might both agree that it's good to live simply, if just on principle you deprive yourself of basic necessities and/or simple pleasures,

you're bound to start to feel resentful, and you may even start blaming each other for the poverty of your lives.

The exercises below will help you and your partner determine whether your Spartan lifestyles are in need of revision. If they are, these exercises will provide you with some ways to try to enact some positive changes:

EXERCISE: FOR TWO SPARTANS

The first step is to decide whether you and your partner are happy with your life as it is now. You can determine this by answering the questions below:

Part I: Is There a Problem?

Are you living in Siberia? Think about your standard of living, including your living situation (your home), your personal possessions, and recreational activities. How do you and your partner feel about your lifestyle? Put one checkmark under "Myself" and one under "My Partner." (Fill in the "My Partner" column based on what you know about your partner, or better yet, have your partner do it.)

Myself	My Partner	
_____	_____	Very satisfied. I have everything I want and need.
_____	_____	Satisfied. A few things could be better, but this is fine.
_____	_____	Mixed. It's okay for now, but I'd like to make some changes.
_____	_____	Dissatisfied. I can stand it, but things need to get better.
_____	_____	Very Dissatisfied. I don't think I can stand living like this.

Are you parishioners at the Church of Frugality? The next rating is quite simple. Even if you're happy with your lifestyle, do you play the game "More Frugal Than Thou" with your partner? Circle the appropriate answer below:

____ Yes ____ Sometimes ____ No   I criticize my partner for spending to much money.

____ Yes ____ Sometimes ____ No   My partner criticizes me for spending too much money.

Part II: Lifestyle Changes for Those Living in Siberia

If either or both of you is dissatisfied with your style of living, it's time to think of making some changes. The habits and routines that make up your frugal lifestyle can be classified into two groups:

1. *Activities that make sense:* Some of the things you do to save money may be very sensible. You can do things that don't take up much of your time, are not too inconvenient, and don't cause a lot of discomfort. For instance, perhaps you shop at discount stores, clip coupons in your spare time, turn out lights whenever you leave a room, and so on. There's no need to change these habits and routines; in fact, they may be very helpful to you.

2. *Senseless habits that die hard:* Some of the things you do to save money may not make sense anymore. You may be hanging on to old habits that are now causing more distress and inconvenience than they're worth. It's time to take inventory and to discard money-saving techniques that have outlived their usefulness.

To test the usefulness of a time-consuming money-saving technique, you need to place a value on your time. One way to do this is by looking at how much you earn for working. But you also can consider what your time is worth in other settings. You must weigh the money-saving activity against what you would do with your time if you were not spending it on the money-saving activity. Then, you have to consider which will add more to your long-term sense of well-being: doing something to save money or doing something else.

Frugal Living

Think about the things that you and your partner do to save money. Here are some examples:

- Buying cheap: Looking for special deals, shopping at discount stores, clipping coupons.

- Staying home: Not going out to movies, restaurants, or other activities you would enjoy.

- Doing-it-yourself: Doing housework, clerical work, home maintenance, or car repair yourselves, rather than hiring someone.

- Cutting down the use of utilities: Switching off lights, turning down heat, keeping down the phone bill, no (or minimal) cable TV.

These are all good money-saving ideas for some people some of the time. They may or may not be good for you. If car repair is your hobby, and your partner doesn't mind, then this may be a fine way to spend your time. But if you're like me, changing the car's oil is a four-hour, very dirty, unpleasant project, and I'd much rather pay an expert $19.95 to do it. If I spend those four hours with my wife, my son, or being paid to practice psychology, I feel much better, either because I have some extra money, have done something I'm good at, or because I've invested time in my family.

Here's a way to decide whether or not you want to keep practicing a money-saving activity:

Money-saving activity   Mowing the lawn myself.

How much do I save?   I would need to pay a gardener $40 per month.

How much does it cost?	*Time:* Including everything, preparation, clean-up, supplies, lawnmower maintenance. I use eight hours a month to do this.
	Actual expenses: $10 a month.
Hourly Wage Equivalent	I save $40 minus $10, or $30 per month. $30 for eight hours of work is $3.75 per hour. [This is how much you save by mowing the lawn. In other words, this is how much you are paid for this time.]

Value Added by Other Activities

1. I could work overtime. This would be no more or less enjoyable than mowing the lawn. After taxes, I would get $12 per hour.

2. I could have one whole extra day a month to spend with my partner. I'd enjoy this a lot and it would improve our relationship. It's hard to put a dollar value on this, but I'd say it would make me about as happy as having an extra $200 per month.

Conclusion: Hire someone to mow the lawn!

By carefully applying this exercise to the money-saving activities you engage in, you can decide which activities to continue and which to discard. Be sure to include all the time spent in money-saving activities. Also, be sure to consider any pleasure/and or non-financial benefits you receive from the money-saving activities versus other activities. Try to put a realistic value on the other things you might be doing. If you were writing a song, you might write, "One day spent playing with my child is a day worth all the riches in the world." But, since we live in the real world, you need to strike a balance, and you need to compare the benefits of spending time together against the benefits of financial stability.

Now, think of something you do to save money and put it to the test: fill in your answers in this workbook, or in your separate journal.

Money-saving Activity: _____

How much do I save? _____

How much does it cost? *Time:* _____

    Actual expenses: _____

Hourly Wage Equivalent: _____

Value Added by Other Activities:

    Money-earning activities: _____

    Other activities: _____

    Conclusion: _____

Two Monarchs: We Deserve It All!

Tania and John had come to me for counseling. They were drowning in deep waters, financially speaking, and needed some help. At our first session together, Tania said, "Of course, no one can live around here without borrowing money and using credit cards to the max." When Tania made this declaration, her husband, John, nodded in agreement. It didn't make sense to me then and still doesn't. But, when two Monarchs are together, it makes perfect sense to both of them.

Living Beyond Your Means

Living beyond your means is a strategy similar to getting drunk to forget your troubles. It starts out being fun, soon seems like a necessity, and eventually becomes a disaster. If you are both Monarchs, the risk is that you will live beyond your means because you value your present lifestyle over future security. As John put it, "I spend money whenever I've got it. If I didn't spend it on something I wanted, it would just end up disappearing anyway."

You are living beyond your means if you have increasing debt or dwindling savings. Sometimes, this occurs because of planned and temporary circumstances, such as going back to school, or staying home with a new baby. If that is the case, and you have a clear and reasonable plan for financial recovery, then there's little cause for concern. But what if your day-after-day and year-after-year routine is draining your financial resources more and more? Then, your dual-Monarch lifestyle is clearly headed for disaster.

EXERCISE: FOR TWO MONARCHS

Circle "Y" for Yes, or "N" for No

Y   N   For at least a year, our savings have been dwindling, and/or our debt has been increasing.

If you answered "Yes" to the statement above, then circle "Y" or "N" below.

Y   N   This was not caused by a temporary circumstance. We have no plan for financial recovery.

If you answered "Yes" to both questions above, you are on a dangerous financial path, perhaps you are even traveling on the road to ruin. Repairing your finances requires swift action. Your immediate task is to balance your expenses with your income. Start to develop your plan now. Follow the directions below:

1. On average, how much do you overspend each month? Think about how long your assets have been decreasing. Over this period of time, by how much has your debt increased and by how much have your savings decreased?

The calculations below are an example of how to do this. Rough estimates of your debt and savings are fine, but if you can dig up old credit card and bank account statements, you'll get a more accurate estimate of how your financial situation has changed over time. You may not have any money in savings, especially if you and your partner are true Monarchs. If this is the case, just examine the change in your debt over time, without including figures for savings.

Assets have been decreasing for: three years (36 months)

Over this period of time we have had:

Increased debt: $15,000

Reduced savings: $3,000

Average gap per month:

$15,000 plus $3,000 equals $18,000.

$18,000 divided by 36 equals **$500 per month.**

You can do a similar calculation with your numbers, and write in the figure below:

Our assets have been decreasing by $ _____ per month.

2. Now, fighting against your Monarchist instincts, decide how you will bite the bullet to make up your monthly shortfall. Note that you will need to save more than this amount to get back on the road to recovery. Remember, the more you can save, the faster your recovery will be.

   Here are some ways to think about saving more money:

   Do you have any options for increasing your income? Be sure to include any expenses (child care, transportation, meals) that are associated with increased income.

   We can increase our income by $ _____ per month.

   Do you have any relatively easy options for reducing your expenses? Think about what you pay for dining out, movies, vacations, cable TV, and other activities that are nice, but not essential. Write everything you can think of on a separate piece of paper, add them up, and estimate what your savings would be if you eliminated some of them from your monthly budget:

   We can reduce expenses by $ _____ per month.

   If your increased income and reduced expenses are sufficient to recover, then congratulations. You have diverted a disaster with relatively easy lifestyle changes.

   If this sum is not enough to make ends meet, then you have some more difficult decisions to make. Your options include the following relatively drastic measures:

   - Consider dealing aggressively with your debt load, through nonprofit credit counseling associations such as AmeriDebt (800-408-0044) or the Consumer Credit Counseling Association. These organizations will negotiate with credit card companies to work out a reasonable payment plan. They can also help you to prevent the problem from happening again. Bankruptcy can be considered as a last resort, but options such as credit counseling are often a better solution.

   - Lifestyle changes: Consider trading in your luxury cars for less expensive models. Think about buying a less expensive home in the same area, or moving to an area with a lower cost of living. Of course, these are radical solutions. But, remember, you are charting a financial course which will lead to an inevitable financial shipwreck. It is far better to make the changes now, before they are forced on you.

   At this point, it is essential to talk to your partner about what you've discovered about your finances, and figure out what the two of you are willing and able to do together. Write your plan below or in a separate journal:

_____

_____

_____

A Spartan and a Monarch: It Cost How Much?

As you might guess, this combination of money personalities causes more relationship problems than any other. For example, consider Maggie's story. Maggie is a forty-five-year-old Spartan who struggled unsuccessfully with her Monarch husband, Philip, for nine years.

> I was thirty-six and pregnant when I got married. I almost stayed single, and I could have raised my child on my own, but my values persuaded me to marry, so I could give my daughter her father's name. Before I married, I had always supported myself. I had two 401(k)s with about $13,000 in them. I had a new car that I made regular payments on, and a student loan that I was paying down slowly but surely. I also had a VISA card with a $5000 limit. I had a few thousand in savings and a checking account. I rented my home. I lived within my means, had good credit, and I was comfortable.
>
> After I married Philip, everything changed. I quit working because we both wanted me to stay at home to raise our daughter. Then he decided to go into business for himself—which he did. He insisted on doing everything in high style. Everything started to change.
>
> I look back on the last three and a half years, and I'll tell you, I wish I knew what happened to me. I co-signed for almost everything Philip wanted. I took all the funds out of my 401(k)s, which are now considered a gift to the marriage. It got to be too much for me to tolerate. I filed for a divorce last August, and am now trying to get everything back on track. I wish I knew what happened to my sense of self. Did I believe I wasn't entitled to more of a say about where my money was going since I wasn't working full-time? I honestly don't know the answer to that.
>
> I started working at two part-time jobs a couple of years ago. I think I was very depressed, but I was also trying to help my husband realize his dream, but his dream became my nightmare, and I am still trying to wake up, and get out from under it.

As previously stated, Monarchs and Spartans disagree about what constitutes a reasonable lifestyle and how their money should be spent. Remember, the Spartan values security and simplicity above all. The Monarch focuses on having the good life. The biggest mistake a Spartan can make is to become a tyrant about saving money, taking frugality to the point where it causes needless discomfort or an unnecessary sense of scarcity. The biggest mistake an unchecked Monarch can make is to focus exclusively on the present, without ever thinking ahead to the inevitable rainy days.

When there are bad feelings in a relationship, these Monarch/Spartan financial personality differences are used as weapons. The Spartan attacks the Monarch as self-indulgent and irresponsible; the Monarch attacks (or defends) by labeling the Spartan as stingy and withholding. Spending habits become the target for expressing anger and exercising control. The Monarch can always rant about how limiting spending causes intolerable hardships; the Spartan can always point an accusing finger at outrageous indulgences.

How Monarchs and Spartans Quarrel

In the heat of an argument, communication becomes distorted. You might start out with simple facts. But a conversation turns into an argument when the facts are given meanings that may or may not be accurate. Then, the facts are expressed in ways that hurt, because they are seen as evidence of all kinds of other failings. You can communicate more effectively if you can state the facts as facts and can separate them out from the other issues. Let's see how this works with Cecilia and Randy, a typical Spartan and Monarch:

Cecilia the Spartan

Facts: "My partner spends more than I would like him to. He buys things we don't need. I'm used to doing certain things to save money, and I can't get him to do any of those things."

Reasonable Assumptions: "My partner is used to a different lifestyle than I am. He didn't develop the same habits as I did when he was growing up, and it's hard to change habits."

Irrational Assumptions: "My partner doesn't care about our future. He only cares about himself. He doesn't care about what I want."

Underlying Issues: "I feel insecure about our relationship. I feel powerless. I wonder if he really cares about me."

Cecilia's facts get mixed up with her underlying issues and come out as irrational assumptions. She'd do much better to express the facts as facts, and her underlying issues as separate issues. Think about the different reaction you would have to the two statements below:

"I've been feeling insecure. Sometimes, I'm not sure if you really love me."

"You only care about yourself. You're like a spoiled little boy, buying your expensive toys all the time."

Randy the Monarch

Facts: "Cecilia complains a lot about the things I buy. I like nice things. We can afford them, and I'd be more comfortable if she stopped harping about my spending habits."

Reasonable Assumptions: "Cecilia was always worried about money growing up. She feels guilty about indulgences, but this has very little to do with our relationship. I know some wives who spend like crazy. I should be pleased that she's concerned about our future."

Irrational Assumptions: "She's trying to control me. She wants to march me around like I'm her little toy soldier. She doesn't want me to have any fun or pleasure."

Underlying Issues: "I hate having someone try to control me. It makes me feel like rebelling. It reminds me of my dad, who always acted like a drill sergeant."

By separating the facts from the underlying issues, Randy and Cecilia can have a much more productive conversation. Here's an example of how such a conversation might go:

Cecilia: Randy, we really need to talk about money.

[This is a good opening. It's neutral and prepares Randy for a discussion about this topic. Notice that Cecilia isn't accusing him of anything.]

Randy: [Sighs] Oh no. Not this again.

[Randy is bracing himself. He knows that every time this topic has come up in the past, it escalated into a go-for-the-jugular argument. Cecilia doesn't take the bait, and thus avoids an argument.]

Cecilia: No, I love you and don't want to argue. I'm not going to criticize you. I really just want to talk about my feelings about money.

Randy: Oh. Okay.

[This is something completely new for Randy. Cecilia caught him off guard. He was waiting for some finger-wagging attacks from her, and was getting ready to come back with a "You're not so great yourself" rebuttal. He's intrigued but still a little apprehensive.]

Cecilia: I've been thinking a lot about it. I've been fighting with you whenever you spend any money. I guess I've seemed pretty controlling. But when you start buying too many things, I start to feel insecure. I wonder if you love me?

Randy: I don't understand. Of course I love you. When I spend money, that has nothing to do with my feelings about you. They're completely unconnected.

[Randy is sincere at this point. He really doesn't understand what Cecilia is saying. This is Cecilia's opportunity to educate him. She's careful to explain that this is just her own perception. She doesn't get angry just because he doesn't understand right away. Remember from chapter 3 that men and women frequently express themselves differently from each other.]

Cecilia: That's the funny thing. In my mind they are connected. I guess it goes back to the way money was treated when I was growing up. There was never enough to go around, but my dad always seemed to have enough to get the kind of car he wanted or to buy fancy hunting equipment. Sometimes, he would get a new model car, when we kids needed school clothes. A lot of times it seemed like he didn't care about us.

Randy: You really have done some thinking about this. You have to understand that things are different now. We do have enough money to go around. You're just more of a saver than I am, and I'm used to a certain lifestyle. I love you to pieces. I wouldn't mind at all if you spent more money on yourself. In fact, I wish you would.

[There's the essence of their misunderstanding. Randy, the Monarch, thinks it's just a matter of spreading the wealth around. Cecilia wishes they could put more money into the bank.]

Cecilia: I know you wouldn't mind me spending more money, and I appreciate that. And I know part of my problem is due to my own insecurities. But I really do think that it's reasonable to have some kind of a buffer in case there are financial problems ahead. I think it's a good idea to put some money in savings.

[Cecilia provides a good balance in her statement above. She knows that she feels very intense emotions about spending, and some of that comes from her past. But she also knows that she has some reasonable ideas about money management that she wants Randy to consider.]

Randy: So what do you think we should do?

[When Cecilia discusses money issues in this way, Randy feels like her valued partner. He doesn't need to defend himself, and he is emotionally open to Cecilia's opinions.]

Cecilia: I'd like us to set some financial goals. I'd feel a lot better if we could work out a budget and plan on putting about two month's income into savings. We'd figure in discretionary money, so we'd both have money to spend on whatever we wanted. I don't want us to feel deprived, but I do want us to be able to handle any financial surprises that might come along.

Randy: I'm comfortable with that.

Irrational Assumptions and Underlying Issues

Examining your irrational assumptions and underlying issues is a powerful method for sorting out communication with your partner and getting it back on track. This method is particularly useful for Monarchs and Spartans because couples with these opposite financial styles are at high risk for misunderstandings. But you can apply it whenever you don't see eye to eye with your partner.

In all relationships, you're dealing not just with what's happening at the moment, but also with how your past experience colors the way you understand what's happening. This effect is magnified a hundredfold in intimate relationships. Because you know each other so well, and because you evoke such strong emotions in each other, everything you do takes on added meaning. You can barely scratch your nose without having an effect on your partner. That's why it's so important and helpful to figure out the irrational assumptions that you make about your partner's statements and actions and where those irrational assumptions come from. When you work on problems with your partner, you want to get the ghosts from the past out of the room. You're not dealing with the teacher who made you feel stupid, you're not dealing with a parent who nagged you, and you're not dealing with the boss who fired you. You're dealing with the person who is committed to a relationship with you, who wants to have a good life with you, but who also struggles with ghosts and irrational assumptions of his or her own.

EXERCISE: SORTING OUT THE ISSUES

Think about a recent disagreement you've had with your partner over spending money. In your argument, both of you probably had some reasonable positions. (After all, you wouldn't have chosen a completely irrational partner.) On the other hand, your argument probably was about a lot more than just money. The following exercise can help you to sort it all out. Go through the same process as Cecilia and Randy did:

Facts: These are cut and dried: What your partner did or does, and what you'd like to see happen. Write down the facts in the space below, or in a separate journal.

_____

_____

_____

Rational Assumptions: Forget about the underlying issues. You will deal with those separately. Remember that your partner's money style was probably around long before you were, and it is not necessarily a message to you. Now, write down some clearheaded assumptions about your partner's money habits:

_____

_____

_____

Irrational Assumptions: These are the things you say to your partner when you are mad about the facts of a particular issue. Try to separate out the irrational assumptions you might have made about the facts you described above.

_____

_____

_____

Underlying Issues: You may have to dig deep to get at these. Underlying issues can be found by asking yourself these questions: (1) What do your partner's money habits mean to you? (2) What do you think they say about your relationship? (3) What do your partner's money habits remind you of from your past? (4) What do you think (or fear) your partner's money habits might mean to your future together as a couple?

_____

_____

_____

The next time you talk to your partner about money, apply what you've learned from doing this exercise.

If you and your partner are both Monarchs, you like living in the fast lane. You may be headed for disaster, though. You both need to take a good look at your financial course, and make adjustments before the adjustments are forced on you by circumstances.

Two Spartans have a good chance of staying afloat financially—but you can drive each other crazy in the process. If you practice thrift as though it were a religion, there is no end to the creative criticisms you can come up with. It you find that you're haranguing each other over every penny spent, you need to start sorting out money-saving strategies that make sense from the strategies that serve only to control anxiety—or for you and your partner to control each other.

A Monarch and a Spartan can really make sparks fly. They are at the two extremes when it comes to ideas about lifestyle. If your partner's lifestyle ideas are quite different from yours, it's important to deal with these differences carefully. Because you and your partner have such different views about how to live, there's a lot of room for misunderstanding. By sorting through irrational assumptions (the assumptions that don't make sense, but that are triggered by your partner's behavior) and your underlying issues (past experiences that color your thinking now) you can talk about your differences and keep your relationship intact.

You can reread Cecilia's dialogue with Randy as a guide. Remember that real conversations are unpredictable, and that when you talk with your partner there are likely to be some twists and turns. But now that you've identified some of your underlying issues, and your rational and irrational assumptions about your partner's behavior, you can talk to your partner with a clearer head. Start out gently, in a way that will minimize defensiveness. Present what you wrote under "Facts" above: what your partner does and what you want to happen. Keep your rational assumptions in mind and don't give in to your irrational ones. As a rule, this is not a one-conversation process. It may take many conversations. Share what you've learned about yourself, explore these insights with your partner, and, if you both feel comfortable with this, encourage your partner to start exploring with you.

$ \quad $ \quad $ \quad $ \quad $

Decisions about lifestyle and spending can affect your financial survival and the quality of your life. By completing this chapter, you've learned how to strike a reasonable balance, and to understand what's behind your arguments over spending.

CHAPTER 7

Dependence: The Homesteader/Pioneer Dimension

CHAPTER GOAL: To learn how to deal effectively with problems associated with financial dependence and independence.

Financial dependence reflects your attitude about where your money should come from. If you feel you are primarily responsible for supplying the cash to take care of your own needs and those of your dependents, then you're a Pioneer. If you feel that most of your money should come from sources other than your own work, then you are a Homesteader.

Before money was invented, the work that one person did to make another person's life easier was more obvious. Thog did the hunting for the family, and his partner, Thogia, gathered the wild grains and berries that supplemented their food supply; she prepared the meal, and took care of their cave. Everyone's contribution to the household was out in the open.

When work is converted into money, and money is traded for possessions and services, matters start to become confusing. It's easier to hide where the money comes from, and where it goes. It becomes more difficult to figure out how much work, paid and unpaid, each person in a relationship is contributing and should contribute.

Work in and out of the Home: Who Does What?

It may seem to you that negotiating home and work responsibilities with your partner is more complicated today than it was for your parents. That's not just your imagination: There's more work to be done, and less time to do it. A study by the University of Michigan Institute for Social Research (New York Times 2002) found that women still handle the lion's share of housework: an average of twenty-seven hours per work week versus sixteen hours for men. On the bright side, these figures do show that more parity has been achieved than existed in 1965. The researchers found that in 1965, the ratio was women did forty hours of housework to men's twelve hours.

So what are women doing with those thirteen extra hours? According to the United States Bureau of Labor Statistics, in 1998, 51 percent of all married couples were both working; by the time you read this, the percentage will probably be higher. Taxes, real estate prices, health care costs, and other social changes in the past forty years have made it more and more difficult to support a family with only one partner's wages. So, at the same time that many women are out in the workforce making ends meet, they are also doing the grocery shopping, the laundry, the vacuuming, and driving the kids to soccer practice and the dentist.

These social changes have been confusing and frustrating for both men and women. Unpaid household labor is often more troublesome to track than paid work. No one keeps timecards to record the hours put in. A few spills or muddy feet can nullify hours of cleaning within minutes. Phone calls and doctor visits that "should" take minutes can stretch into hours, once you've navigated past the voice mail menus, receptionists, doctor's office paperwork, and other roadblocks to a smooth day.

Even though men are slowly coming to realize that they need to pitch in at home, this still remains a sensitive subject between genders. Men are working as much as they always did outside the home. They are also doing more housework, and they are having trouble understanding why their partners want even more time from them for the upkeep of their homes.

Women are trying to balance their work at home with their jobs in the work world, and they are feeling more exhausted than ever. There's no doubt that the pace of life has accelerated over the past few decades. Regardless of whether you and your partner are basically "Pioneers" or "Homesteaders," nowadays you're likely to be forced into roles that feel uncomfortable. Even if (I've heard this line from both men and women) you're just "not the type of person who likes housework" or you "don't like to worry about making a living," the chances are good that you'll have to share these roles with your partner. Negotiating a fair division of responsibilities and finding time to enjoy yourself and each other has become harder than it ever was in the past.

The Attitudes of Pioneers and Homesteaders

The old-fashioned, traditional arrangement had men as Pioneers, and women as Homesteaders. Although this has changed to some extent, housewives are still more common than house-husbands.

On the other hand, it is not unusual for women to earn more than their partners. Statistics from a report by Winkler (1998) showed that, in one-third of dual-career couples, the wives earned more than their husbands. Another study by Heckert, Nowak, and Snyder (1998) demonstrated that the divorce rate goes up when a wife earns more than her husband. It takes a particularly strong, secure relationship, and two responsible and secure people, to reverse the traditional arrangement between gender and work.

It's not better to be either a Homesteader or a Pioneer. The most important thing is for both partners to feel comfortable with their arrangement. Both should feel that they and their partner make contributions to the home that are valuable and valued. When each person's contributions are valued, this can lead to a very happy living arrangement. Unfortunately, too many couples are not comfortable with their arrangement, and some very destructive attitudes emerge when a Homesteader and a Pioneer quarrel about money.

Destructive Attitudes

Here are some examples of destructive attitudes held by Homesteaders and Pioneers:

George, a thirty-nine-year-old husband has a Pioneer personality. He summed up his attitude with these words: "I make the money and pay the bills. That gives me certain rights. It means that whatever I say goes! I call the shots! Work around the house, or earning some pin money with odd jobs, is just not the same as what I do. I have a career. I don't have choices. I can't take a nap in the middle of the day."

Enid, a twenty-two-year-old wife, has a Homesteader personality. She summed up her attitude like this: "My father always treated me like a princess, and I expect to be treated that way by my husband. Besides, I'm just not very good at dealing with responsibility. Men are our protectors; my job is to let my husband take care of me."

Charlie, a thirty-one-year old, is a cohabiting partner. He has a Homesteader personality, and this is how he summed up his attitude: "I could go out and earn a living, but that's just not what I'm about. Nelly pays the bills right now because I need more time for my acting career to get off the ground. I don't think Brad Pitt would waste his time washing dishes, and I'm not going to do that either.

Constructive Attitudes

The combination of a Pioneer and a Homesteader does not have to lead to destructive attitudes. Sometimes, healthy and constructive attitudes emerge when these two different money personality types live together. For example, Sally, is a twenty-nine-year-old with a Pioneer personality. She summed up her attitude this way:

> I have a big investment in my career as a book editor. I was very excited about getting this job, I'm good at it, and I expect to move up with this publisher. Bill is staying home with our four-year-old now. He loves being a house-husband. He doesn't like the pressure and competition of the business world. I'm grateful to him because I know our daughter is well taken care of. What's he's doing isn't any less important than what I'm doing. In the big scheme of things, it's probably more important. Sometimes the neighbors make catty comments about our arrangement, but that's just ignorance. I'm very happy with things the way they are and so is Bill.

My own research has demonstrated that Homesteaders are more likely to be Monarchs than Spartans. In other words, when people expect someone else to take care of the finances, they also expect a higher standard of living. This combination of high financial expectations and low personal contributions can be deadly to a relationship.

On the other hand, the Homesteader/Spartan combination has much more potential for happiness. For example, Regina is a Homesteader who sees herself as an equal partner. Although she is a stay-at-home mom, she takes responsibility for managing the household finances. Her husband is responsible for getting the bringing the money in, but she feels responsible for tracking it and using it wisely. Regina described how it works in her household:

> We kept separate accounts until our first child arrived. Then, we decided that since I was choosing to stay home with the kids, I would have the responsibility of managing our household finances. It has worked well for us. We are both frugal by nature, so I rarely get a surprise when the monthly statements come. When I mention low account figures to my husband, he listens to me, so we have never overdrawn our household checking account in the ten years we've had this arrangement. Trust plays a large part in how well this arrangement works. I think that money problems are caused by sticking your head in the sand and ignoring reality.

Two Pioneers: Shared Ambition, But Nobody's Home

Two-career couples have become increasingly common. To a large extent, this is due to the economic realities of modern-day life. Housing affordability, increased taxes, inflation, and other economic realities often make two careers a necessity for a household where the partners aspire to have "the good life."

When both partners are working to support the household, it is not necessarily the same as having two Pioneers in one household, however. Pioneers see themselves as having a primary obligation to earn money and to develop a career while they support themselves and their dependents. This is a quite a different mind-set from those who are working to provide extra money, or working temporarily in times of need.

There are certainly advantages when both partners see themselves as Pioneers. These advantages include the following:

- Less economic stress. Both partners share the economic responsibilities.

- Two careers can give a couple interesting and stimulating subjects to talk about with each other.

- More empathy for economic problems.

- Less potential for resentment over the other partner's spending.

But two working Pioneers in one household can also encounter problems:

- Some couples compete with each other. Studies have shown that marital problems are more likely to occur when a woman earns more than her husband does (Heckert, Snyder, and Nowak 1998).

- There's no one home to manage the household. This can be particularly difficult if there are children.

- There's less time and energy to spend together as a couple.

- When one partner is stressed at work, the other may be less able to provide emotional support.

EXERCISE: FOR TWO PIONEERS

If the two of you are Pioneer personalities, you must first decide whether your arrangement is causing problems. Put a checkmark next to any statement below with which you agree.

_____ Our career focus has drained too much time and energy from our relationship.

_____ I think that matters at home are neglected because of our focus on our careers.

_____ I find myself envying or competing with my partner's career success.

_____ I think my partner envies or competes with my career success.

If you didn't check any of the statements above, and these issues don't cause any problems for your partner, then, clearly, your Two Pioneer arrangement works. If there are big changes in your life, such as starting a family, your new responsibilities could create a need to reassess your situation. In such a case you might want to look at these questions again.

If you checked *any* of the statements above, then you have some work to do. You can approach these problems in two ways: change your thoughts or change your circumstances.

Changing your thoughts: As you discovered in chapter 2, the things you tell yourself about your situation can cause a great deal of distress. It's important to distinguish between problems that you can have an impact on by making changes in your life, and problems that are caused by distorted thoughts and resentment. Sometimes, you can change both your thoughts and your circumstances.

Here are some examples of the type of thoughts that might cause you distress:

"Our lives are nothing but work, there's no time for any enjoyment."

"I hardly know my partner anymore, it's just work, work, work."

"I feel like I'm going nowhere with my career, compared to my partner's success."

"I feel bad because my partner resents my success."

Now, write your own thought(s) here: _____

_____

_____

Next, you will rewrite your thought(s) so it can be more helpful to you and your partner. Here are some examples of more productive thoughts:

"We're working hard to build a future. Limited time makes the time we have together even more precious."

"I'm not competing with my partner's success, I'm sharing it. Some of her/his success comes directly from some of my ideas and encouragement."

Rewrite your thought(s) here: _____

_____

_____

Changing your situation: Sometimes you need to do more than just change your thoughts, you need to change your situation. Here are some examples of things you can do to change your situation:

- Hire help to take care of neglected tasks at home (this assumes you can comfortably afford to do this).

- Schedule time together for relaxation, recreation, and intimacy.

- Take action(s) to change your work situation to reduce stress or the number of hours you are on the job, to give your life and your relationship more balance.

- Work out a chore schedule with your partner to make sure that needed tasks get done.

- Talk to your partner about your competitive feelings.

Write down something you will change in your work life and/or home life: _____

_____

_____

Write down some of the details (i.e., times, specific details) about what you'll do: _____

_____

_____

Pioneer and Homesteader: A Delicate Balance of Power

A Pioneer and a Homesteader can create a very workable arrangement. Trust is the crucial element that makes this arrangement work well. Here are some of the reasons why this traditional arrangement works.

- Clear role definitions: one person brings the money in, the other manages the home.

- The partners' interests emphasize different issues, providing each other with more balance in their lives.

- Each partner experiences different types of stress, giving each the room to be both objective and supportive of the other's problems.

- Problems with running the home are less likely to be ignored.

- There is more time to spend together as a couple.

A Pioneer and a Homesteader view work and responsibility differently. The partner making most of the money might feel weighed down by responsibility, and resent the fact that the other person carries less of the financial burden. The partner taking care of the house and the kids might feel just as burdened, and might frequently complain, "I never get any help at home."

Here are some of the issues that can arise in a Pioneer/Homesteader arrangement:

- When only one partner brings in the money, there is often less money.

- One partner feels resentful or superior because she/he sees their role as more important than the other's.

- One partner feels resentful because she/he sees their role as more unpleasant than the other's.

EXERCISE: FOR A PIONEER AND A HOMESTEADER

If you're a Pioneer/Homesteader couple, you may or may not be having problems because of your money personalities. Put a checkmark next to any of the problems listed below that apply to you:

_____ I feel that my partner doesn't appreciate the work I do (either paid work or housework).

_____ I feel that I have too much financial responsibility and I wish my partner would share some of it.

_____ I feel that I have too much responsibility around the house, and I wish my partner would share some of it.

_____ I feel that what I do is less important than what my partner does.

_____ My partner thinks that what I do is less important than what he/she does.

If you didn't check any of the statements above, and none of these issues is a problem for your partner, then your Homesteader/Pioneer arrangement is working. If you checked anything above, you can approach these problems by changing your thoughts, changing your circumstances, or both.

Changing your thoughts: Here are some of the thoughts that you might have in a Pioneer/Homesteader partnership:

"I have all the responsibility, while my partner plays."

"What I do doesn't count for much, compared to what my partner does."

"My partner is taking advantage of me: what I do is a lot more stressful."

Write your own thought here: _____

_____

_____

Now, you will rewrite your thought so it's more rational. Here are some examples:

"I'm grateful for what my partner does. It helps both of us."

"My work is every bit as important. We function as a team and support each others' efforts."

"My partner experiences stress, too, just over different things. He's helped me deal with some very difficult matters, just like I've helped him."

Rewrite your thought in more rational language here: _____

_____

_____

Changing your situation: In addition to changing your thoughts, maybe you need to change your situation. Here are some examples of changing situations:

- The Homesteader can do some (or more) work outside the home, and hire or barter with someone to do the less pleasant tasks at home.

- Express appreciation for the work that your partner does. If you struggle a lot in your relationship, it may, at first, feel as if you are giving something up, or that your partner has "won." However, putting positive feelings into the relationship eventually will increase the positive feelings you get back.

- Switch roles occasionally with your partner.

- Take vacations and breaks together, seeing them as necessities that strengthen your relationship rather than luxuries you can do without.

Write down something you will change in your life to change your situation: _____

_____

_____

Write some details (times, specific details) about what you'll do to change some of your circumstances: _____

_____

_____

Two Homesteaders: The Responsibility Hot Potato

When two homesteaders live together, this forms the combination of money personalities with the greatest potential for problems. When neither partner feels responsible for bringing the money in, there's a vacuum. The result can be that someone from outside their home takes responsibility for them, or the couple accepts a very low standard of living. Either way, there's a potential for resentment and instability.

Jim and Betty, both in their twenties, were typical of a "double Homesteader" arrangement. They had a two-year-old daughter and were living with Jim's parents. Jim worked part-time in his father's store. Betty complained bitterly about the arrangement. "We can be in the middle of having sex, and his mom will call, and he jumps up and runs to her. This is ridiculous. We don't have any privacy at all."

Jim countered Betty's statement this way, "I'm just waiting for my dad's store to start doing more business. He's going to move me up to full-time then, and Betty and I will be able to afford our own place."

As with most double Homesteader couples, Jim and Betty viewed money as something that should come from other people or from lucky circumstances, like winning the lottery. Such couples usually end up resenting not only each other but also the people who help fill in the vacuum, i.e., by paying the rent, buying the groceries, or providing free child care.

But all of the struggle and resentment this couple goes through is often not enough to produce a change in their thinking. When neither partner is willing to take financial responsibility, often there are deeper problems, such as substance abuse or mental illness. I discuss problems like this in chapter 21, "When Self-Help Is Not Enough." However, on occasion, the problem stems from simple immaturity, and the belief that someone else should pick up the slack. The couple might be two people who saw marriage as a way out of financial responsibility, each expecting the other person to take over. Sometimes dual-Homesteader couples see their problems as external, and they start fighting with each other only when the going gets really rough.

EXERCISE: FOR TWO HOMESTEADERS

If you are both Homesteaders, you might find yourself thinking thoughts like these:

- People keep trying to control our lives, I wish they'd leave us alone.

- Other people have it a lot easier than we do.

- Other people have so much; they're being selfish when they refuse to share.

- I'll get out and make it on my own, when I get my lucky break.

- I wish my partner (or parents, friends, the government, etc.) would do something to help us out of this awful situation.

Write down any thoughts you have that are similar to these: _____

_____

_____

Here are two thoughts that can promote your own and your partner's success more effectively than the thoughts you may think habitually:

- I have control only over my own life and actions; I need to stop depending on others to make me successful or happy.

- I made this bargain some time in the past: less control over my life in exchange for less responsibility. I'm not happy with this bargain now, and I need to change.

Write down a similar thought that will start moving your life forward: _____

_____

_____

Write down a way in which you are willing to take on more financial responsibility. Think of a way that you can try to balance your financial needs better (your spending) with your financial responsibilities (your earnings). _____

_____

_____

Tell your partner about your plan to take on more responsibility, explain your goals, and see if he/she is willing to match or raise you.

$ \$ \quad \$ \quad \$ \quad \$ \quad \$ $

In this chapter you gained a better understanding of your own and your partner's expectations and beliefs about who is responsible for bringing the money into your household. When you know what each of you expects and believes, you can deal with the financial demands on your household as a united team. This knowledge also will enable you both to work on any resentments or disagreements you may have had about unequal responsibilities.

CHAPTER 8

Where Does the Money Come From?

CHAPTER GOAL: To learn about the three places you can find money, and how to maximize income without sacrificing happiness.

Your parents probably told you where money doesn't come from. Like many other parents in the world, they probably told you not to look for it growing on trees. As an aside, they might have mentioned that you could getting it by working hard. That's where financial education left off for many of us. Trees: no. Hard work: yes. However, work is only one of the three avenues that can provide you with money. And, if you're lucky and work things right, the work needn't be that hard. The two other places to get money from are love and risk.

Work

There's a lot to be said for getting money through work. It's dependable and respectable. In short spurts it might even be enjoyable. Frankly, though, if you expect work to always be enjoyable, you can get yourself into trouble. If you prepare well and are clever, you might be able to find paid employment along the lines of something you might do for free. But to make a career of it, you probably need to do more of it than you'd like, with people you wouldn't choose to work with, under circumstances that are not always appealing.

If you're like most people, most of your money comes from work. At some point, almost everyone realizes that their work "ain't all that grand" when it comes to the realities of the day-to-day grind.

Take Phil, for instance. He was a good student. He graduated from medical school at twenty-six, and, after completing his residency, he began his career as a family practitioner at the age of thirty. He is now thirty-six, married, and has a one-year-old son. He said:

> I remember wanting to be a doctor ever since I was in elementary school. It seemed like the greatest thing you could possibly do, using your knowledge and skill to help people get well. I also figured having a good income and prestige couldn't hurt either. But the reality isn't quite what I imagined it would be. I start work very early in the morning, and frequently I have to work evenings. When I'm not working, I'm on call. Most of the work is very routine, doing physicals, making referrals to specialists, writing prescriptions for antibiotics or analgesics.
>
> No one's all that impressed with physicians anymore. I really enjoy some of my patients, but some are angry and demanding, and can color my whole day with their negativity. Moreover, I have to worry about keeping up with my office expenses, billing different insurance companies, insurance audits, and malpractice liability. I feel like I'm scrambling just to keep up with expenses. The amount of paperwork I have to deal with sometimes seems overwhelming.
>
> I guess I need to keep it in perspective. I'm lucky to be able to do this sort of work, and I don't want to sound like a whiner. But, to tell the truth, a lot of what I do isn't all that exciting. Often, it feels dull and repetitive, and I wish I could spend more time watching my son grow up.

Faced with the reality of routine work, most people take one of two paths: they either look for an escape route, or they accept what they see as their grim fate. The Pioneers accept what they see as inevitable. They leap headlong into work, figuring that "as long as I've got a career, I might as well make the best of it." The Homesteaders often lament that they were very unlucky with their work experiences, and encountered one terrible work environment after another. As a result, they jump onto the first train out of the work depot that they see. Some dabble in one profitless business venture after another, while someone else, often a spouse or parent, picks up the financial slack and pays the bills.

A few people find another, much more satisfactory solution. They decide to actively manage their careers. This could mean lots of things. It could mean using their skills to run their own business instead of working for someone else. It might mean finding a niche that's uniquely satisfying, one that allows them to make use of their special talents and show those talents to the world. It could mean reviewing what they do during an average workday, and figuring out how to eliminate the scut work (the routine and or menial parts of their work) that makes it unpleasant. Believe it or not, it is often possible to eliminate the unpleasant parts of your work and just keep what you like to do. That way, you end up giving yourself a raise. This is because the things you like to do are probably the things for which you have a special talent. And talent has value.

Take a moment to think about the things you've done over the course of your work life, and what you do in the job you have now. Then fill out the lines below:

EXERCISE: MY PERFECT WORK SITUATION

In my job and/or career, these are the things I enjoy doing. (Be specific. For example, don't write a vague phrase like "helping people," but be specific, as in "helping people to create more beautiful living areas," or "helping people by fixing their computers"): _____

_____

_____

In my job and/or career, these are the things I dislike doing. (Again, be specific. Don't write just "paperwork," but "the paperwork involved in billing, and following up on unpaid accounts"): _____

_____

_____

In my perfect work situation, I would be doing the following things: _____

_____

_____

Now, consider how close or far away you are from your perfect work situation. Then look at chapter 15, "Work II: Creating Your Ideal Work Situation," to help you figure out how to get there.

Love-Money

Most of us get some money from love. If you continued your education after high school, and your parents footed some of the bill or provided you with a place to stay, you got a love dividend. You most likely didn't earn this money, it just came to you because of the important role you played in someone else's life. Marriage and inheritance are the two other traditional channels for love-money.

In fact, though, very few people will receive substantial amounts of money through inheritance. In the United States, 92 percent of the total population receive no inheritance at all, and less than 2 percent receive an inheritance worth more than $50,000 (Gokhale and Kotlikoff 2000). Note that for a typical middle-class family, $50,000 is not even the sum of one year's worth of work.

Other people become wealthy through marriage. Ivanna Trump and Jackie Onasis are two fairly recent classic examples. You can even find adult education classes in some schools that will teach you how to find and, hopefully, marry a rich man or woman.

Getting money through love is a tricky business; it often comes with a lot of emotional baggage attached. As a general rule, work rewards effort and talent fairly and impartially. This is not so with money gained through love. As a result, love-money leaves a lot of room for feelings of envy, jealousy, and resentment to arise.

Money inherited from parents after their death, or money given to adult children during their parents' lifetime may be viewed as a form of validation; as a measure of the parents' love and as a yardstick of how much they value their children. Furthermore, when money is bequeathed unequally, it may rekindle old feelings of rivalry.

I'm reminded of the story that Regina, one of my former clients, brought to her session. She came into my office sobbing, and I braced myself for a tragedy, but she announced, "I'm only going to inherit one house. My brother is getting two, but my parents are leaving me only one." She started to sob again with renewed vigor.

At the time, I was a newly licensed psychologist, living in a small condominium, and struggling to support a new family. I strongly experienced the dynamic process that psychoanalysts call "countertransference." Countertransference is the complex of feelings that a psychologist feels for the client in the course of therapy. In this case, what I was experiencing was negative countertransference. For most people, owning a house represents a lifetime of toil. Regina took what should be a very positive event—inheriting a house—and saw it as a cause for grief. She saw it as much more than just a house. She saw it as the yardstick of her parents' love for her, and compared to the love-money given to her brother, she came up short.

Love and Marriage

"Marrying rich" is an age-old method for climbing up the social ladder. You've undoubtedly heard the expression, "It's just as easy to marry a rich man as a poor man. So you might as well marry rich." This would make sense if money were the only ingredient that counted for achieving happiness, or if the dynamics in all relationships were the same, no matter what people brought to them. But neither of these statements is true.

Marrying is the pivotal decision in life. When two people choose each other, they are making a profound decision, and they're saying a lot about each other and about themselves. Both people are bringing something to the relationship and committing to each other because, among many other feelings, they feel that they're getting a good deal. Or, at least, the best deal they could get, compared to their other options.

So, when you marry someone with a lot more earning capacity or a lot more money than you have, you're expected to bring something to the relationship to make up the difference. That "something" might be physical beauty, youth, great charm, spirit, or wit, a willingness to keep your opinions to yourself, or a willingness to put up with a spouse that few others could endure.

In a marriage you're interdependent and have a lot of power over each other. You can bring each other a lot of happiness or you can plunge each other into a murky pool of misery. No amount of money can compensate for an unhappy marriage (you can argue this point, but I'm sticking with it). The greatest joy in life is to have a partner you love and respect as an equal; someone you can share your ideas with, feel close to, and build a future with. Your best shot at achieving lasting happiness is with someone you see as an equal.

For example, a study of lottery winners demonstrated that the winners felt happier only for a year or two after winning, but after some time passed, they settled back into feeling exactly the degree of happiness that they felt before they won the lottery (Brickman, Coates, and Janoff-Bulman 1978). Other studies show that the quality of your primary relationships is one of the main ingredients for happiness (Argyle 1998). So, what happens after the thrill of having lots of money wears off, and you're left with an unhappy relationship? If you marry just for money, the chances are good that you'll end up paying for it!

What's the bottom line with love-money? Inherited money is a happy bonus, although it's not something you should expect. If you try to win it by changing your behavior or relationship, you can end up disappointed and lose your self-respect in the bargain. It's the same with acquiring money by entering into a committed relationship. If you think that you can get more money by entering a relationship than you could get for the work you do, you may find yourself giving up more than you bargained for.

EXERCISE: DANGEROUS THOUGHTS ABOUT LOVE-MONEY

Listed below are some thoughts that people often have about love-money. These thoughts can cause a lot of unhappiness. Check any thought that you agree with—then read the discussion about what that thought entails, and what to do about it.

_____ **My parent (or someone else) tries to control me with his/her money.**

Being controlled by money is not unlike being used for sex. You go into the deal with ulterior motives, and it makes you angry that the other person was just as underhanded about his/her motives as you were. Being "controlled by money" means that you were trying to get money without much effort on your part, and you're frustrated that it's not as easy as you had hoped it would be.

When you let yourself be controlled by money (and letting yourself be controlled by money is the only way that this can happen), you risk resenting the person who has the money, and, more importantly, you lose respect for yourself. You would be better off developing your skills, making your lifestyle match what you can earn yourself, and letting go of your quest to weasel money out of Daddy (or Mommy, or Grandma) Warbucks. Try to imagine what you'd be doing to get money if this "controlling" person weren't in your life—and then do it.

_____ **Because of who I am (cultured, educated, good-looking, important, talented) I deserve a better lifestyle than I can earn for myself, and I expect someone else (like my spouse or lover) to make up the difference.**

The question is, what do you do once you find this other person? One of my clients, Edna, was a woman in her seventies. She had never had paid employment, but her recently deceased husband had been a hardworking professional who had provided a very comfortable lifestyle for her. Edna's every other sentence began with, "My husband was the type of man who. . ." and ended with a statement intended as an indictment, "didn't like to remodel the house," "was more loyal to his Army buddies than to his family," "worked twelve-hour days, and had very little time left over for me." As far as I could tell, none of her criticisms justified the intense anger she felt for him.

Edna made it clear that she felt cheated by life; that she had married beneath herself. Her other recurring statement made clear why she felt that way, "I was a *beautiful* woman, just beautiful." She described herself as a "bird in a gilded cage." This seemed quite apt to me. A loveless marriage, entered into for money, is very like a cage—or a prison.

The ability to earn money is not a trivial one. It is a free-market, unbiased evaluation of your skills and your willingness to apply yourself. If you believe your partner's ability to earn money is much greater than yours, you are admitting that, on this important dimension, you are not your partner's equal. This is an unpleasant thought to admit, so your mind is likely to juggle things around to make you feel better about yourself.

Like Edna, you can claim that you're superior in the ways that count. You can claim that your partner's moneymaking abilities are similar to the skills of a trained seal, and really don't matter much. You can even claim that you could have made lots of money yourself if only (choose one or more): you had been more materialistic, your ethical standards had been lower, or you'd been willing to give up what's really important in life. Do you see where all this is headed? Instead of a joyful, intimate relationship between equal partners, you now have a formula for anger, resentment, and unmet expectations.

You have the most potential for a happy, intimate relationship when you consider your partner as an equal, and you both respect each other's assets and abilities. Choosing the right partner gets you off to a good start. Once you're in a committed relationship, it's essential to respect your partner's abilities and assets, and to work to develop your own.

____ **I stand to inherit some money, and I'm depending on this to retire (or go back to school, start really living, do what I've always wanted to do, take off time to write a screenplay, etc.).**

Here, "depending on" is the key phrase. You've already decided that the money is yours; as far as you are concerned, your job is just to wait it out. But think about what happens while you're waiting. Other people are going on with their lives, while you have put your life on hold. And while you are waiting, your potential benefactor is spending "your" money. This person, perhaps an aged parent, aunt, or uncle, could serve as a valuable link to your past, and be a source of wisdom and comfort for you. Instead, you start monitoring this person's budget and resenting every pleasure he or she spends money on. You may even find yourself wishing that this person's death would come sooner rather than later.

Put your focus back on your own life. Waiting on someone else to die before you move ahead with your goals is a sure formula for resentment. The struggle to accomplish against difficult odds is an integral part of the process that leads to emotional growth and depth in people. If your desire is to write a screenplay (or any other big goal), and the desire doesn't burn strong enough so that you want to write it at night and on weekends, then an inheritance won't make any difference. It may even squelch your drive and creative fire.

____ **My parents have a responsibility to help me until I'm able to "get it together." or whenever I have unforeseen financial problems.**

If you hang onto this belief, you may never reach a time when you "have it together" or will be prepared for financial problems. Furthermore, if you remain a dependent child financially, your attitude can't help but bleed over into other relationships and situations.

Every time you're faced with a problem, you have a choice: you can solve it yourself, or you can find someone else to solve it for you. Solving a financial problem yourself may be uncomfortable. It may produce stress. You may have to wrack your brain to come up with solutions, you may have to deal with hardship, or have to work harder and longer. But every time you solve a problem yourself, you'll be strengthening your faith in your personal competence. And your faith will be justified, because you'll be learning invaluable skills for navigating through life.

Risk

At the beginning of this book, you discovered whether you and your partner are Gamblers or Bankers. You found out about how you feel about risk. It's possible to live decently with very little risk. You go to your job every day, put some money away, and at some point, you retire. But, as stated in chapter 4, most people who became wealthy took some risks to get there. Well-calculated risk can let you skip a few spaces on life's game board.

What's a "well-calculated" risk? OK, let's have a brief math lesson. Eyes front, stop fidgeting. I promise this will be quick.

In Las Vegas, some casinos boast that they have "loose" slot-machines. They use the word "loose" to suggest that their machines have trouble holding onto money, and will frequently dispense jackpots.

Some even tell you that they have payoffs like "98 percent." That means every time you put in a dollar, they'll give you back 98 cents. Great deal, huh? So, if you dump $10,000 into their "loose" one-armed bandit, they'll take only $200 of it. Of course, if you take the $9,800 you have left and put that in, too, and keep doing this all day long (while they ply you with free rum and Coke), you'll eventually lose it all. Now, you'll win a few times, and there might even be some moments when you have more than $10,000, but if you make a habit of gambling you'll end up losing it all, sooner or later. That's why the casino owners are much richer than most of the casino visitors.

On the other hand, if you could find a bet that returned 101 percent, you could make playing the slots your full-time job, and you'd soon be able to buy the casino. If you started with $100, and played the slot machine once a minute over a forty-hour week, you'd end up with more than two *trillion dollars*.

For the interested reader, the math works out like this:

Each bet increases your money by an average of one percent. In other words, it multiplies your money by 1.01. Betting every minute for forty hours is forty times sixty (minutes per hour) or 2400 bets. This means that the money you start with will be multiplied by 1.01 2400 times, or by 1.01 to the 2400th power, which equals 23.5 billion. So, if you start out with $100, $100 times $23.5 billion equals $2.35 trillion.

The trick is being able to tell the difference between 98-percent bets and 101-percent bets. A lot of times, the 98-percent bets look pretty good, because sometimes people come out ahead on them. Companies that sell special stock market systems on late-night television often rely on this fact: Some people make money with their system and are happy to give them glowing testimonials. But you don't hear from the losers.

Here are a few basic rules about risk:

- Good risks usually include more personal responsibility, control, and decision making. Examples are: owning your home rather than renting it, owning a business rather than working for someone else, investing in the stock market instead of a fixed-interest account, and getting more education.

- Even good risks can go bad. That's why they're risks. Whenever you make a risky decision, you need as much information as possible to make sure that it's at least a 101-percent bet. Risk for the sake of thrill and adventure is just that. Like putting money in a slot machine, it's a way to have fun, not a way to get rich.

- Take fewer risks when you have less time to recover. Take more risks when you'll have more time to get a return on your investment. For example, training and education makes more sense when you're young, and can get back your investment. Shifting retirement funds to more stable, fixed-interest investments makes sense when you're nearing retirement.

- Take risks within your comfort zone, or perhaps just a little beyond. If your investments cause you sleepless nights, you're too far out of your comfort zone.

Where Should You Find Your Money?

Here are the messages in this chapter to take home with you:

- Work is a reliable, honorable, and time-tested way to make money. But there's nothing wrong with working smart. Do everything you can to maximize the value of your work, and to reduce those parts of it that you don't like.

- During your lifetime you may get some love-money, i.e., money that comes to you because of a loving relationship that someone has with you. If you're fortunate enough for this to happen, be grateful and appreciative. But if you use love-money as a measure of your worth, or try to win it by ingratiating yourself, you're likely to be disappointed.

- Risk can help you to skip ahead a few spaces on the financial game board. But you need to choose bets carefully; choose bets that will come out in your favor, avoid risks that cause you to lose sleep, and pull in the reins as you get closer to retirement.

CHAPTER 9

Where Does the Money Go?

CHAPTER GOAL: To learn how to make informed lifestyle choices, those that construct solid foundations for the future.

Winged Money

Ever hear someone say, "I wonder where it all goes? or "Some days, my money seems to vanish into thin air." Probably we've all lamented the distressing fact that money just seems to evaporate. There are even seminars and costly programs that take advantage of our money-tracking difficulties. They tell us, "Think positive," and money will flow to us from the generous universe. On the other hand, they also tell us, if we allow negative thoughts into our consciousness, our money will sprout wings and seek out the pockets of all those positive people wearing smiley-face T-shirts.

Books like *The Millionaire Next Door* (Stanley and Danko 2000) make a simple but important point: many millionaires aren't that much better than we are at making money. They're just better at hanging on to it. When the "rich and famous" appear in magazines and on TV, we see their ostentatious lifestyles. The media keep confronting us with examples of what it means to be successful: owning beautiful objects, having a beautiful partner, and being beautiful yourself, even if it takes some surgical revision to get there.

Images like these can mess with your mind—and your wallet. If you don't make conscious choices about your lifestyle, you're likely to be swept up in the giddy, "shop-'til-you-drop" whirlwind of American consumerism.

Princes and Paupers

Most people fall into their lifestyle, they don't choose it. Your *baseline lifestyle* is what you experienced when you lived with your family; this becomes your point of comparison.

You might change this point of comparison as you grow up. For example, you see how some of your friends at school live—either more Spartan or more Monarch than the way your family lives. Eventually, you may see that your partner has different financial priorities than you do. But no matter where your life journey takes you, what you grew up with stays with you as a constant reference point.

That baseline lifestyle, the one you grew up with, becomes a "given." You probably don't think much about how it compares to other people in general, you just assume that's where you belong. If you do worse than your baseline lifestyle, you feel as if you've fallen short; if you do better, you feel that you're "making it." Here are two stories to show you how this works.

The Frustrated Construction Worker

Randy's father was a plumber. His parents were divorced when he was three years old. After the divorce, Randy's mother finished her college degree, and she remarried five years later. Her new husband was a physician. They lived in an upper middle-class suburb and had a lifestyle to match. Randy is now twenty-five. This is how he talks about his career:

> I tried college, but I just didn't fit in. I really like outdoor work. I guess I'm just not a book person. It's weird, 'cause my mom and stepdad are both well-educated, and they like to read. I've been working construction, but I don't seem to fit in there either. The guys I work with are crude. They cuss all the time, and they tease me about not being manly enough. I feel like I should have been a professional; that's what I'm used to. I'll probably never be able to afford the sorts of things I had when I was growing up. I'm doing good, honest work, but I just don't feel like I'm making it.

If he had had a different upbringing, Randy might feel fine about his career. But when his mother remarried, Randy's point of comparison changed.

The Happy Electrician

Now read Calvin's story. His career and level of success are almost identical to Randy's, but his point of comparison, his baseline, is different. Here's how he describes his life:

> It was crazy growing up with my mom. She had problems with drinking. With drugs too, I think, but she never did them in front of us. Anyway, we just had to move from place to place all the time to beat the rent and the bills. Sometimes, we were even homeless.
>
> I started working construction when I was seventeen, and I'm a journeyman electrician now. I'm making good money. My mom's doing better now, too. She's with a good man, and she feels bad about her past. I help her out with some money now and then, and I'm living good. I bought a car, and I'm saving for a down payment on a house. Things worked out great for me, I'm feeling really good about where I am.

Forget About the Joneses: Keep Up with Yourself

Randy and Calvin both ended up in more or less the same place in life on the economic ladder, but they feel very differently about where they are because of where they came from. The key is not to let your past define you, and not to let the people around you define you, either. If you compare yourself to that "whiz kid" you knew in school, you might easily feel that you haven't lived up to your potential. If you compare yourself to the guy who dropped out and got involved with drugs, you may feel that you've done pretty well.

People's lives are so complex that comparisons are meaningless. If you dig deep enough, you might discover that the whiz kid's life is littered with rocky relationships, and he is filled with self-doubt, even self-loathing. If you wait long enough, you might see the drug addict "failure" reform himself, and go on to achieve an exceptional level of personal depth and great success in a helping profession. As the saying goes, "It ain't over, 'til it's over."

You have certain talents and potential. There are probably things that you can do exceptionally well. Maybe your skills include making money, and maybe they don't. Or maybe you know how to make a lot of money, but you decide there are other things in life more important to you than the time and energy you would need to invest to make money.

As stated above, "Most people fall into a lifestyle instead of choosing it." Because of this, they may be haunted by feelings of failure because they don't measure up to where they think they should be, or they may always be scrambling to keep up. This is a trap into which you and your partner need not fall.

Choosy Humans Choose Happiness

Together with your partner, you can consciously choose a lifestyle. We make so many assumptions about the "right" lifestyle that this idea may sound silly to you. But think about the possibilities. What would it feel like to have a lifestyle where you had complete control over your finances, or where you could work only as much as you wanted to, or do only the things that you enjoy doing?

For a moment, stop thinking about the type of car you *should* drive. Perhaps you are drawn to a simpler lifestyle than the one you are currently living. Maybe you could simplify your life so that you wouldn't need a car at all! Maybe a bicycle and public transportation can satisfy your need for transport. (Now I've really gone off the deep end, haven't I?).

Or maybe you want to shift your thinking toward the other direction. *What if* you started that business, invested in real estate, temporarily took on more work, or wrote that screenplay you've always been thinking about? What would it look like if you imagined yourself and your partner "living large"? Imagine what your life would be like if you were extremely successful—a life in which you achieved all of your dreams.

In choosing a lifestyle, you're not making a decision about your value as a person. You're making a decision about what it is that you value. Valuing your free time more than earning a lot of money is a reasonable decision, one that says nothing about your value or your abilities. Living your life in a manner that matches your desire to earn money, and in a way that is a good fit with your abilities, is a reasonable and responsible way to live.

EXERCISE: LIFESTYLES OF THE HAPPY AND CONTENT

Chances are, you've never reviewed most of your assumptions about your lifestyle. By the time you were a teenager, you had a pretty good notion of what life was supposed to be like. In some areas, this turned options into necessities: that is, you felt as if you had to have certain possessions and had to live a certain way to measure up to your peers' lifestyles. On the other hand, these "options" may have limited you. You may have believed that certain things were out of your reach, or that you didn't deserve to have those certain things. But that was then, and this is now.

As an adult, you even may have stumbled into what seems like the perfect lifestyle for yourself. But, as perfect as it may seem, for *lasting* happiness you want to *choose* your lifestyle as a conscious decision, one that fits with your and your partner's values and desires.

Your current lifestyle decisions came from four sources:

1. Your history: what you grew up with, and how you have seen your friends and family living.

2. Your partner's history.

3. Your conscious, current decisions.

4. Your partner's conscious, current decisions.

The goal of this exercise is to encourage you to examine your assumptions about your lifestyle: that is, to make conscious choices. You've been riding the same train for so long, you may have forgotten that there are other trains, going in different directions, with different fares, and different amenities.

1. **Where You Came From:** Describe the lifestyle you grew up with. Were your parents struggling financially? Comfortable? Or did they seem well-off to you? How did you compare to others in your neighborhood or school? How did your family's lifestyle compare to the national average? Describe what you know about your partner's upbringing. Was it similar to yours? Did your partner's family have more or less money than your family?

_____

_____

_____

2. **Where You Expect to Be:** Now describe what you assume your lifestyle should be like. Most people assume it should be similar to what they grew up with. If your parents were professionals in a middle-class neighborhood, then that's likely to seem "right" to you. Do you assume your going to live about like your parents? Has your partner changed these ideas at all? Or have you come up with a picture that's completely different?

_____

_____

_____

3. **Where You Are Now.** Okay, what does your current lifestyle really look like? Maybe you're still struggling to reach what you described in step No. 2 above, maybe you're already there, or maybe you've exceeded it. Where are you compared to where you

assume you should be? Describe any feelings you have about where you are. Do you feel as if you're on track? That you've "made it"? Or that you've fallen short?

_____

_____

_____

4. **Where Your Dreams Could Take You.** This step is the important part of the exercise; it is also the fun part. You've reviewed where you came from, you've reviewed your ideas about where you're supposed to be, and you've described where you really are. Now, what if you threw out all of your preconceived notions? What if you stopped using your upbringing, your neighborhood, and your friends as points of reference? What if you and your partner rewrote your life stories? Think about where you'd live, how much and what kind of work you'd do, what you'd give up to get what you want that you don't have now. Keep yourself within the realm of reality, but describe a life that you really could have. Don't limit yourself by comparing yourself to others, or by your past.

_____

_____

_____

$ \quad $ \quad $ \quad $ \quad $

In this chapter, you began first to examine your assumptions about your lifestyle and then to free yourself from those assumptions. These may have been assumptions that controlled you and your partner without either of you ever knowing it. By examining your unspoken assumptions, you give yourself the freedom to explore new possibilities. In chapter 19, when you work on your financial plan, you will do this exercise again, in a way that focuses more closely on your specific financial situation.

CHAPTER 10

Your Money Circle

CHAPTER GOAL: To learn where you draw your financial boundaries, and how these "lines in the sand" affect your relationships.

The Circle Starts Out Small

Your money circle changes throughout your life. When you were an infant, you had no need for cash and no pockets to put it in. That blissful state didn't last too long. By the time you were three, you were beginning to understand that some things are yours, and some things belong to other people. This was quite an exciting concept when you first learned it. Even though you were smaller than the lumbering giants who surrounded you, you could declare your superiority in small, but imperial, ways by declaring ownership. You could clutch a nickel in your sticky little hand, loudly declare "Mine!," and it was yours.

In the years that followed, you learned to modify your concept of possession. The "Mine" routine annoyed your friends and brought out the worst in your siblings. A big part of kindergarten was learning to share. And ever since then, you've had to negotiate the boundary line between selfishness and generosity. If you're too selfish, others respond in kind, and you wind up losing friends. If you're too generous, there will always be people who will take advantage of you. By the time you were a teenager, you were still figuring out which people you could share with, under which conditions, and with what expectations.

Home Economics

By the time you've figured out whom to share with, whom to trust, and whom not to, you've arrived at your "Money Circle." Along the way, you undoubtedly noticed that money isn't too easy to come by, so you had to learn to be selective about whom you shared it with.

The concept of your "Money Circle" is intended to give you a way to picture your financial boundaries. All of us have invisible borders around our wallets and bank accounts. For some of us, the circle is small, including only ourselves. If this is the case, your money is just what you earn; other people's money is just what they earn. Events such as marriage, having children, and entering into other intimate relationships tend to expand the circle, allowing money to flow freely, without keeping track of who is earning what, and how much.

In early adulthood, most people just take care of themselves. As a young adult, you might buy a birthday gift for a friend, or spring for a dinner here and there, but your money is pretty much your own. But when you enter into a long-term, intimate relationship, it's a whole new ball game.

Misers Aren't That Much Fun to Live With, but They Sure Make Great Ancestors

If you and your sweetie choose to live together, you might start out by sharing the rent and other living expenses. Here is where the differences between your money style and your partner's will take on new significance. A financial style that might have seemed attractive at first looks different when it's affecting your own bank account.

Celia experienced just such a shift when she moved in with Paul, about eighteen months into their relationship. Here is her description of her rude awakening:

> When we first started dating, it was really exciting to go out with Paul. The way he spent money was something new to me. He always had to have the best—the best car, the best seats at the theater, the best clothes. He'd take me on trips; and we'd go to really expensive clubs and restaurants, and order anything we wanted. Spending like that was new to me, I was raised to count every penny. When I was with Paul, it was like I was learning to give up my old inhibitions, to be freer and not so worried about money, and about not having enough of it.
>
> When we moved in together, things changed, though. We opened a joint checking account and I found I couldn't stand the way he went through the money. I was used to always having a cushion, but he didn't mind spending everything, and letting the overdraft protection take care of it if he went over. We started fighting, and his extravagant spending was the subject of most of our fights. I think my parents went overboard with their thrifty ways, but I was beginning to see the wisdom in what they taught. It's one thing to feel free, and not worry about every dime. It's another thing to be reckless. And I could see that what Paul was doing wasn't going to bring us freedom; it was just reckless and stupid.

The next story describes a couple who were far more successful when they merged their separate financial styles.

Jeanette had kept a separate bank account for some time after she married Stephen, but when they had a child, it made sense to merge the accounts. Even though both partners are frugal by nature, they went through some real financial difficulties. Here is how Jeanette described it:

> We kept separate accounts until our first child arrived. Then, we decided that since I was going to be a stay-at-home mom, that I should take the responsibility of managing our finances. By and large, this worked well for us, since we are both frugal by nature so I rarely got a surprise when the monthly statements came. Stephen always listened to me if I said our account was low, so we've never had an overdrawn check in the account in the ten years that we've had this arrangement.
>
> Trust has played a large part in how well our arrangement works. When I first started taking responsibility for our finances, I kept accountant books so that we could both see where every penny was going. This meant having a budget in place for everything. We had to set money aside for gifts, winter fuel, insurance, taxes, and so on. One big benefit of our system is that our account balance is always above $1000, so we have the advantage of a bank account with no fees.
>
> The only time that money was ever an issue for us, and we had a lot of arguments then, was when Stephen was unemployed for one and a half years. He was laid off from his job in the recession of the early Nineties, and he decided to strike out on his own and start a small business with our savings. That business fell apart really fast. It was a very difficult time for both of us. Our stress levels were both going through the roof. Our arguments escalated to the point that we were blaming each other for the financial mess we were in.
>
> Well, Stephen finally found a new job, and we stood by our frugal ways, and we came out of that awful time with a new appreciation for financial security. Sticking your head in the sand and avoiding reality just causes more money problems. Stay 20–30 percent within your budget, and there will always be some surprise bill that will chew into your savings. But you will be much less stressed using those savings than maxing out your credit card.
>
> I think that some luck goes into achieving financial success, but it also takes a whole lot of personal willpower. I came from a family that had no savings and no equity, due to one parent always living on the edge. It is extremely stressful for kids to hear terrible arguments about money. It makes them feel terribly insecure. We are providing security and stability for our children and, hopefully, for their children.

An intimate, long-term, committed relationship will force you to bend and reshape your ideas about money. Sometimes, you luck out and you find someone who matches your financial style. If this is the case, consider yourself one of the fortunate few. Usually, you and your partner will handle money differently. If that is the case, then, you're faced with three choices:

1. Change the way you think about money, so your way of thinking is more in line with your partner's attitudes.

2. Change your partner (good luck!).

3. Work out a compromise arrangement that both of you can live with.

There are two other possibilities: silently simmer or endlessly bicker, but these are not on my list of good ideas.

And Baby Makes Three

Having a child is one of life's most profound experiences. It's like stepping through Alice's looking glass to Wonderland. Having a child changes the way you see yourself, your work, and your relationships. Furthermore, it will produce the last big change in your money circle.

A new baby does a lot of work to get you used to your new role. She (or he) will be relentlessly insistent about getting her needs met. If you do things right, you're rewarded with smiles, cooing, and cuddling. If you do things wrong, or neglect your child care duties, retribution is swift. Your ears (and your heart) will be assaulted with heart-rending screaming and crying, and the baby's look of horrible consternation will consume you with guilt.

So, through your baby's hard work, your partner's admonitions, and your own feeling of love for your child, your money circle is given a new shape and size, big enough to include your progeny.

How you include your children in your money circle starts out pretty simply for responsible parents. The baby needs something and you go out and get it. You either buy it, or someone with a small child has what you need and is glad to give it to you, because their baby has outgrown it.

As your baby grows from infancy to adulthood, however, more and more subtleties and decisions about how to include your child in your money circle will arise.

Children and Money

The things you teach your children about money are among the most important lessons they'll learn in life. Their knowledge about money will affect their future standard of living, the quality of their relationships, and it may be passed down for generations to come.

Early on, your money decisions about your baby are just between you and your partner. As long as your baby is comfortable, she really won't care whether her stroller or outfits have brand names. But during your child's infancy and toddler years, you set the stage for how you will include the baby in your money circle.

Not too long after learning how to talk, your child will learn something about money. At the very least, she will know that you have some, and that it is used for such delights as balloons, candies, and ice cream. Most kids quickly figure out what behaviors are needed to get you to spend it according to their preferences.

The money you spend on your children can be divided into three areas:

1. There are the things that you get for your children because you're a responsible parent. You provide food, clothing, shelter, and an education for them. As for the education, you have a wide range of discretion here. There are fancy and plain clothes, private and public schools. What you get for your children will reflect your own financial status, your ideas about spending money, and the things you want to teach your children. Your kids will become accustomed to your lifestyle, and, hopefully, you'll teach them what they need to know to attain that lifestyle for themselves eventually, or better yet, to better it.

2. There are things you get for your kids for no reason in particular. These are the things they don't need, and that they don't do anything specific to earn. Such things include

toys and treats. Toys and treats can make them happy, and seeing them happy makes you happy. Giving kids treats (in moderation) is a way to express your love, and it gives them a sense of security and of being valued, but it also gets them used to a certain lifestyle.

3. Then there are the things that you get for your children based on their behavior. These items are a crucial part of your children's financial education. When your toddler screams for candy in the supermarket checkout line, and you cave in and buy it, you've taught the child an important lesson. The child will have successfully used what psychologists call "negative reinforcement" on you. That is, you stop something unpleasant (your child's screaming), if you do what the kid wants you to do—buy candy. If you project ahead a few years, you may think twice about buying that candy.

Imagine a teenager insisting that you must buy him a BMW ("but everyone else drives a 'Beemer' to school, Dad. Do you want the other kids to laugh at me?"), or a thirty-year-old whining for rent money because he hasn't managed to find a steady job for the last five years. (Just writing that makes me feel queasy.) On the other hand, giving money and other rewards to children based on their *good* behavior can be a valuable way to teach them about the relation between work and money. Completing chores, taking the initiative, and showing a positive attitude are, most likely, the behaviors you want to reward in your children.

How you deal with your children's money will affect not only them, but also their children. In fact, what your children learn from your example may be passed on for several generations.

Anne, a married, fifty-four-year-old woman, described how her parents catered to her financial irresponsibility when she was young, and how, decades later, she wants to rescue her adult children from similarly irresponsible habits:

I had to unlearn a lot of what I learned about money when I was growing up. My parents didn't have much money when I was a child, but they were generous with what they did have. When I got into college I didn't know much about managing money, and my parents covered my overdrafts. So I deal with our kids the way my parents dealt with me. It's a lot different from the way my husband deals with them.

I believe that finances are a source of contention for every couple. My spouse is very good with money. He saves, he invests, he pays bills on time. He thinks through purchasing items—that is, he plans for them and sets money aside. I, on the other hand, buy at a whim. I am impulsive, and want what I want when I want it. One part of our recent arguments has to do with giving money to our college-age children, and bailing them out of their financial mishaps. I am willing to part with our last penny to help our children out, but my husband says they need to learn responsibility and they can't come running to us each time they are broke. Theoretically, I agree with him; however, I still give them money, or I badger him into giving them some.

When my husband served in Korea for a year with the military, I wrote checks like there was no tomorrow. It took me four years to get our finances back in order. I had to go to consumer credit counseling, have my bank balance my checkbook, and take an allowance from my husband. I felt terrible that I messed up that way, but I did pay off all the debts I accrued, and I took a money management class and now I am doing well.

I still have spendthrift impulses, but they are in control. The key to financial success is planning, setting aside the money for what you want, and, most of all, talking about finances. Every little bit helps.

This kind of situation can become even more complicated when the kids are stepkids. This is what Mayryl, a forty-three-year-old computer engineer, had to say about the situation with her husband:

We fight mostly about giving gifts to my stepdaughter. He wants to buy very expensive gifts for her to make up for his guilt about leaving his former wife. He admits that, in this area, he is overcompensating.

Raising children is the most challenging task you'll ever share with another person. It will continue for at least twenty years, even if your relationship with your partner doesn't survive. Teaching your children to be responsible with money makes the difference between "a job well done," allowing you to send them out into the world as self-sufficient adults, and a job that never ends.

EXERCISE: MAPPING YOUR MONEY CIRCLE

This exercise will help you and your partner see where each other's financial boundaries are drawn. Many different kinds of arrangements can work. For instance, some couples draw a financial boundary line by keeping separate bank accounts for their personal expenses, while sharing joint expenses, like the rent. The most important thing is to work together with your partner, so that your financial circles work well together. If your boundaries are very different from your partner's, you're bound to have disagreements.

As always, your partner can complete his or her own chart, or you can complete it for your partner. Now, take your pencil and darkly shade any area of the circle where your money flows freely, i.e., where you have complete trust. The areas you shade reflect people who don't need to ask you for money, and who don't earn it—your money is their money. Perhaps there isn't anyone else whom you trust so completely. If that's the case, you will just shade the "Me" area.

Next, lightly shade areas where you have flexible boundaries. Sometimes you would give this person (or people) money, or they might give you money, but not without conditions. You might describe these people as dependent on you or you on them. Or money might flow back and forth between the two of you, making you interdependent.

You can use different shades on your chart to show different levels of interdependence. People whom you never exchange money with (except to pay fair-market value for their work or to give them small gifts) would be left unshaded on the chart.

Understanding your charts: *There is no ideal chart.* Your boundaries change over the course of your life, depending on the type and stage of your relationships. Doing this exercise will give you a better picture of how you and your partner see things. It also can give you a better understanding of the source of some of your money-related arguments.

For example, your partner might think and say that there should be no boundary lines drawn between your money and his or her money. But if that is really the case, then your partner has no business being surprised when you become upset about the purchase of a $2,000 stereo system without your knowledge. Or your partner's boundary line with friends may be more fluid than yours is, and your partner can't understand why you'd

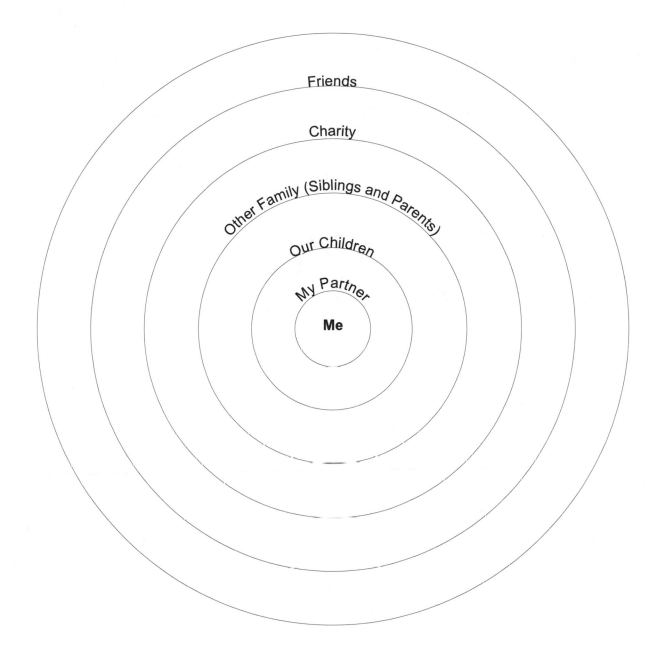

Figure 10.1A: Your Money Circle

object to his or her generosity. Note that very few couples are comfortable with completely fluid financial boundaries between themselves. At the very least, you probably need to talk about big-money decisions before making any by yourself.

Your money circle charts are just a starting point for further discussion. They'll give you some insight into some of the frustrating or confusing money decisions that your partner makes. They will also help you and your partner decide whether looser or tighter boundaries might work better for the two of you.

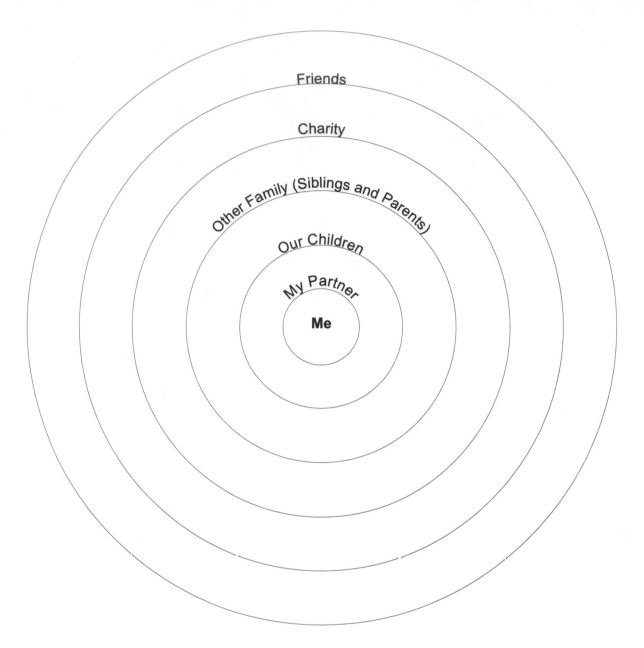

Figure 10.1B: Your Partner's Money Circle

EXERCISE: CHILDREN AND MONEY

There's no "standard" good way to deal with money and kids. The following exercise will help you and your partner understand where you stand on this important and confusing issue. Moreover, today, more and more people are forming blended families, where one or both partners have children from a previous marriage. This situation can be a real setup for some nasty arguments about spending, since there's always the fear, felt by both parents and their children, that the biological children of one parent will be favored over the stepchildren of the other parent.

Whether kids are in your future, you're raising them now, or you've already launched them into the wider world, it's important to have a clear idea of what you consider your financial limits and responsibilities, as parents, to be. Unless you and your partner are quite sure that you'll never have any children, doing this exercise will be helpful for you.

Babies (Before They Can Walk and Talk)

What's your policy on getting things for your baby? Check the statement that is the closest fit with your attitude. Then have your partner do this, or fill in the blanks depending on your knowledge of how your partner would answer.

	Me	My Partner
My baby gets the best of everything: the luxury stroller, newest toys, a great crib.	_____	_____
I want to find a reasonable middle ground. I want nice things for my baby, but I don't want to break the bank.	_____	_____
Hand-me-downs are fine. A baby cares more about being loved than about wearing name brands.	_____	_____

Comments: If you're going all out for your baby, that's fine. It's natural to want the best for your baby. But make sure you aren't paying for material goods by sacrificing time or the baby's college fund. If you and your partner disagree here, you'd better resolve this issue before you go much further. The discrepancies will only get larger as your baby grows.

Childhood and Adolescence: Lifestyle

	Me	My Partner
I want my child to have the very best that we can buy in every area.	_____	_____
I want a modest lifestyle for my child; I want her to have some nice things, but nothing too fancy.	_____	_____
I think it's best that my child has the minimum and learns early that money doesn't grow on trees.	_____	_____

Comments: Again, it's important to figure out a level with which you and your partner are comfortable. Remember that you're teaching your children about what life is like. Making life seem luxurious can lead to some unhappy surprises when they're grown. If they can't earn the same kind of lifestyle you provided when they were young, there's the risk that they will feel like failures, or drive their spouses crazy with their demands. On the other hand, you don't want them to remembering their childhood as if it had been a sentence at boot camp.

Childhood and Adolescence: Contingencies

	Me	My Partner
If my kids want something, I'll get it for them, if I can. I don't expect them to work for "pin money" allowances, or treats like comic books, action figures, records, or movies.	_____	_____
I'll give my kids some extras, but I expect them to do some work, too. A part-time job for a teenager is great preparation for the future.	_____	_____
There are no free rides in life. If my kids want something, they have to earn it.	_____	_____

Comments: To be sure, when you have kids, there are a lot of details to be worked out that aren't covered above. What chores will you expect your kids to do, at what age? How many hours is it reasonable to work at a job? Do you expect you children to help with their college expenses? Striking a balance is essential.

If life is too easy, that first low-wage job will seem pointless. But don't give your seven-year-old the fear that he'll be homeless if he doesn't get his chores finished before supper. You and your partner should figure out what you're both comfortable with. Then, when you're in agreement, and when your kids are of a suitable age to understand such matters, you should both discuss your financial arrangements with your children.

Adult Children: Contingencies

For our purposes, the typical age in our society to call a person an adult is somewhere around twenty-two, give or take a year in either direction. This allows for four years after graduating from high school to attend college, or otherwise get established in the adult world.

	Me	My Partner
If I have the money, I'll get my kids whatever they need. I'll always help out my children financially if they need it.	_____	_____
I'll provide my grown kids with a place to stay or extra money in emergencies, but only after setting clear limits and conditions.	_____	_____
This is what I'll tell my grown kids: "Once you're grown, you're on your own."	_____	_____

Comments: It's a fact of human nature that there will be more "emergencies" and unexpected problems if there's a safety net that adult children can depend on to cover their problems. The transition between adolescence and adulthood is one of the most treacherous phases of child rearing. Grown children can present enormously complex and difficult problems to their parents. It's important for you and your partner to decide what your boundaries with your adult children will be *before* problems occur, and to let the big kids know what you are and aren't willing to do.

$ $ $ $ $

Your financial boundaries or "Money Circle" changes throughout your life. Entering into a marriage or other intimate partnership and having children are the two big events that can dramatically change your boundaries. Arguments can arise over misunderstandings about these boundaries. By defining your own and your partner's Money Circle, you can come to a better understanding about how money affects your relationship with your partner and other important people in your life.

CHAPTER 11

Your Financial Life Path

CHAPTER GOAL: To discover the roots of your financial beliefs, and learn how to challenge unwanted ghosts from the past.

Carl and Chelsea: Different Pasts, Different Expectations

Thirty-two-year-old Carl had been married to Chelsea for five years. She was twenty-eight. They had two children, one two-year-old and a four-year-old. Lately, they had been arguing about money a lot, and their arguments had brought them to see me for counseling.

In my office, Carl leaned forward and spoke to me in a soft, almost conspiratorial tone. He said, "What my wife doesn't understand is that we have to plan for the future. We have the retirement fund, a separate account for college money for the kids, and we're saving for the down payment on a house. If only Chelsea would be patient, things will get a lot easier in a few years."

In contrast to Carl's cool demeanor, Chelsea was visibly upset. I could see the anger she was holding in, and hear the anger and frustration in her voice, when she exploded with, "When do we get to live our lives? We can't go out to eat. We never go to the movies. I can't buy anything for myself, all the money has to go to one of our accounts. But retirement may never come! We could drop dead at fifty—and what could we do with the money then? And he's always working. The kids and I never see him. When are we ever going to have some time to be a family?"

Clearly, Carl and Chelsea had different viewpoints as to the financial trajectories their lives should follow. If he were to plot it on a graph, Carl saw the graph with the line that represented their finances gradually inclining upward. He believed that self-denial now leads to satisfaction later. So, in accord with his belief, he accentuates their future needs over their present desires.

Chelsea, on the other hand, feels that their life together now is a nearly intolerable exercise in self-deprivation. She believes their future should be a continuation of what she had always known. Before she married Carl, she pictured her financial future as always moving upward in a straight line, continuing the comfortable life she had grown up with in her parents' home.

She felt it was unacceptable for the line to dip below what she had known in her past. Yet that's what Carl was proposing: to start out way below the level of comfort that she had come to expect. She had her doubts about their lifestyle ever improving. Even if it did, she believed that it would be "too little, too late."

Because Chelsea and Carl were following different scripts for their financial future, each saw the other as unreasonable.

Where Did They Get Their Ideas?

How did Carl and Chelsea develop such different points of view concerning their mutual finances? Much of the difference can be explained by their personal histories. Carl's parents had been in their early twenties when he was born. He remembered them as being very frugal when he was a youngster. They frequently admonished him to save his money and always look to the future. Throughout their lives they promoted thrift as a virtue, and played down the importance of outward appearances. By the time Carl was a teenager, his parents had, in fact, established financial stability for themselves. They had substantial savings, home equity, and a comfortable lifestyle.

Chelsea was the youngest of three children. When she was born, her parents were already middle-aged, and well established in their community. Her mother was a home-maker, comfortable in her role, and her father owned a furniture store which did well. There was not much talk about money in her home, but there always was enough for everything that was needed, and for some luxuries, too.

After graduating from college, Carl had moved into a small apartment where he took pride in living modestly, working hard, and accumulating savings and investments. Chelsea, on the other hand, remained at home with her parents after college graduation. She worked part-time, and, with her parents' help, maintained the lifestyle that she had known all her life. After the couple married, Chelsea had experienced a much more dramatic shift in her lifestyle than Carl. He simply continued his save-and-build strategy.

For the first time in her life, Chelsea had to rein in her spending habits. Whenever they quarreled about money (and their quarrels were always about money), she had the uneasy feeling that her marriage was in danger.

Gaining Insight

In the course of therapy, Carl and Chelsea became aware of several key issues. Both had expectations about the future that were based on their pasts. Now, all of us try to learn from and be guided by our past experiences; there's nothing wrong with that, and it's often a good strategy. However, too often, our internal scripts, which are laid down by our histories—our past experiences—guide us unconsciously and are seen as unchangeable reality. To change their internal scripts, Chelsea and Carl were encouraged to work on the following steps. You, too, can study these steps and do them, first by yourself and then with your partner.

- Become aware of how your individual histories shaped your beliefs about your financial futures.

- Talk about your different financial pasts with each other.

- Talk about how your pasts influenced your thinking about your financial futures.

- Discuss what was useful and valuable about reviewing your financial histories. Carl was challenged to find the value in Chelsea's financial views, and Chelsea was challenged to see the benefits in Carl's way of thinking.

- Discuss your common goals and where they differ; for example, financial security versus a comfortable lifestyle now.

- Discuss with each other what you want to change or modify about your financial beliefs.

- Discuss your plans for implementing the changes you and your partner decide to make in your day-to-day lives.

Plotting Your Financial Trajectories

Much of your financial behavior is controlled by your experiences in your past and the expectations you have about your future. By bringing these hidden assumptions out into the open, you may gain the power to change the ideas that may not be working for you. You also can plot your partner's path, based on what you know about him or her, or invite your partner to plot it, too. The simple exercise below can help you to better understand your financial path. This can be a map for your financial past and future.

EXERCISE: YOUR FINANCIAL PATH

First, you'll see how Chelsea and Carl completed their graphs, then you will have your turn to create a graph of your own projections for your financial future.

In figure 11.1, Carl graphed his financial path with a dotted line, and Chelsea used a solid line. Remember that Carl's parents were struggling financially during his early years, but they had become comfortable by the time he was a teenager. So, Carl shaded in the "Struggling" circle under the "Early Childhood" column and the "Comfortable" circle under the "Late Childhood" column. Because of his early life experiences, he thought it was perfectly reasonable to live frugally during his early adulthood. So, he shaded in the "Struggling" circle under the Early and Late phases of his "Pre-Relationship Adulthood" and he carried this lifestyle over into his current situation—where he is now in life, in the early stage of his marriage ("Early Relationship"). He drew a circle around this point in the graph to show that it is where he is now, like the "You Are Here" marker on a shopping mall map.

Figure 11.1 also shows that Chelsea thought of every stage of her life before marriage as "Comfortable." Because of this consistency she hadn't given much thought to how her lifestyle would change when she married. Nevertheless, she had some strong expectations about what her life should be like. When she began married life with Carl, the change in lifestyle was a shock. What he viewed as "Struggling" felt more like abject "Poverty" to her.

You can see this on the chart: Chelsea's solid line dips down to the "Poverty" circle in the "Early Relationship" column. She didn't think their financial status would get better anytime soon, either. She pictured poverty extending through the "Middle Relationship" stage of their marriage, and saw her life becoming only marginally better, moving into "Struggling," by the "Late Relationship" stage, when their kids are grown and she and Carl are ready for retirement.

In figure 11.2, you can see that Carl and Chelsea were able to make some adjustments, and arrive at a vision of their future that worked for both of them. Carl was able to loosen up a little, and he agreed to make some concessions. He admitted that it wouldn't break their bank to order out for a pizza or rent a video, every now and then. Chelsea softened, too. She knew that it wasn't realistic for a young couple just starting out to have all the luxuries that her well-established parents had had.

They settled on a lifestyle that was better than "Struggling" but not quite at the "Comfortable" level that Chelsea had been accustomed to. Chelsea felt much more hopeful; she could see that a comfortable lifestyle wasn't too far off in the future. Both she and Carl anticipated that they'd have a comfortable lifestyle by the middle stage of their relationship. Because they would be spending more money now, Carl thought they wouldn't quite reach the "Plentiful" lifestyle he had been aiming at previously. But the two of them believed that they could accept a lifestyle that fell somewhere between "Comfortable" and "Plentiful" in the late stage of their relationship.

Now, you are ready to do this exercise to plot your own financial future. Take a look at figure 11.3, and follow the directions below.

Directions: Look at all of the column names at the top of figure 11.3, "Early Childhood" to "Late Relationship." Then, look at the different lifestyles on the left-hand side of the figure. Then, shade in the circle in each column that best describes your lifestyle at each stage of your life, including all the stages you already have experienced, and your expectations about the life stages that are still in your future. Draw a larger circle around the stage that you are currently experiencing. Use the following definitions to define your life's stages:

Early Childhood: This stage is generally considered to be the time from birth to age ten or eleven. However, if there was a major event that led to a dramatic change in your family's financial status during your childhood, count the time before this event as your "Early Childhood" and the time after this as "Late Childhood." Such major events might be a parent's death, divorce, remarriage, or a business failure or success.

Late Childhood: This period lasts from about age ten or eleven until late adolescence, or follows a major economic shift in your family.

Pre-Relationship Adulthood (Early): This period is considered to take place in your early twenties, or the age when you moved away from your parents' home and began building your separate financial independence.

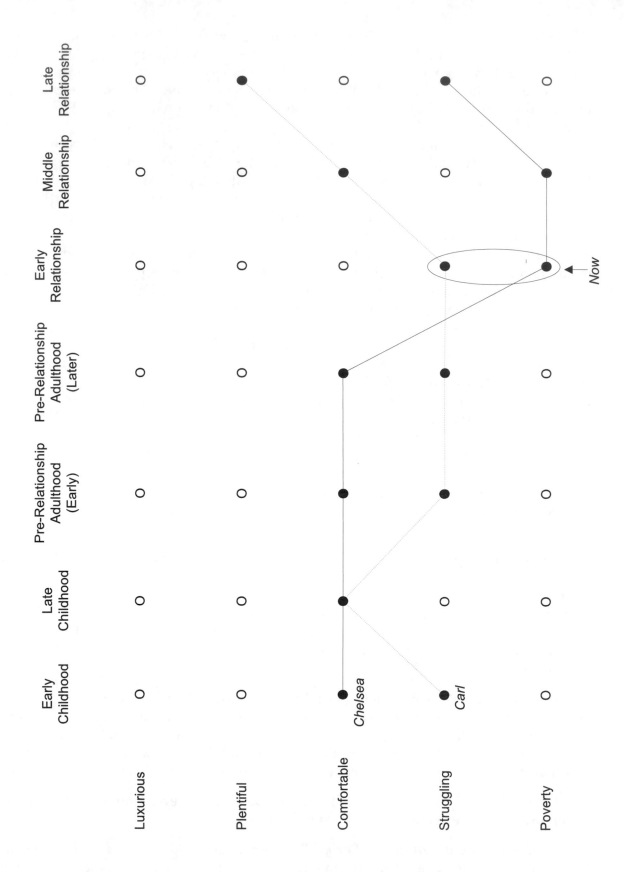

Figure 11.1: Chelsea and Carl: The First Graph of Their Financial Path

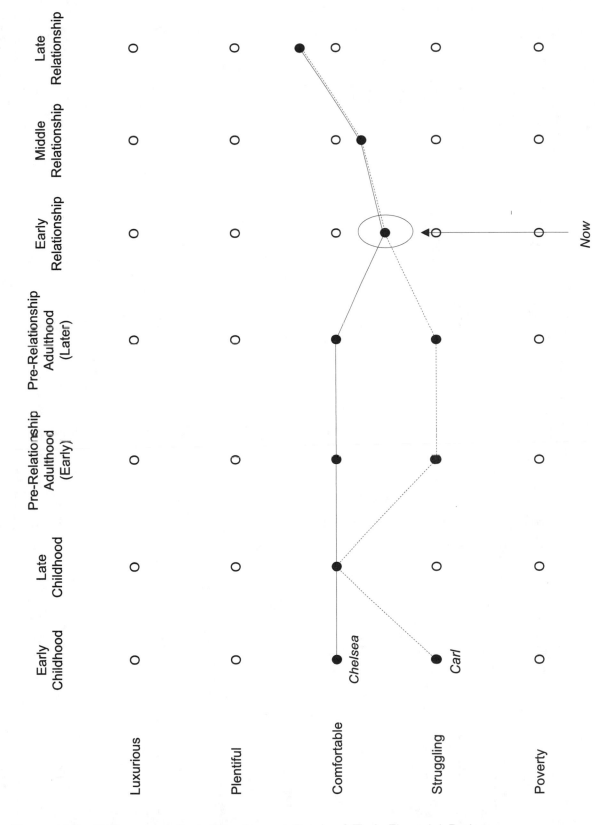

Figure 11.2: Chelsea and Carl: The Second Graph of Their Financial Path—
        After Their Discussions

	Early Childhood	Late Childhood	Pre-Relationship Adulthood (Early)	Pre-Relationship Adulthood (later)	Early Relationship	Middle Relationship	Late Relationship
Luxurious	○	○	○	○	○	○	○
Plentiful	○	○	○	○	○	○	○
Comfortable	○	○	○	○	○	○	○
Struggling	○	○	○	○	○	○	○
Poverty	○	○	○	○	○	○	○

Figure 11.3: Your Financial Path

Pre-Relationship Adulthood (Later): This is the point just before your current relationship. It might be marked by the completion of your education and/or the beginning of your career.

Early Relationship: This is the period after marriage (or after you have made a commitment to your partner), and the two of you have begun entering into joint financial arrangements.

Middle Relationship: At this point you are establishing or have established routines and understandings with regard to finances and responsibilities. As a rule, if raising children is to be a part of your relationship, that takes place during this stage.

Late Relationship: Grown or adult children and retirement are the events associated with this stage.

Now, connect the filled-in (shaded) circles for yourself and your partner using different colored lines. Note that it's possible that one or more stages will be missing for one or both of you. For instance, you might have gone directly from late childhood to marriage, without a period of independence. If so, just leave the column blank, and restart your colored line below it. This blank spot is important information.

Understanding Your Graph

When you complete your graphs, do the following steps:

- Examine your recent financial pasts, that is, the period before you entered your committed relationship. Talk about whether your childhoods were similar or different, financially speaking. What beliefs about money did each of you receive from your childhood experiences? If there was a financial shift from early to late childhood for either of you, did you draw any conclusions from this shift? How did your financial experiences differ in your adult stage, before your relationship began? Did you see yourselves as responsible for your finances during this period, or was someone else responsible? How did your childhood experiences contribute to your experiences during your early adulthood?

- Look at how each of you evaluates your current financial status. Is there a difference? If so, what is the source of this difference? Where and when did your expectations originate?

Now, look at how each of you views the future. Do you expect your finances to get better or to worsen? Do you trust each other to make good financial decisions? Does the financial path you hope to follow for your future have any relationship to what you've experienced in the past? (This is probably the case.)

EXERCISE: CHANGING YOUR THOUGHTS

Now think about whether you learned something in the past that you'd like to "unlearn." Some of your experiences may have been beneficial, and provided you with useful information for dealing with your current financial life. Other experiences may have been unique to a certain time and place in your life, but you may have exaggerated them well past the point where they are still useful.

Some assumptions you have about money may have worked for you in the past as a single person, but they may not apply to your current relationship.

All of your past experiences have been incorporated into your life's script. The exercise below will help you to rewrite those parts of your life's script that may not be work well for you anymore.

First study figure 11.4. The top row in the figure, under the names of the columns, provides an example of how to complete the exercise. Now, in the first column, under "Old Thought" write down one of your financial assumptions, preferably one that your partner does not share. In the next column, write the source of your belief in this assumption. Think about when you first began to think this way and how you got this message. Perhaps your belief is based on something you were told directly. Or maybe it comes from what you saw going on around you when you were a child. Or maybe it's based on your direct experience with money. Think about how this assumption or belief influences your daily financial decisions, and think about whether there is anything you'd like to change.

Old Thought	Where the Thought Came From	Want to Change the Thought?	New Thought
We'll always have financial problems, so we might as well spend money whenever we get it.	I first recall my parents complaining about no money when I was 7. Nothing they did made a difference.	Yes.	It's a good feeling to save money. My own experience tells me I can control my financial future.

Figure 11.4: Changing Your Thoughts

$ $ $ $ $

Moving along a financial path that's different from your partner's, or a path that doesn't fit your current reality, can cause conflict and lead to faulty financial decisions. By understanding where your financial ideas came from, and where they are leading you to, you will gain the power to change them, so they can work better for you and for your partner.

PART II

Money-Growing Strategies

Financial security and prosperity are possible for nearly all couples to attain. If you've been struggling with money up to now, this may be hard to believe. You may feel as if your own particular financial problems are too huge to deal with effectively. You may feel that your partner is too difficult to deal with in regard to money issues. Or you may feel as if you can make it from day to day, but you'll never really experience prosperity.

Part II of this book contains effective strategies for moving ahead financially. These strategies do require work and commitment, but they are effective and they will move you forward. If you completed Part I of this book, you've done a lot of the work already. You're starting to change the way you think, and you've gotten rid of some of the problems and thought patterns that were holding you back.

Now you're ready to start the exciting process of dreaming and planning for your future, and to start taking actions that will make real improvements, both in your day-to-day life and in your relationship with your partner.

CHAPTER 12

Shared Dreams

CHAPTER GOAL: To help you develop the ability to think of your finances from a joint perspective, creatively visualizing how the two of you can work together to create a better life than either of you could create independently.

You were attracted to your partner for certain unique and special reasons. Often the life partners we pick are similar to us in many ways. For instance, they may share our religion, or have similar levels of education, or other background similarities. These similarities provide a sound basis for your relationship. You can talk with this person because you understand many things in the same way. But then you may have been brought together by some attractions that operate at a deeper level. There was a reason why you were brought together with this particular person and not all the others with the same similarities.

People are often drawn to their partners because those people complement their personalities; parts of their psyches fit together like the pieces in a jigsaw puzzle. Someone who wants to be taken care of may find someone who wants or needs to be a caretaker. Someone who is cautious might be drawn to a risk taker. It's also not uncommon to pick someone who recreates the dynamics of the relationship that you had with a parent when you were growing up.

However, what attracted you initially often can lead to difficulties later on. For example, the outgoing, funny, and very sociable person you were attracted to might begin to seem loud and overbearing a few years later. When the going gets tough, the sympathetic, sweet person you were attracted to might seem too passive and nonassertive.

But the differences between you can also function as a powerful positive force, and can allow you to do things together that neither of you could do alone. Some of the great partnerships in history illustrate this. John Lennon and Paul McCartney were both good song writers: Lennon was a hard-driving rocker and McCartney a sweet balladeer. As the Beatles, the two of them together created songs that changed the musical landscape, something neither could have done by himself.

Both you and your partner have skills and attitudes that have allowed you to reach the point you are at today. As partners, you now have common goals and dreams. By combining your skills and talents, you can work on those dreams together. And you can do this work better together than either of you could do alone.

Goals and Dreams

A *goal* is a realistic objective that you can reach by following careful, consistent steps. A *dream* is more ambitious; it is something that will take a leap of faith and an extra push to attain. (Publishing this book has satisfied one of my dreams.)

You can think of the progress of your life as a series of stepping stones. Once you realize one goal, the next step becomes easier. In fact, in many instances, you can make a dream come true by completing a series of goals. For example, let's say your dream is to own a beautiful home. Your goals along the road to achieving this dream might be as follows:

1. Create a work situation that generates enough income to save some money every month.

2. Save a small down payment.

3. Buy a starter home or a "fixer-upper."

4. Accumulate equity in your starter home.

5. Use the equity in your starter home and other savings to purchase your dream home.

Each of these five steps can be broken down into even smaller steps, so that every step will seem reasonable and easily attainable.

When you share dreams with your partner, you double your potential to do great things. You and your partner can help each other in many ways. You can offer each other emotional support, encouragement, and inspiration. One of you can earn the money, while the other does the footwork, paperwork, and negotiations. One person can pick up extra responsibilities while the other puts more energy into achieving the goal.

Here are some examples of financial goals and dreams. They're organized from basic to ambitious. Pick one to start with, or come up with one of your own:

- Pay off your debts.

- Free up time so you can spend evenings with each other.

- Take a short vacation together before the end of the year.

- Save 5 percent of your income every month.

- Change to a job that pays better, or switch careers.

- Do a type of creative work (i.e., paint, act, write, teach) that will bring you greater emotional satisfaction than just earning money.

- Buy a home together.

- Start a small business that you can run from home.

- Earn all of your income from self-employment.

- Totally support yourselves by investments and by generating more passive income.

(Passive income is income that you get without working. It may be money that you get from investments, such as bank interest or stock dividends, or it may be money that you get from work that you did in the past, such as royalties on book sales.)

EXERCISE: FINANCIAL GOALS AND DREAMS

As with all of the exercises in this book, you can complete your partner's section based on what you know about him or her. You can complete it after you talk it over with your partner, or you can have your partner complete it.

A good way to start would be to complete the exercises yourself. This will help you to organize your thoughts about "the Dream," and provide you with a springboard for discussing the Dream with your partner.

1. *The Dream.* Write down a dream that you have for yourself, and you'd like to share with your partner. Starting small is fine. But if you'd like to make this exercise more exciting, pick something right on the edge of what you think is possible. Don't choose something completely unrealistic, such as becoming a world class athlete or a movie star, but pick a dream that is a stretch when you consider your current circumstances, such as owning your own business, instead of working for someone else.

The Dream: _____

_____

_____

_____

2. *Whose dream is it?* Circle a number below to show to what degree this is your dream, your partner's dream, or a dream shared by both of you. If you don't know your partner's feeling about it, it's likely to be more your dream than his or hers. But even if this is the case, after discussing it with your partner, you might be able to turn it into a shared dream.

   The scale below ranges from 1, "My Partner's Dream" to 5, "My Dream." If the dream is entirely yours, then you'll circle 5. You would also circle 5 if your partner has no interest in your dream and can't see any personal benefits coming out of it. If you rate your dream a 5, you'll be going it alone. You'll want to consider whether this dream will be feasible for you and your partner, or whether it will put too much strain on your relationship. Investing a lot of energy into a dream that your partner doesn't share at all can be very frustrating and potentially it could cause conflict. You'll need either to convince your partner that achieving your dream would benefit both of you, or you'll want to modify your dream to include your partner.

   Many of your goals and dreams would be rated "2." This means that, although you came up with the idea, your partner can see some benefit to it. Circling "3" means that the dream is equally shared by the two of you: you are both equally motivated to work for it. A "4" indicates that it is more your partner's dream than yours, and a "5" indicates that it is exclusively your partner's dream.

My Dream		Shared Dream		My Partner's Dream
1	2	3	4	5

3. *How our lives will change*. When you're trying to bring a dream into reality, it helps to clarify what the realization of that dream will mean to you and your partner. For example, will it mean more money, more free time, more personal fulfillment in your work, or a more enjoyable life? Now, write what you think will happen if you realize your dream.

Realizing the dream will change my life in these ways: _____

_____

_____

Realizing the dream will change my partner's life in these ways: _____

_____

_____

_____

4. *My Involvement/My Partner's Involvement*. Your partner might actively share your dream and completely share in the effort that it takes to make your dream become a reality. Buying a house often is a shared dream. Some dreams are more individual, and your partner may be less directly involved. What kind of involvement do you anticipate your partner will contribute? Consider what you wrote above, and remember that the more your partner benefits from the dream, the more you can probably expect of him or her.

Circle a number on the scales below to show how much you and your partner will contribute to each of the following items in the realization of the dream:

Circle "1" on the *Money* scale below if you expect your partner to entirely finance the dream, "2" if you'll make some contribution, with your partner carrying the bulk of the finances, "3" if you'll share the financial part equally, "4" if you'll finance most of it, and "5" if you'll provide all of the money.

On the *Time and Work* scale, rate from "1" if you expect your partner to put in all the work, to "5" if you'll do all of the work. Rate the *Emotional Support* scale in the same way: from "1" if you expect your partner to provide all of the encouragement and enthusiasm, to "5" if you expect no support at all from your partner.

Money (For example, if you're buying a house, whose income or savings will furnish the down payment, and who will be responsible for the mortgage payments?)

My Partner		We'll Share		Myself
1	2	3	4	5

Time and Work (For example, if you're buying a house, who's going to find an agent, look at houses, talk to appraisers, negotiate with the seller, contact a loan agent, be responsible for raising the down payment, and so forth?) Circle the number that seems most appropriate.

My Partner		We'll Share		Myself
1	2	3	4	5

Emotional Support (If attaining the dream begins to seem harder to accomplish than you had originally thought it would be, who's going to keep the dream going?)

My Partner		We'll Share		Myself
1	2	3	4	5

The ratings you made above show how much involvement you expect to have in achieving the dream, compared to how much involvement you expect your partner to have. These ratings should be fairly consistent with the rating you gave to *Whose dream is it?* For instance, if you indicated that it's mostly your dream by giving a "4" or "5" rating to "Whose dream is it?," then you can't expect your partner to provide most or all of the money, work, and/or emotional support (ratings in the 1 to 2 range).

Let's say, for example, that you would like to return to school for a graduate degree, and your partner reluctantly agrees. If you expect your partner to pay your tuition, help with your homework, and to listen sympathetically when you're overwhelmed by final exams, you're bound to be disappointed. If you want to keep the peace, you'll either need to make it a shared dream by selling your partner on the benefits of your dream, or drawing deeper on your personal resources to achieve your dream. Or you may need to modify your dream.

5. *How will we get there?*

   Consider the actual steps you'll need to accomplish to realize your dream. You'll start out with small steps that you can do easily; for example, doing research, contacting people for information, regularly setting aside a certain amount of money. These small steps make the next steps possible, and will allow you to realize your dream eventually.

   First Steps: What will you do over the next few months? Consider what you need to do to start moving toward the dream. When you take these first steps, you are laying the foundation for your dream. Do you need more information? Personal contacts? How will you involve your partner? If you are buying a house, you'll need to do some research to find out what you can afford, where you'd like to live, and how much you will need to save.

   Write down the first steps that you will take on the road to making your dream a reality. Be sure to include dates for accomplishing these first steps:

These are the first steps that I'll take toward realizing the dream: _____

_____

_____

_____

Middle Steps: This stage is often the "nuts and bolts" or hard work of moving toward your dream. This may happen over a period of time, possibly years. What do you need to do, and what do you anticipate your partner doing? If you're planning to buy a house, saving a down payment will be a large part of the work. In the First Steps you found out how much you need to save for the type of house you want. Now you'll need to figure out a way to save for this goal by setting aside a certain amount of money each month. In all likelihood, you will either need to cut back your expenses or increase your income to accomplish this.

These are the intermediate steps that I (we'll) take toward realizing the dream: _____

_____

_____

_____

Final Steps: By the time you've completed all of the middle steps, the momentum will almost carry you though the final steps. Once you've made all the preparation and investment, what will you need to do to nail down your dream? If you're buying a house, in this stage you'll contact a real estate agent and sign up for the agent's services. Then you will look at houses, and make your bids.

These are the final steps that I (we'll) take toward realizing the dream: _____

_____

_____

_____

Example: Writing a Book

Here's my personal account of how I made a dream of mine come true. I knew that I enjoyed my work as a psychologist, but helping one person at a time is a slow and sometimes frustrating process. I found teaching exciting, but being badgered for grades and dealing with administrative problems made this frustrating, too. In high school, I had loved writing for the school paper, and enjoyed being read by a large audience. One of my fellow news reporters from the paper went on to become a screenwriter and director. After seeing his latest movie, I felt a mixture of admiration and envy, and became aware of a burning desire to write.

This is how I worked the steps to realize my dream:

1. *The Dream:* I wanted to write and publish a book. I knew this wasn't anything that would be easily accomplished. It was definitely more of a dream than a goal. Clearly, it was something I'd have to work a number of steps to reach.

2. *Whose dream is it?* My wife was reluctantly supportive. She knew this would take time away from our family, and she also knew that there are a lot of unpublished authors. This was definitely more my dream than hers.

My Dream		Shared Dream		Partner's Dream
1	X	3	4	5

3. *How will our lives be changed?*
Realizing the dream will change my life in these ways: I will receive recognition from my peers. I will feel a sense of accomplishment. I might experience a measure of fame. It might be the start of a new and exciting career. I will receive some passive income (the book's royalties) that might eventually allow me to spend more time with my wife.

Realizing the dream will change my partner's life in these ways: It might generate at least enough money to allow us to spend a few more days together every month. It will provide something fun to talk about with colleagues and relatives. It will generate feelings of excitement about future possibilities. It will create some passive income that eventually will allow us to spend more time together.

One common goal that my wife and I shared completely was to work less and spend more time together. So, my writing a book is actually a shared dream from that perspective.

4. *My Involvement/My Partner's Involvement.* Because this was mostly my dream, I didn't expect much more than understanding and some occasional encouragement from my wife.

Time and Work

My Partner		We'll Share		Myself
1	2	3	4	**X**

Money

My Partner		We'll Share		Myself
1	2	3	4	**X**

Emotional Support

My Partner		We'll Share		Myself
1	2	3	**X**	5

5. *How will we get there?*

First Steps: I read many books and articles about writing and publishing books. I chose a topic, and I did some research to find a market I could realistically break into. I spoke to editors, sent out query letters. I got my wife's ideas and feedback.

Middle Steps: I wrote a book proposal. I submitted it to various publishers. I revised my manuscript in ways that the publishers suggested. I did follow-up, and negotiated until I got a book contract. I got my wife's feedback about my writing.

Final Steps: I wrote the book, revised it, figured out ways to market it. I told my wife how much I appreciated her bearing with the loss of my time and energy for my family. I shared my dreams for our future with her.

$ $ $ $ $

Next Steps

As you work through the steps to accomplish your dream, you can keep coming back to this chapter with new dreams. Creating, sharing, and building dreams with your partner is one of the great joys of being in a committed relationship. By doing this, you'll not only increase your prosperity and happiness, you'll also learn a lot about each other. Achieving a dream together will enhance your relationship and your individual lives.

CHAPTER 13

Spending and Debt

CHAPTER GOAL: To learn how to tame the debt that is eating you alive. Learning how to tame the financial monster called "debt," and getting your finances under control can eliminate the tension over money that you may be experiencing in your relationship.

I Spend, Therefore I Am

How you spend money says a lot about you. Spending money is a form of self-expression. You can spend to reward yourself, to give yourself the material goods that you feel you deserve. Or, you can buy gifts for others, perhaps hoping to get a certain response from them, or to make them think a certain way about you. You also can buy consumer goods to impress others and make a statement about your level of success. Your personality style, Monarch or Spartan, regulates how you spend money. Having a financial personality style different from your partner's may be a big source of conflict. Even if you agree on how much to spend, you may still disagree on what's important.

Caution: Bottomless Money Pit Ahead

A large debt is often a warning sign that you're spending more than you make. For example, consider George's situation. He is a fifty-two-year-old man who was divorced because of money issues. Observe how central the issue of debt was in his marriage. Here is what he had to say about it:

> When I was growing up, it was important not to make a purchase if you couldn't afford to pay cash for it. Getting into debt was for buying a house or a car, but that was it. After we got married, my fatal financial mistake was falling prey to my wife

and her family's philosophy that, if you can afford the monthly payment on it, whatever it is, then there is no reason why you shouldn't have it. That philosophy was the reason we took on a tremendous debt load, and some very unrealistic expectations.

My wife's family's philosophy seemed to be that when you reach the point where you're so financially strapped that you can't make payments on your debt, then the only solution is to earn more money. I know that this was the main reason my marriage ended in divorce. Money was the key issue. It is sometimes impossible to carry the burden of always making too little money. I learned to hate the phrase, "But everyone is in debt!" It still haunts me today, and it's been twelve years since I got divorced.

Reasonable Debt

Occasionally, debt is reasonable. It makes sense to incur debt if any of the following is true:

- The debt is for a reasonable investment, such as a business, that will return your money with a profit.

- You're "going in the red" for a short, time-limited period, and you have a plan for getting yourself out of debt. For instance, one parent might stop working to stay home with a pre-school child, knowing that the other parent's income won't be enough to cover expenses during this time. Student loans also can be a reasonable type of debt to assume.

- You're buying a house, an investment that increases in value and provides you with tax breaks.

- Most people still consider it reasonable to borrow money to buy a car. But the monthly note should be well within your budget.

Short-term Fixes for Long-term Problems

You might take on debt because you feel as if you can't make ends meet any other way. But if you think your financial affairs are bad now, wait until those monthly loan payments are added onto everything else you're paying. Debt's a lot like a drug addiction: It starts out by giving you a high—a sense of relief, even happiness, and ends up being a noose around your neck.

Cheri, a twenty-eight-year-old homemaker, has a good description of what life is like once you start to fall behind on your debt payments. She's scrambling to make it every month, and starting to see her husband as the source of the problem. Her husband is starting to blame her, too:

Financial problems are a huge element in my marriage. My husband will ask me to stop at a store to pick something up on my way home, when we can't afford it. I've tried to keep up with our spending, but we have so many overdue bills and termination notices that there is no way to schedule payments. Usually, when we get cut-off notices or threatening letters, we pay the minimum amount required to keep the account open or the service on. I'd like to use our checking account only to pay bills, and to put my paycheck in a savings account. That way, I would not be able to write checks on what's not in there. That would also help with not using our debit card, which we often use as a check card for store purchases.

We don't get too many extras. We have basic phone and cable, and I buy groceries at a warehouse outlet store to save money. But we have a mortgage, and the utility prices seem to be going up every day. And once we're short of money one month, we're short every month thereafter. Unfortunately, we are in the position where we make too much money to get help of any kind, but not enough where we can actually afford to pay for everything.

It would be a great help if I could go to school and get a degree so I would be qualified for a better-paying job. However, I work full-time already, and I cannot afford any out-of-pocket costs to better my education. So, unless we win the lottery or something miraculous like that, I am canceling our cable service, and I'll tell the kids to keep wearing their sweats so I can keep the heat down, and we will continue to be broke. By the way, did I mention that we are ready to split up over all the stress this financial mess has caused? Unfortunately, that would mean the mortgage wouldn't be paid at all, and then the house would be lost, too.

When you're in debt, it can seem as if the debt is going to eat you alive. Every day you wake up thinking, "What bill is overdue today?" Every time you put some money into the bank, you just watch it disappear into the mouth of the hungry debt-monster.

Did We Take a Wrong Turn Somewhere?
We Have Too Much Debt

It's all in your head. No, not the debt. You know from opening your mail every day that the debt's real. But what's in your head, or maybe your partner's head, is a thinking style that allows you to spend more than you make. If you want to get out of debt, then you need to examine your thinking, and change some of your thoughts.

EXERCISE: ARGUING WITH THE DEBTOR WITHIN

In this exercise you will see some of the types of thoughts that accompany overspending and getting deeply into debt. By slowing down long enough to pay attention to your style of thinking and learning to recognize the habitual thoughts that you or your partner have about spending, you can stop the debt-monster in its tracks.

Put a checkmark next to any thought that fits your or your partner's habitual style. (As always, your partner should do this exercise, too. And, as always, you may answer for your partner if you wish, basing your answers on your knowledge of your partner's spending habits):

Me   My Partner

_____   _____   If I can afford the monthly payment, I can afford to buy it. The actual price isn't too important.

_____   _____   Money goes quickly, so I need to buy what I want before my money runs out.

_____   _____   After I take out a loan, I feel a sense of relief.

_____   _____   There's no point in making more than minimum payments on debts.

_____   _____   I make my spending decisions based mostly on what I feel I need and want, not on whether I have the money.

_____   _____   Everyone I know is in debt. Getting into debt is what you need to do to survive these days. It's patriotic to spend money in hard times.

_____   _____   If my debt load becomes intolerable, I'll get a second job or just declare bankruptcy.

_____   _____   My motto is "Live for today!" Who knows if we'll even be alive tomorrow?

Now, look over the statements that you checkmarked. If there are several checkmarks, then thoughts like these have had a powerful influence over how you've dealt with money in the past. Did you ever see a cartoon character with an angel perched on one shoulder, encouraging good deeds, and a devil on the other, encouraging the character to go down the wrong road? Well, you are in a similar position. These ideas come from the "debtor devil" within you. Such ideas can be very strong, strong enough to bulldoze the reasonable concerns you should have about getting into debt. If these thoughts are the "tapes" you listen to when you want to make a purchase that you can't afford, they allow you to spend and charge feeling only a minimum of guilt.

Now, let's see if you can come up with a few more of the tapes that you run for yourself; that is, what are some of the things you tell yourself that allow you to run up your debt to credit card companies:

Example: "It's patriotic to consume. I'm helping the national economy every time I make a credit card purchase."

_____

_____

_____

How do you squelch a debtor devil? You get into an argument with him, and you argue him down! And don't be afraid to use a lot of energy when you make your argument. Those devils are nasty customers (Note: These are examples of how to argue with *your own* thoughts—this is *not* an example of how to argue with your partner!).

Here's some examples:

Debtor Devil: Money goes so fast! So I need to buy what I want—before all my money vanishes.

Argument: Oh really? Of course, you know that if you spend it on what you want, it won't be there to pay the bills you need to pay. Hey, what a great strategy—if you want to wind up in the poorhouse. How about trying to pay for necessities first, and the luxuries only if there's money left over. How about getting your finances back on track, and acting like a grown-up for a change?

Debtor Devil: After I take out a loan, I feel a sense of relief.

Argument: That's another brilliant strategy. Lying in bed all day instead of going to work or shooting up a little heroin would also provide some relief! Taking out a loan means more is going out than is coming in. That can be a heavy-duty danger sign! It should cause you to feel concern, not relief.

Now you try it. Write down what your own personal Debtor Devil tells you, and then write down an argument to rebut the Devil:

My Debtor Devil: _____

_____

_____

_____

My Rebuttal: _____

_____

_____

_____

With some practice, you'll get better and better at "arguing down" your Debtor Devil. If you want to involve your partner, and he or she is willing, get him/her to help you challenge these thoughts and you do the same for your partner.

Knowing how to argue with debtor thinking provides the verbal "willpower" you need to help you to resist problem spending. It can help you to change your "tapes." But, to reinforce your arguments, you also must commit to making concrete changes in your behavior, changes like not using your credit cards except for dire emergencies.

(A woman I know freezes her card in a block of ice. She defrosts it only for emergencies, and by the time it's okay to use, she has given herself enough time to think about whether she really needs to use it or not.)

- You don't have to freeze your card in a block of ice, but it's a good idea not to carry it in your purse or wallet. If it's not there, it's harder to make impulse purchases. Put the card in a safe place and carry it with you only when you have given the purchase a good deal of thought. Think about whether using the card fits into your current budget. That is, how much will your monthly payment to the card company be after you buy the item? Can you pay it off in one month? Two? Three? How much interest will you wind up paying for the item? Is it really worth that?

- You also need to make a commitment not to do things or go places that lead to spending problems. You know where your "problem" places are. If you like to walk in the mall and window shop, just don't go there. Take a walk in the park instead.

- You also can make a commitment to lower your credit card balance by a certain amount each month, and to pay it all off in a certain amount of time.

Write down some things that you're willing to do differently.

I will take the following actions to decrease my spending and to lower my debt:

_____

_____

_____

$ $ $ $ $

Debt, like most human problems, starts with your thinking. In this chapter, you learned how to argue with the self-destructive thoughts that allow you to fall into debt. You learned how to prevent old thoughts from controlling your behavior by arguing with them. Using these techniques, you and your partner can work together to take back control of your finances. Taking control of your debt gives you financial freedom, and starts you on the road toward a life with less stress and more options.

CHAPTER 14

Work I: Time for a Change?

CHAPTER GOAL: To help you decide whether a career change would be good for you. A career change can open new doors—but it's a big decision that takes careful thought. This chapter will help you think about the issues that are involved in changing careers.

If you are like most people, by far the greatest portion of your income will come from the work you do. If you work full-time from your twenties through your sixties, you will have earned $800,000 at an average of $10 an hour. At $40 an hour, you will have earned more than three million dollars. You'll also have spent nearly a fourth of your adult life with your nose to the grindstone. Since for most people, there's no way around work, you should create the best possible work situation for yourself that you possibly can. Here are some of the important variables to consider:

- Will I work with what I have, or do I have to get more training and education?

- Will I be self-employed, or will I work for someone else?

- Will I work at home, or will I go out to work?

- Will I involve my family in my work?

This chapter discusses ways to determine whether it's a good idea for you or your partner to change careers. Chapter 15 focuses on ways to change and manage your work situation, without the necessity of changing careers.

Change Careers or Keep Your Job?

Big career changes may involve risk and sacrifice, and can put a considerable strain on your partner and family. If you can pull it off, the ideal situation would be to settle on your career before you enter into a committed relationship. But what if you're already in a committed relationship and you find yourself wrestling with a desire for a new career?

Getting more education and making career shifts are not always completely positive moves. When you are considering a career change, it's important to consider *all* the benefits and risks of such a change. The factors to consider depend on your stage of life, and whether you're single, with a partner, and whether you have children.

David's Story

David is forty-four. He was forty-two when he decided to make a career change. As his story shows, even with a supportive spouse, the transition was not easy:

> I started out as a real estate agent when I was twenty-two, and then got my broker's license when I was thirty. At that point, I felt well established and I was ready to settle down. The next year I married Shelly. We started a family; Harrison and Dustin are five and six now. By the time I was forty-two, I'd been in real estate for twenty years. It was a decent career and I was doing well, but I was beginning to feel bored with it. My dad was an attorney, and if I had been more ambitious when I was younger I think I would have pursued law back then. I've always thought that it's never too late to go after your dreams. I told Shelly about my plans, and she was very supportive. She agreed that we could take out student loans and she was willing to take over some of the things that I'd been doing with the boys, like picking them up from school and getting their bath at night.
>
> I was fortunate to get accepted into a local law school, and I've just started my second year. It's beginning to take its toll on my family. I cut my real estate work to half-time, and that means our budget has been a lot tighter. And we have those student loans looming. I'm not home too much and when I am, I'm studying. Dustin is starting to have some behavior problems at school, and it's up to Shelly to deal with the teacher because I don't have the time. I can tell she's overwhelmed, and getting tired of this whole idea. I'll be halfway through in a few months, but it doesn't end there. I'll have to build a law practice, and that means more time and money problems. I'm wondering if it isn't time to just admit this was a dumb idea. But I've never been a quitter.

Clearly, David feels torn. His ambivalence is common among people making midlife career transitions. When you're single and are responsible only for yourself, career advancement is much easier decision than when you're middle-aged, and your decisions have an impact on other people.

Teri's Story

Teri, a thirty-two-year-old woman who is in a committed lesbian relationship, related what it was like for her to shift careers:

For years, I had no one to answer to and I spent money as I wished without any concern for tomorrow. After becoming involved and committed in our relationship we eventually combined finances. While I was working it was all right, but then we decided that I would stop working and go back to college to complete my degree. So, now my partner is the breadwinner. The past year has been a lesson in being humble, taking suggestions, and reining in my shopping impulses. It has been much harder to do than I thought it would be, but I have made some huge changes. I think the most important thing that has helped me to make these changes has been to remember that nothing is more important to me than my healthy and loving relationship with the one person I love.

EXERCISE: MAKING A CAREER SHIFT

Shifting careers can be costly in terms of the money and the time taken from your important relationships. But, clearly, a shift to a more enjoyable or higher paying career also has obvious benefits. The following exercise will help you to weigh the costs and benefits of a career change. If you need specific information about a career you're considering entering, such as typical salaries and working conditions, go to the Web site for the Bureau of Labor Statistics, http://stats.bls.gov/oco/, or look at the *Occupational Outlook Handbook* (U.S. Department of Labor 2002) in your library. If you or your partner is thinking of a career change, here are some of the subjects you need to study and discuss.

Financial Costs

Depending on the type of career shift you're making, there are many potential costs. If you need to attend school or get other training to make the shift, you'll have costs for tuition and supplies. You'll also be investing your time. This is time that you could have devoted to earning money. So, the element of lost or unpaid income should be factored into your considerations. Think about how much a career shift will cost you, and how long these costs will continue. Consider, too, that when you're starting a new career, you may need to invest a lot of your time for a relatively low income. Before you reach an income that's average in your new field (or better than average), you will need to build your clientele base, and/or your reputation, and gain a certain amount of experience.

With all of these factors in mind, think about your earning capacity now, and project ahead to what your earning capacity will look like in your new career. What if David could roll back time to the point when he was considering going to law school? Figure 14.1 provides an example of how David could have assessed the effect that changing careers would have on his family.

When David made the decision to enter law school, he was earning $85,000 a year as a real estate broker. That was his starting point. That point is marked on the graph as "The Same." Before he began the shift to change careers, his earning capacity was "The Same" as it had been up to that point. He already had a college degree, so completing law school will take three more years. During this period, he will be cutting his real estate work back to half-time, so he will be earning only $42,500 per year. So, at the six-month point and the one-year point, he would have graphed his earning capacity as "A Lot Less."

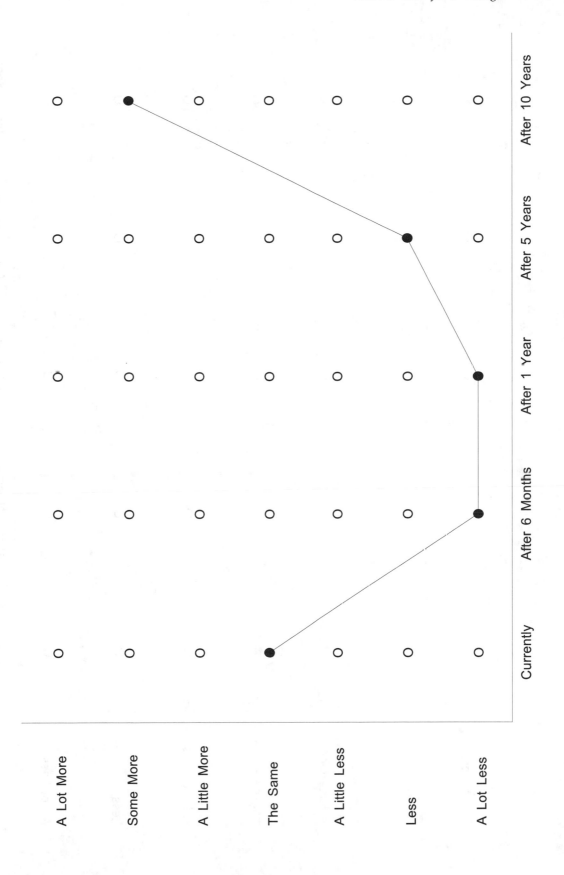

Figure 14.1: Projecting Earning Capacity (David's Graph)

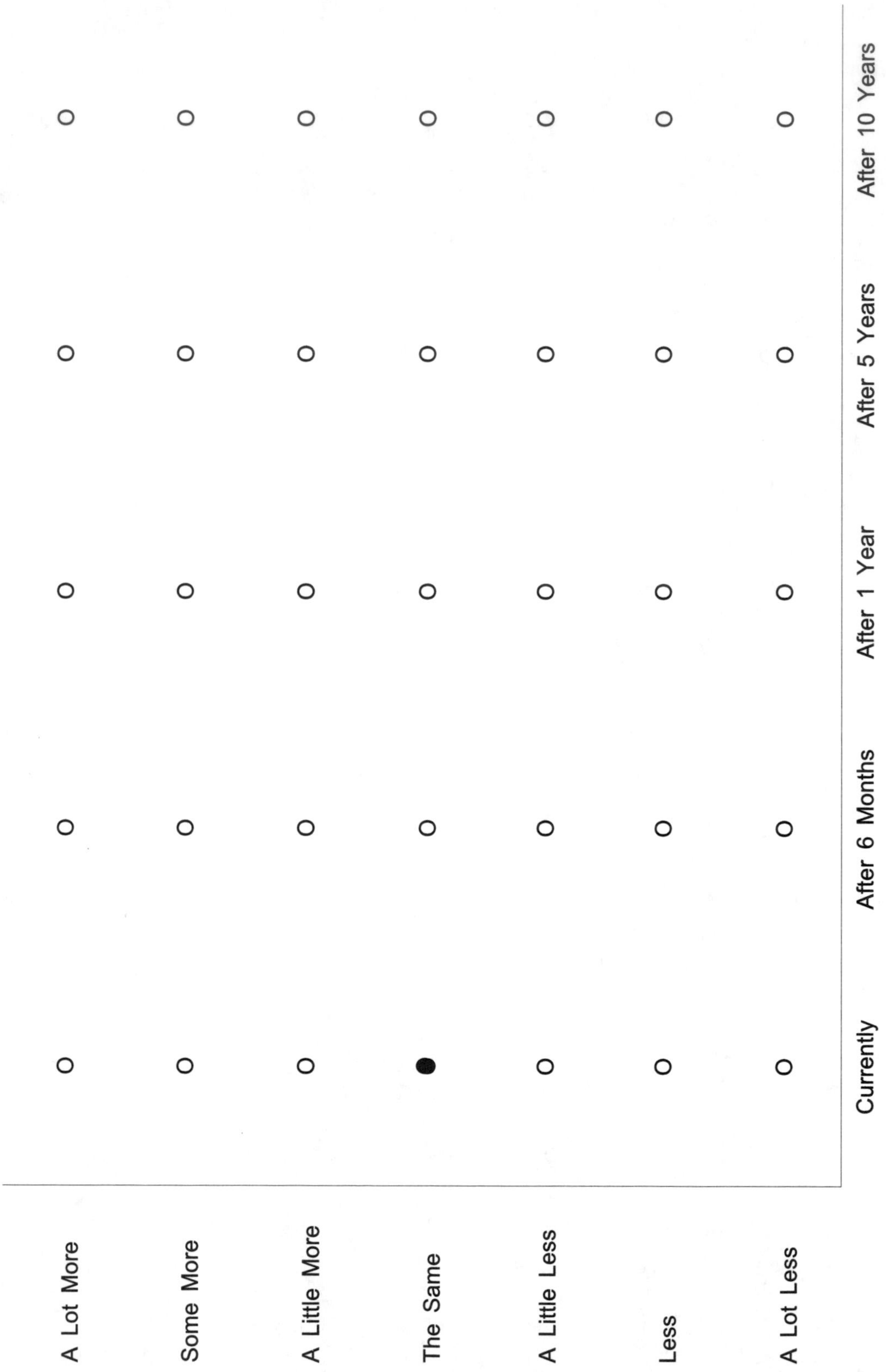

Figure 14.2: Projecting Your Earning Capacity

At the five-year point, he will have been out of law school for two years. He will just be starting his new career. He found out that his local county employs new attorneys at a starting salary of $55,000, so he could have assumed that he would be starting out with an annual income of $55,000. He could also have figured that he'd be paying back $3,000 a year for his student loans, so that would bring him down to $52,000 a year in income. He would have graphed that as "Less" than he was making previously.

Projecting out ten years, he might have figured that he'd be earning $125,000 per year—more than he would have made if he had stayed in real estate, but not spectacularly more. So he could have graphed this as "Some More" at the ten-year point.

If you are considering changing careers, use the graph in figure 14.2 above to chart your own earning capacity over the next ten years. At each point, compare what you think you'll be earning to what you would have earned if you had not changed careers. Remember to subtract any additional costs that would result from the additional training you might need.

For instance, if you pay tuition as you go, you will subtract your tuition for the period that you're in school. If you take out student loans, you will subtract your loan payments (as David did) during the period when you start paying them back.

With most career shifts, your graph, at first, will show a dip, followed by a rise. If you're changing careers to increase your income, the line you graph should rise higher than it is now. Of course, if you're changing careers only for greater career satisfaction, and not for a higher income, you should not expect to see the line you plot rise.

If you are changing careers to increase your income, look at how much time will elapse before you reap the benefits. Think about the total number of years that you will practice your new career. Consider the amount of time that you, your partner, and others will have to deal with the effects of reduced income before receiving positive benefits. Then check one of the appropriate responses below.

From a financial standpoint, changing careers would be a good idea:

_____ Yes

_____ Not Sure

_____ No

Time and Emotional Costs

Now, consider the time you will have to spend away from your important relationships to train for a new career, or to get a new career started. Think about the impact your training will have on your important relationships, and the emotional stresses it might create.

Consider your partner, and think about what possible effects the loss of your time could have on him or her. What kind of stress and how much of that stress will your partner have to endure alone, if you change careers? Then, too, if you have children, disrupting your career might have a significant impact on your relationships with them, and also on their future. Are you prepared to deal with those consequences? How can you prepare yourself and your family for such big changes?

A career change can also have a positive impact on your state of mind and your relationships. If you feel better about your work, you are likely to be happier and have improved relationships. And, of course, if you're making more money, that does have the potential to provide a better life for the people you love.

There are a great many factors to consider when trying to add up the potential emotional costs of changing careers. Let's suppose that David is still considering these factors. The four questions below are questions that he could ask himself. David's possible responses to these questions are set indented type.

1. While you're training for your new career, what sort of changes might happen in your life? Describe factors such as time, money, and your mood:

   Money will be tight, I'll make about half as much as I did before. My time will be tight, too, I'm going to keep up my brokerage business and go to school in the evening. For three years I'll be almost invisible to my family. We'll be like "ships passing in the night." I'll be stressed. Law school is intense, and real estate is no cakewalk. I'll also worry about whether I can keep my real estate clients while I'm working half-time and I'm stressed by school.

2. Describe how these changes will affect your partner and children (if applicable):

   Shelly is excited about me becoming a lawyer, but it's going to be a real test of our relationship. She'll be working more hours to help with finances, and helping more with the boys. I know she's a real trouper, but she's going to be pulling for my time and affection, and I anticipate more than a few arguments and hurt feelings. This is a crucial time for our boys. I really want to be involved with them. I'll have to push myself to the limit to make time for them. My worst fear is that they'll stop seeking me out and end up not feeling as close to me as they do now.

3. When you complete your training for your new career, what sorts of changes will take place in your life? Describe factors such as time, money, and your mood. It's tempting to be Pollyannaish when you describe this, but try to be as realistic as you can.

   As I develop a law practice or when I take my first law job, it will be tough going at first. I remember what it was like starting out in real estate, and I know it's going to be a lot like that again, establishing a reputation, getting a client base. Five to ten years from now, I might see things starting to look really good. As my practice builds, we'll have more money. I'll enjoy the prestige of being a lawyer, and that will make me feel good about myself. Time will be tight for a long time, though. When I'm on a case, it's bound to take time away from my family. But that's the way it is with real estate, too. The demands on my time will be similar to what they are now.

4. Describe the long-term effect on your partner and children (if applicable):

   I think Shelly will be relieved and happy when I complete school. She's always been supportive of my goals. I hope I'm being realistic, though, and that the three years won't cause damage to our relationship. The boys will be eight and nine. I think it will be good for them to see their daddy reach a goal like this, but I fear we won't be as close as we could have been with more time together. On the other hand, my law practice will be going strong when they get to college, and the extra money will really open up some opportunities for them.

Financial and Emotional Costs of Your Career Change

Now, use the space below to explore your own possible career change:

1. While you're training for your new career, what sort of changes will take place in your life? Describe factors such as time, money, and your mood:

_____

_____

_____

2. Describe how these changes will affect your partner and children (if applicable):

_____

_____

_____

3. When you complete your training for your new career, what sorts of changes will take place in your life? Describe factors such as time, money, and your mood. It's tempting to be Pollyannaish when you describe this, but try to be as realistic as you can.

_____

_____

_____

4. Describe the long-term effect on your partner and children (if applicable):

_____

_____

_____

You can get an even better picture of the impact your career change would have on your relationships by drawing a graph, just as you did with your future earning capacity. Figure 14.3 shows the graph that that David might have constructed.

The starting point or baseline for the graph is just before you start making your career change. Above "Currently," the "Same" circle would be marked on David's graph, just as it should be pre-marked in figure 14.4, the graph you will use. Six months into his career change, David would be in his first semester of law school. He would expect this to be a particularly difficult time. Money would be tight and the family, both his wife and sons, would be getting used to new routines. He and his wife would be negotiating new roles, and both would be strapped for time. So above "After 6 Months" he would have marked "Worse." He would have considered marking "Far Worse," but because Shelly is so supportive of his decision, and they have a good relationship, he would not expect the emotional climate to get that bad.

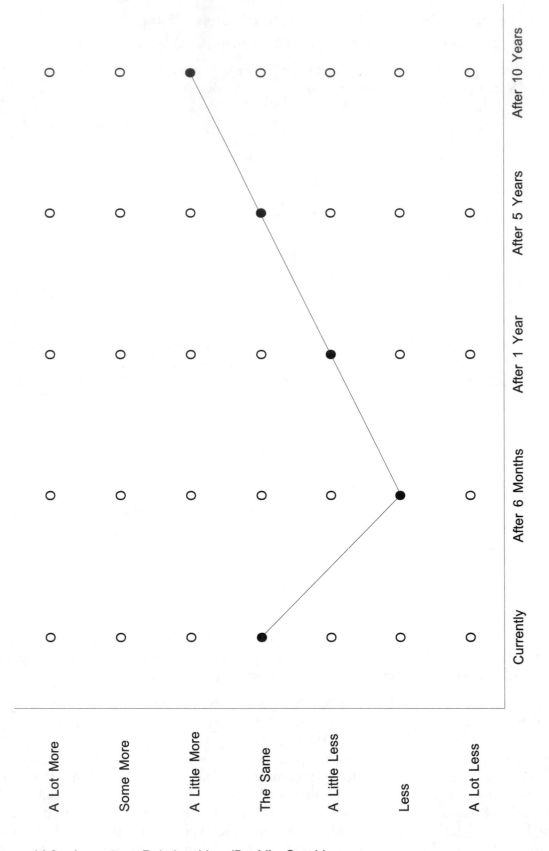

Figure 14.3: Impact on Relationships (David's Graph)

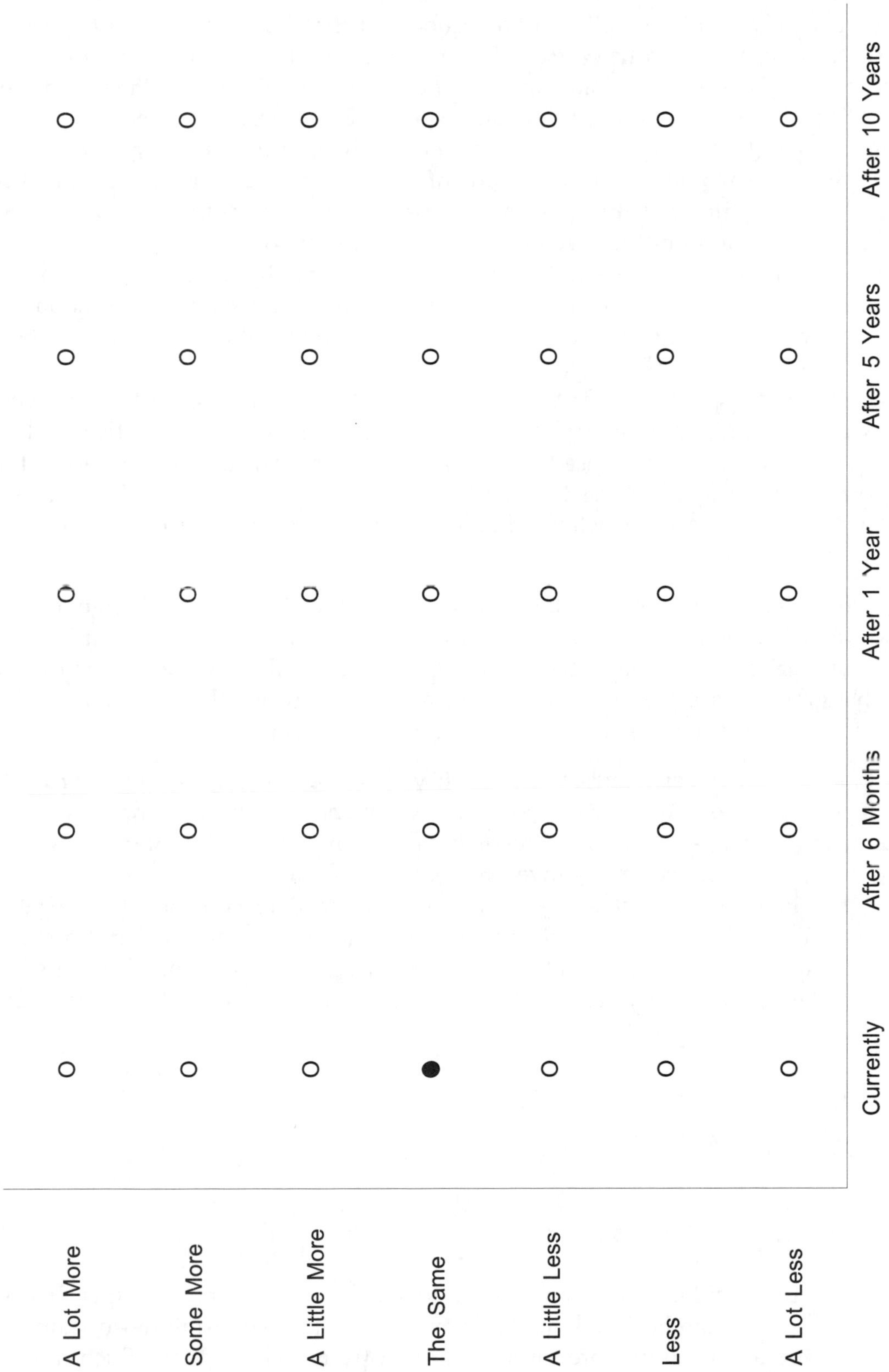

Figure 14.4: Impact on Your Relationships

At one year, he would be well into law school. At that point, he would expect his relationships to be only "Slightly Worse." There would still be a lot of extra work and some strain, but by then he would anticipate that everyone would have adjusted to their new roles. At the "One Year" point he would expect these problems to be only slightly greater than normal. (It is possible that he would be overly optimistic in his assessments.)

At five years, he would expect to be out of school, and starting his law practice. Their income would still be a little lower than previously, but both time and money would be more available than they were when he was in school. In spite of these negatives, he would be a lawyer at this point, and he, along with Shelly, would be anticipating a bright future. In the balance, he would expect that his relationships would be about the "Same" as they were before he started school, so he would mark the "Same" circle above "After Five Years."

At the "Ten-Year" point, his first impulse would be to mark "Greatly Improved" because he was thinking about law practice in very rosy terms. He would anticipate having a very good income and increased career prestige. But, realistically, he knows that what's important to his family is his time and love. He would expect that the increased income would give his family a better standard of living, and he would have marked "Some More" to represent that.

Now, use the graph in figure 14.4 below to chart the effect of a career change on your partner and other family members. The current state of your relationship is your baseline or point of comparison. Consider what your relationships will look like at each point, given the changing roles for you, your partner, and children or others in your family. Consider the effects of time demands and changes in your finances.

Now, look at the lowest point on the graph you drew. If the line is moving in the negative direction, ask yourself whether your family can endure your career change without experiencing any long-lasting or unacceptable problems. Think about how long your graph indicates you might be in negative territory.

Even if the long-term effect is very positive, you have to consider any negative "hump" you will need to get past. Taking all of these factors into account, put a checkmark below to indicate how your relationships would fare if you changed careers.

From the standpoint of my relationships, changing careers would be a good idea:

_____ Yes

_____ Not Sure

_____ No

Escape Clauses

One final matter to consider before moving ahead with a career change is this: It's not uncommon for people to go back to school as a way to avoid responsibilities or unpleasant situations, or as a way to prepare for a separation from their partners. Such motivations may be conscious or unconscious.

A new baby, an out-of-control teenager, or an unhappy marriage might make going back to school seem like a particularly inviting alternative. You need to examine your motives thoroughly and be sure that changing your career isn't an excuse for avoiding problems and shirking responsibilities. Consider your long-term situation and that of your partner and family, and address the responsibilities and problems of the long-term situation as best you can, before moving on. The next story is typical of the thoughts many people have before they make a career move to escape an unpleasant situation.

Valerie's Story

At age forty-six, Valerie is considering a career change. She works as a receptionist, and she has been married to Will for twenty-one years. Their son, Dan, is sixteen, and recently he has been having more and more behavioral problems. She is considering a career change, but for all the wrong reasons.

> I got a call from Dan's school today—again. He brought a knife to class and now he's suspended for two weeks. This makes me sick. Dan is so belligerent now; it's going to be intolerable to have him be home from school. And Will is no help. Since Dan has been having problems, he's just been less and less involved with our family. He is spending more time at work and with his buddies. I feel like I need to move on with my life, to take better care of myself. Being a receptionist has been okay as a career, but I'm getting tired of it now. I deal with problems all day long, and then I go home and hear about more problems. I'm looking into a school that trains you to work with computers. I'm so sick of people, I think I need a job where I can work by myself and not have to interact with anybody. And it wouldn't hurt to have a higher-paying skill because I'm not sure my marriage is going to survive.

Valerie sees school as a solution. It would give her a reason to get out of the house. It would also give her a reason to stay busy and to isolate herself from her family when she's at home. Going back to school sounds like a good thing to do; her friends are likely to tell her, "Good for you!" But her situation at home has reached a critical stage and the decisions she makes now could affect her own and her family's life for decades to come.

Unless her son gets strong family support and guidance right away, his problems could intensify and cause greater pain and deeper problems for himself, Valerie, and others for many years to come. Valerie's marriage is on the brink. A new career will bring little consolation if it comes at the cost of a divorce. Even her career decision is blurred by her difficult circumstances.

In the future, she might not enjoy a job with few social contacts, but her frustration with her current circumstances makes it seem like a good option. School may be a reasonable option for Valerie at some point in her life, but not before she tends to the problems at home. At this point, her time, energy, and money would be better spent on family or individual counseling than on a career change.

The important question to ask yourself before you make a career change (or any big life decision) is this: *Why now*? For instance, why didn't Valerie think about returning to school before she was married, before parenting became so stressful, or during the time when her relationship with her husband was better? Uncomfortable circumstances are pushing her toward her decision; she is not being pulled toward it by positive factors.

Here's how Valerie answered three important questions:

1. What (if anything) is pushing you toward your decision to change careers? What is uncomfortable in your life now that you'd like to change or escape from?

My home situation right now is awful. It's so stressful with Dan having so many behavioral problems and my relationship with Will going downhill. I've been irritable at work and no one there is understanding. When I'm snappy, they snap right back.

2. What (if anything) is drawing you toward the career you're considering? What positive changes do you see coming out of this decision?

There's nothing special about computer programming, except that I've heard it's a hot field. It's just so different from what I'm doing now. I'll be the expert instead of the helper who always has to smile at people. I think it will help me to make a big change in my life.

3. What impact will the career change have on the problems you mentioned in question 1? Will it help—or hurt?

I guess at this point I'm trying to preserve my sanity more than anything else. Going back to school won't help my home life. I'm thinking it could make my life less stressful, at least for now.

When Valerie read over her responses, she could see that her prospective career shift is much more of an escape than a well-considered change to something better.

Your Career Change

Now you can answer these three questions:

1. What (if anything) is pushing you toward your decision to change careers? What is uncomfortable in your life now that you'd like to change or escape from:

_____

_____

_____

2. What (if anything) is drawing you toward the career you're considering? What positive changes do you see coming out of this decision?

_____

_____

_____

3. What impact will the career change have on any problems you mentioned in question 1? Will it help—or hurt?

_____

_____

_____

Now, read over what you wrote, and consider carefully what your motives are for changing careers. Remember that developing a new career requires dedication, energy, and interest. If you are more motivated by a desire to escape from personal problems than by excitement about the new career, then you are unlikely to benefit from the change.

Check the statement that applies best to your situation:

_____ Yes, I have addressed my problems and taken care of my responsibilities as best I can before going ahead with my career change.

_____ No. When I honestly look I my situation, I see that there are some things I need to take care of before I make a career change.

Ready, Set, Go . . .

You checked "Yes" or "No" to three questions throughout this chapter: that is, you decided whether or not a career change would be a reasonable decision, first from an economic standpoint, and then from an emotional standpoint. You also considered whether or not you are using a career change as an excuse to escape from problems in your life.

If you checked "yes" three times above, and you were perfectly honest with yourself, then it looks as if you are ready to take the leap. A career change certainly has the potential to bring personal and financial rewards. Anything less than three affirmatives, and you have some more thinking to do. Talk to your partner, and consider the "no" and "not sure" answers. Do some research if you need to, in the library or bookstore, on the Internet, or by talking to someone already working in the field you would like to enter. If you're not ready to go for a complete change, look at chapter 15 for some ideas on how to make your current work situation a better one.

CHAPTER 15

Work II: Creating Your Ideal Work Situation

CHAPTER GOAL: To increase the value of your work, so that the quality of your life and relationships will improve.

When it comes to money, presidents, movie stars, and the CEOs of large corporations have something in common with us: most of their money derives from their own labor and choices. High-paying careers are not just the result of good luck. Generally, those who are highly paid have developed a specific skill or talent. This skill might be the ability to repair cars, or to solve complex mathematical equations, or to perform well in front of a camera.

Like you, highly successful people were better at particular tasks than most other people were. Through training and experience they honed their skill to make it better, and worth more. And then, they applied their skill so that it was properly valued.

Being paid well for the work you do has two elements:

1. You need to offer something valuable.

2. You need to find or create a situation whereby people will pay for what you have to offer.

"But I'm Not in It for the Money"

Most people don't need to be sold on the idea of making more money. Nevertheless there are many people who are different from most people. People who work as psychologists, social workers, teachers, and other "helping professions" are socialized to believe that "we're not in it for the money." Women, more than men, think about work in these altruistic terms.

For example, a recent study (Morgan and Isaac 2001) asked male and female college students to report their career choices, along with the reasons why they made these choices. Women were significantly more likely to report that they made their career choice because of a desire to "help people": 47 percent of the women versus 28 percent of the men listed this as a reason. On the other hand, men were more likely to report extrinsic rewards, such as money and status, as their motivators. None of the women, but 15 percent of the men, reported that they based their choice on such factors.

Moreover, because you're reading a self-help book, there's a good chance that you're the type of introspective, self-sacrificing person who has, at one time or another, denounced materialism, and declared that you're "not in it for the money." I may be overgeneralizing, so if I haven't described you, then you are certainly free to move on to the next section.

Maybe you feel that your work is intrinsically rewarding. This may be particularly true if you do work that is artistic, such as painting or writing, or if you work in fields that benefit society, such as teaching or counseling.

Employers are aware of, and may even exploit, this sense of social consciousness that many people feel. When Jerry Brown was governor of California, he told the teachers employed at state colleges that the state did not intend to raise their salaries because they receive "psychic pay" from the work they do. The message he sent, of course, was that their work is so rewarding, they don't need to be properly compensated. The teachers expressed their gratitude to then Governor Brown by sending him a "psychic" campaign contribution.

In fact, making good money, and contributing to the social good, are by no means mutually exclusive goals. Moreover, accepting lower pay doesn't necessarily mean that you'll get to do work that you will like better. In truth, the opposite is usually true. If the work you do is valuable, then it makes sense to hire other people to do the grunt work. This is true whether you own your own business or you work for someone else. If you're doing work that is not highly valued, the chances are good that that you'll be booking your own appointments and cleaning your office yourself. But if your work is worth a lot, you can focus on practicing your unique talent, and have other people take care of the less interesting chores.

Maximizing the value of your work has other personal advantages. It means that you can earn the same or more money in less time. If you work for an employer, an increased wage means more free time: You can drop a part-time job, your partner can work less, or you can cut back the hours you are working at your main job.

Self-employment often means working longer hours at first. Because you don't have much business or money initially, you often need to work as the receptionist, typist, and janitor. But as your reputation spreads, and there is more competition for your services, the value of your time increases, the actual number of hours you need to work decreases, and you can hire assistants for the more routine or less pleasant tasks.

Here's an example of this from my private practice. When I first started out in my own practice, I was willing to see almost anyone, for any reason, for very little money. I was so excited about being a newly licensed psychologist that I was happy to get paid anything for practicing my new skill. I wanted to keep what little money came in, so I typed my own reports, booked my own appointments, and did my own billing. For every hour I spent with a client, I spent at least another hour with paperwork and other chores.

As I built a reputation, and became more specialized, and better at what I do, I was able to charge more and get paid more.

My own Spartan tendencies made it difficult for me to hire other people to do the routine office tasks that I had been doing. At first it seemed like I was wasting money. But now, when I walk into my office, I know that all the tedious chores have been taken care of; I can do just the parts of my work that I enjoy doing, and I am earning considerably more money in considerably less time than I used to.

Increasing the value of your work gives you more control over your work schedule and your life, and means that you have more time to spend with your partner, family, or in other pleasurable pursuits. It also means you can provide more opportunity for your children, through furthering their education or by other means. If you feel a need to have some kind of social impact, you can do it within your own family, or by contributing to a worthwhile cause, rather than by allowing your work to be devalued.

Offer Something Valuable

"Supply and demand" remains a classic law of economics. A service or product is valuable when a lot of people want it, but it is in short supply. If you can do something that solves a problem for people, makes money for them, or gives them pleasure, you have something that is sure to be in demand.

Curing illnesses, creating stories, songs, or movies that many people enjoy, or helping a business to save or make more money are all services that are sure to have takers. If you have an aptitude or talent, and you develop it through practice or training, you will have something valuable to offer in the marketplace.

Consider the work you do now. If you are working for an employer, you earn your money by improving your employer's bottom line. In some direct or indirect way, you are helping your employer to get richer. Employers take the money that you earn for them, pay their business expenses, give you some of the money, and keep the rest for themselves.

You may think that your employer sets your salary, but this is true only in a very limited and temporary sense. Your work has a specific supply-and-demand value. If your employers can find someone to do the same tasks for less money, eventually they'll do that (unless they're your relatives). The opposite is also true: if everyone else who does your type of work is charging more than you are, then you are underpaid and you have the power to earn more money.

Let's say you teach French, and you're paid $15 an hour. If you quit, the next cheapest French teacher would demand $20 an hour. If you're doing a good job, your employer would be wise to try to keep you and to pay you more. Even at $19 an hour, they would still be getting a good deal, certainly a better deal than they could get if you quit.

You can also think about taking on new tasks to make yourself more valuable to your employer.

There are three basic strategies for making your time more valuable:

- Change jobs.

- Negotiate for a raise, because your employer cannot get the same value from anyone else. This includes making yourself worth more to your employer by learning how to solve specific problems or by offering new and special skills.

- A third way to increase the value of your time is to figure out a payment system that works better for both you and your employer. For instance, you might be able to work from home and be paid by the amount of work you produce. You can try to figure out a way for both you and your employer to make more money than before with an arrangement like this.

EXERCISE: CREATING YOUR IDEAL WORK SITUATION

Part I: Your Motivation

Check any statements that apply to your situation, and fill in the blank lines with anything else of importance that comes to mind.

I want to improve my work situation in order to:

_____ Spend more time with my partner

_____ Spend more time with my children/be a better parent

_____ Get more enjoyment out of my work

_____ Get more enjoyment out of the time when I'm not working

_____ Improve my standard of living

_____ Feel better about my work

_____ Do more creative tasks at work

_____ Do more creative tasks at home

_____

_____

Now look over your list. These are your motivations to change your work situation. Think deeply about the motivations on your list. Picture how your life could be different if your work situation could change, and share your thoughts with your partner. Get excited about how your life could change, and then start planning the changes in Part II of this exercise.

Part II: Making the Changes

Negotiating for a raise: This is a time-honored way of improving your work situation. *Negotiating* a raise is different from *asking* for a raise. Just asking for more money is a little like begging. You hope your situation will be pathetic enough to warrant mercy from your employer. On the other hand, negotiating means you bring something of value to the table and ask to be paid for it. This means that it's up to you to do the research to show your employer that the extra money paid to you will translate into extra value for your employer.

Why *should* your work be worth more today than it was yesterday? Because your boss has more information today than yesterday, and you're the one who provided it. Directly below there are some statements that, if you can make them apply to you, will transform your previously brass or silver talents into pure gold:

"People who do this kind of work are rare." The marketplace sets your value. If you boss can't stay in business without widget makers, and you're the only one for one hundred miles who can make those particular widgets, then you have a lot of value. Even after you negotiate a raise, you will still be saving money for your boss, because she or he will not have to comb the countryside looking for other rare and elusive widget makers.

"People who do this kind of work are expensive." When you sell your house, the agent looks up "comparables." The value of your house, which is determined by whatever people are likely to pay for it, is whatever houses like yours sell for, in the same area. These houses are said to be comparable. It's the same with people. You're worth whatever other people with the same skills are receiving for their work. Find out what your work is worth, and show your employer how much it would cost to replace you. A good resource to explore comparable salary information can be found at www.salary.com.

"I know more than you think I do." Maybe your boss already knows that widget makers pull down big bucks, and that you have to go to Timbuktu to find a good one. But how could anyone know that you're able to make the new, hot-selling pink, acrylic widgets, with handles? You have to find a way to get this information to the right people. Your company's reason for existing is to make money. If you can find a way for them to do this better, and you have the skills and knowledge to pull it off, they'll be all ears.

"There are other fish in the sea." You probably won't use these exact words, but, in the final analysis, having better alternatives is what gives you bargaining power. When you have other options lined up, you are in a strong bargaining position. Don't bluff, but if you know you can do better, then you can do some hard-nosed negotiating. When your boss says "no," if you have another job to go to, you can start walking.

EXERCISE: GETTING THAT RAISE

Option I: Increasing your work value

Step 1: *Find out what you're worth*: Check the library (see, especially, the U. S. Department of Labor's *Occupational Outlook Handbook* 2002) and the Internet at www.salary.com to find out how much your labor is worth. Be sure to take your experience, special skills, and location into account. Then fill in the blanks below.

According to my research, my annual salary should be between $ ____ and $ ____ .

Step 2: *Take an inventory of your special skills:* Do you have any knowledge, experience, or talents that make you more valuable than other people who do your type of work? Can your employer use your unique abilities to make more money?

My special work-related skills are these:

- _____

- _____

- _____

Now, put a value on your special abilities. Can your employer use these skills to make money? If so, how much more per year?

$ _____

Step 3: *Shopping for a deal*: Even if you've been at the same job for years, it's a good habit to check the want ads every other Sunday to pay attention to the market value of your skills. It is also a good way to keep your ears open for opportunities. It is not an accident that people who prepare well experience the best "lucky breaks" in their careers.

Go through the ads in the paper or search the Internet for current opportunities. Search engines like the ones at www.hotjobs.com or www.monster.com make this very easy. You enter what you've looking for, and you get a list of jobs that meet your criteria.

Now, list the jobs that you'd qualify for and that you know you could do:

- _____

- _____

- _____

If you find something that might be better than your current job, call or e-mail the firm for particulars, send a resumé, and try to get an interview.

Step 4: *Making your case*. Once you've gathered the information listed above, you'll come to one of two conclusions: either you're getting a good deal at your current job, or you're not.

If you're already getting a good deal, one alternative is to settle in with what you've got and count your blessings. The other, more exciting, alternative is to develop your skills so you're worth even more, or to develop a business that will better use the skills you already have.

But, first, let's say you're not getting a good deal. You could do what a lot of employees do—complain and grumble about your tightwad boss and the sorry company that hired you. Although this may provide you with some pleasure, it definitely won't develop your career or promote your personal growth. It would be much better to present your case and try to maximize your situation.

Look over what you wrote above, and decide what makes the best case for you. Are other people paid more? Do you have special skills that can make more money for the business? Is there a way that you can redesign your job so that it works better for you and your employer? Do you have other, better options? Now fill in the blanks below:

My research shows that my employer would still get a good deal if I were paid an extra $ _____ per year.

I could arrange my job differently so it would work better for both me and my employer (i.e., I could work at home, work as an independent contractor, use assistants or automation, find my own clients, etc.):

_____

_____

_____

I have some better alternatives. I'll pursue some of them, or try to get my current job to match what one of my alternatives will offer. (List information about any better alternatives you've discovered. List employer names, positions, and salary or other advantages over your current job):

_____

_____

_____

Now, it's time to take some action.

- I will set up an appointment with the person who has decision-making power (your boss, a job interviewer, the Human Resources Department). Specifically, I will contact: _____

- I will present important points based on what I've written above. I'll specifically focus on: _____

- I will ask for (a raise, a change in the way my job is structured, different work schedule, etc.): _____

  _____

  _____

- If I don't get what I want, my next step will be (to make a modified offer, discuss alternatives with my boss, actively pursue another job): _____

  _____

  _____

Option 2: Creating Your Own Work Situation

If you work for someone else, your employer has created a structure that allows you to focus on your work, while the company takes care of all the other aspects of running a profitable business. For instance, let's say that you're a hairdresser. You've been trained to cut and style hair. You have a skill that people are willing to pay for. You work for a firm called MegaCuts.

As an example, let's say you do two $15 haircuts per hour. You're earning $30 per hour for your employer, Megacuts, but your employer is paying you only $12 an hour. Where does the other $18 go? Is your employer ripping you off? Not really. Out of that $18, your employer is paying the rent on the hair-cutting salon, paying for the utilities, buying supplies, and absorbing risk and liability.

If you cut off someone's ear, you won't be doing many more haircuts in that shop, but your employer will pay for the damages and the lawsuit you incurred. The same thing holds true if you slip on some spilled hair tonic; your employer will pay for your hospital bill. If business is slow, you will still get paid. If the business fails, you can walk down the street to find a new job, but your employer will have to pay off the creditors.

One of the most important things your employer does is to find customers for you through advertising and other forms of marketing. People come to MegaCuts because they have positive associations from previous haircuts there, and they know they'll get a certain, predictable service.

Now *think big*. Or, at least, think a little bigger than you've been thinking. There are different ways that you can do your work that will allow you to make more money and have more freedom and control, *if* you're willing to take on more responsibility. If you want to go in this direction, you can do it gradually, both in terms of hours per week and levels of responsibility.

For instance, if you're a hairdresser, some shops will give you your own booth, and you pay them a percentage. That is, you become an independent businessperson instead of a salaried employee. You keep your salaried job until you build up your independent business. If you're really adventuresome, you can rent or buy your own shop, hire a receptionist and other hairdressers, and go into the haircutting business as your own boss, and as an employer of other haircutters. The more responsibility you take on, the more money you can make—and the more money you can lose.

Going into business for yourself can work for almost any job. If you have knowledge that others can use, you can be a consultant. If you have a skill, you can advertise or otherwise find people who will buy your time to make use of your skill. Sometimes, your spouse or partner can become part of your business as an added bonus. The upside to this arrangement is that you will have more contact with each other and, at the very least, part of the work can be done at home. The downside is that such business contact may be stressful, and may interfere with your relationship.

I used to have my wife book my appointments from home. This allowed me to make more money and it made it possible for her to stay at home with our young son. On the other hand, on the days when she had to deal with particularly rude or difficult clients, booking my appointments gave her some serious doubts about the wisdom of my career choice.

EXERCISE: SHOULD YOU GO INTO BUSINESS FOR YOURSELF?

When you own your own business, you take on more responsibility in return for more freedom and the possibility of earning more money. Here are some advantages, disadvantages, and personal characteristics that go along with starting your own business:

To answer the following questions, circle either Yes or No. The more "Yesses" you circle, the more likely it is that you should remain an employee rather than becoming your own boss.

Yes   No   I like to focus on using my particular skills, without having to worry about the business aspects of my work.

Yes   No   I'd rather have a steady income, instead of taking the chance of earning a greater, but unpredictable, income.

Yes   No   It's more important for my job to be dependable than flexible.

Yes   No   Finding clients or drumming up new work is something that I'd rather not worry about, even if I could make more money with my own clients.

On the statements below, the more "Yesses" you circle, the more likely it is that you would do better to start your own business than continue working for someone else.

Yes   No   I'd really like to have more flexibility in my work, e.g., choosing my own work schedules, making my own decisions about how to do things, etc.

Yes   No   I'm very responsible when it comes to tracking and budgeting money.

Yes   No   If I ran my own business, I'd research my options and buy for myself the benefits and business overhead costs that my employer buys for me now, e.g., health insurance, disability insurance, liability insurance, accounting expenses, salaries for assistants, etc.

Yes   No   I don't mind taking a calculated risk if it can help me do better in the future.

$ $ $ $ $

In this chapter, you were asked to consider ways to make your work more valuable. You can negotiate with your employer, or you can set out on your own. You also can look at creative ways to rearrange your career so that you will increase your emotional and financial rewards.

Many couples have a fairly rigid idea of what their two careers are supposed to look like: you go to your job in the morning, I'll go to mine, and we'll see each other at dinnertime. Work can be much more flexible and fluid than that. You can combine salaried work with your own business. You can keep your work life completely separate from your partner's, or you can look at ways to merge them. You don't have to let your career be defined by your employer(s); you and your partner can define your work lives for yourselves.

CHAPTER 16

Investments

CHAPTER GOAL: To learn how to decide where to put your extra money, once you've defined your tolerance for risk and your vision for your future.

Investing: Easy; Spending: Easier

Making investments is the opposite of going into debt. If you've ever carried a balance on your credit card, you know how quickly debt can snowball. Buy a lot of small things, and a few big ones, and before you know it, your "easy monthly payments" have turned into a monster.

Investing works in the other direction, and allows you to accumulate lots of money. Given enough time and enough consistency, you can make investments with hardly any financial pain.

If you had money in the stock market in 2000, you probably experienced a considerable amount of financial pain, and you had lots of company. When the stock market dips, however, that doesn't mean investing in the stock market is senseless or that you were a fool for putting your money in the market. But your experience does emphasize basic fundamentals about investing; i.e., investing is for the long haul and it is essential to diversify your investments.

If you look at a graph of the stock market over the last seventy years or so, you'll notice a few characteristics. Sometimes it dips or even crashes. Everyone knows about the big crash in 1929 and the early thirties. The market didn't fare too well in the mid-1970s, there was a big drop in 1987, and the early 2000s haven't looked too good so far. But the overall trend has always been upward, and the dips create opportunities to pick up stocks at a discount.

Variations from day to day and even year to year reflect all kinds of factors, such as the mood of the country and the latest news stories. But over long periods of time the trend reflects the fact that corporations earn a profit (to survive they need to), and this profit makes their stock go up. No one can predict when the market will go up or down or when an individual stock will take off. But if you invest for the long haul, and make regular investments in a wide variety of different industries, you will be taking advantage of the market's long-term success.

Spending Money

Spending money is a lot easier than saving it. (Hey, you needed a psychologist to tell you that?) That's because when you spend, you get a reward right away. Having less money doesn't have to cause you much immediate pain or stress, but whatever you buy for your money usually feels pretty good.

On the other hand, putting money away where you can't see it isn't particularly exciting. Your reward is far off in the future, and faroff rewards govern our behavior a lot less powerfully than immediate rewards do. So, in our consumer-oriented society, spending and incurring debt take place easily, without much effort or thought, but saving and investing have to be thought about and planned.

Almost every human problem (and some animal problems, too) are caused by the general tendency to seek short-term rewards over long-term ones. Alcoholism and drug addiction certainly fit this description. The desire for the immediate good feeling caused by the substance is stronger than the bad feelings that inevitably come later. So it is with saving and investing money. In the short run, stashing money where you can't see it, or use it, just isn't that much fun. It takes a highly evolved human brain to figure out that what you do today will make your life easier a few years down the line.

What Kind of Investor Do You Want to Be?

When it comes to investments, these are the things to consider:

1. How much risk are you comfortable with? This is the dimension of the Gambler/Banker that was discussed in chapter 4.

2. What's your vision for your future? Do you see a steep incline upwards, with a lot of money in the future? Or do you see a flatter course, medium work now, medium work later, and not much change in your income? What kind of financial life path did you and your partner map out when you read chapter 11?

3. What's your situation now? If you're in debt, then your main investment goal is to pay off debts. A credit card balance, with interest charges in the range of 18 to 21 percent, is like a gaping hole in your financial ship. As you move toward a sound financial future, paying down this debt needs to become one of your primary goals.

What to Invest In

There's a lot to know about investing your money, and there are many other books that can fill you in on the details. I particularly recommend *Lifetime Financial Strategies* by M.

Loeb (1996), and *The Wall Street Journal Guide to Understanding Personal Finance* by K. Morris and A. Siegel (2000).

Here's the back-of-the-hand, cheat-sheet version:

Stocks

Buying stocks are what most people think of when they think "investment." When you buy stock, you buy a small piece of a corporation. There are fairly low-risk ways to invest in the stock market. You can make regular investments in tried-and-true "Blue Chip" companies. Or you can invest in large groups of companies, through a mutual fund, and let a professional pick your stocks for you. If you buy-and-hold for many years, you will weather the ups and down of the market, and you're likely to make some money over time.

There are other ways of investing that can make things very risky and exciting. When the stock market was soaring in the late nineties, day trading was very popular. People would sit in front of their computers and make big bucks in short-term trades. Some of these people sold all their stocks at high prices and stopped trading before the bubble burst. They are now living the life of Riley. Most day traders didn't stop (there's really no way to know when the market's going to turn around), and now they're living the life of "Poor-Me."

Bonds

Bonds are less glamorous than stocks. You don't make fortunes with bonds, but then you don't lose your shirt either. When you buy a bond, you're lending your money to a corporation or a government. They pay you a certain fixed interest rate over a specified length of time, just as you would if you were borrowing money from a bank or a credit card company.

Real Estate

Owning your own home has been a classically good investment for hundreds of years. For most people, it's a natural step as they move ahead in their lives. The advantages of owning your own home are these: (1) by deducting your mortgage interest, you receive a tax savings on your income tax, and (2) you accumulate *equity* as you pay off the loan, and as your house rises in value. (Equity is the difference between what you owe on your house and what you can sell it for.)

The disadvantage to owning your own home is that you have less mobility. Because you have to keep paying your mortgage until you sell your house, it becomes harder to move. In a slow real estate market, it could take months to sell your house. You also risk losing money, because in a recession, the value of your house could fall, and you could even wind up selling it for less than what you paid for it.

Another disadvantage to owning your own home is that you also have to pay for all of the maintenance and home repairs that your house might need. The plumber, the electrician, the guy who cleans the gutters on your roof after a big storm—they all work for money. If it is your house, you have to pay for these services yourself.

Buying property and renting it out can be an excellent way to make money, but it, too, has definite risks. A bad tenant can cause a lot of stress and can cost you a lot of money. If you have problems with exercising authority, having one or two bad tenants will cure you of this.

As a landlord, you'll find yourself in a position of natural authority, and you are likely to start hating irresponsible people. If you own rental property, you have to be able either to keep it fully occupied, or be able to pay the mortgage when it's unoccupied, or worse, when it's occupied but your tenant isn't paying rent.

Bank Accounts

Banks are good places to store money; they are much safer and cleaner than old mattresses. The interest rate is low, usually just enough to offset inflation, and sometimes even less. But it's easy to get to your money when you need it, and unless there's a nuclear holocaust, you won't lose any of it and you aren't risking any of it.

Money Market Accounts

In addition to a standard passbook savings account, your bank also offers money market accounts. They usually require you to invest a certain minimum amount, and they limit the number of withdrawals you can make. The interest rate is generally better than a regular savings account.

Certificates of Deposit

You can also invest in certificates of deposit at your bank. These require a certain minimum deposit, often several thousand dollars. They also require that you keep the money on deposit for a certain amount of time. The longer the period of time you are willing commit to keeping your money in the account, the higher your interest rate will be.

Your Debts

As I pointed out above, you can hardly find a better investment than paying off your debts. Unless you can get rid of your debts in a bankruptcy proceeding, they have to be paid, and the interest you're paying on them just vaporizes your money. As a general rule, put extra money toward your highest-interest debts, and start paying off the next highest-interest loan when the first one is paid off.

Consolidation Loans

If you have one or more high interest debts and reasonably good credit, a consolidation loan might make sense for you. A bank, credit union, or savings and loan institution can loan you money to pay off your existing debts. As a result, you will make one monthly payment which will be lower than the payments you were making on several loans.

However, it is important to look over the terms of the loan very carefully because it is possible to lower your monthly payment without improving your overall financial condition. The crucial factor when taking out a consolidation loan is the interest rate. To save money, the interest rate on the new loan must be lower than the rates you were paying on the debts you consolidated. Otherwise, you've only lowered your payments by stretching them out over a longer period of time.

Education

Putting money into your education is often cited as a classic good investment. It's hard to argue against the quest for greater knowledge and further self-development, but from a financial standpoint, more education is *not* always better. If you're young and you learn a well-defined skill at a state subsidized institution, you'll come out ahead. So, a twenty-two-year-old entering medical school at the University of California at San Francisco will see her initial investment in higher education returned many times over. However, a forty-five-year-old attending an expensive, private art institute to study art history is going into a money-losing proposition, and should consider the cost of the higher education only for personal growth and enrichment, not as an investment.

EXERCISE: PLANNING INVESTMENTS

You'll need to do some library research for this exercise. The two books I mentioned above, *Lifetime Financial Strategies* by M. Loeb (1996) and *The Wall Street Journal Guide to Understanding Personal Finance* by K. Morris and A. Siegel (2000), are excellent places to start your research.

Let's say you have $500 a month to invest. (If you haven't got $500 on hand that you can invest right now, try doing the exercise in chapter 19, "Financial Planning," and perhaps that will help you to find that money.) Look at the investment possibilities outlined in the sections above, and try to come up with other possibilities of your own, or with variations on the possibilities above. Think about your risk tolerance, your long-term goals, and your current financial situation. Then start planning your investment portfolio below. Start simple. If you have a lot of credit card debt, then paying off your debt might be your only investment option, but it would certainly be one worth doing. Now, fill in the blanks in the exercise below:

Out of $500,

I would put $ _____ into paying off debts

$ _____ into stocks

$ _____ into fixed-interest investments

$ _____ into my education to increase my skills and job potential

$ _____ into real estate, i.e., saving for a down payment, if I don't already own my home; or saving to buy a rental property, if I do own my home.

Take notes. Keep a notebook devoted only to your investment research. Jot down specific details from your research. Collect information about the types of investments that are a good fit with your financial personality and your partner's. Investigate investments that would work with your current financial situation, not with the situation you hope to achieve in the future, but right now. What can you afford to invest now?

Planning Investments Together

I wanted to give this section the subtitle, "Skipping Hand-in-Hand Down to Easy Street," but my editor thought that was too frivolous. Clearly, investments are not the sort of thing you talk about over a quiet, candlelit dinner. But there is some romance to be found in investing together. By planning your investments jointly, you're committing to a future together. You're sharing your dreams and your visions for how you want your life together to look in one, five, or forty years.

There are two things you need to decide:

1. What are your goals for your life together in the future?

2. What are you willing to sacrifice now—this year—to get there?

This exercise will help you and your partner to clarify these two very different but completely interdependent components. You'll probably arrive at some shared goals and the willingness to share some sacrifices jointly, while other goals and sacrifices may be more specific to one of you. Nevertheless, since you're already sharing your lives, whatever you decide to do as individuals will affect your partner.

EXERCISE: PART I—DEFINING YOUR GOALS FOR THE FUTURE

Here are some reasons why people invest money. Check your top two or three goals. Then, consult your partner to find out his or her top goals (or make your best guess):

Me   My Partner

_____ _____ To have more control over our lives (so we can make decisions with less need for concern about work and work schedules)

_____ _____ To spend more time together or with family

_____ _____ To have more time to pursue my own interests

_____ _____ To have enough money to finance children's education (now or in the future; children we currently have or plan to have)

_____ _____ To further my own or my partner's education (to change careers, advance careers, or for personal enrichment)

_____ _____ To have enough money for retirement

_____ _____ To achieve a better lifestyle or accumulate wealth

_____ _____ To buy a house (or move up)

_____ _____ To experience less financial stress

_____ _____ Other: _____

_____

_____

When you have completed this exercise, you're likely to find that you have some shared goals, and some that are more individual. There are some goals that you'll definitely want to commit to achieving, but you'll negotiate about whether to go for the deluxe or economy version. For instance, at some point you'll both need to retire, but will it be in a mansion with servants, a one-room studio apartment, or somewhere in between? The kids will need an education, but whether you're saving for the local state college or Harvard is definitely something to discuss.

You're making big decisions about your future, so you'll need to sit down with your partner. Set a time to meet and a time limit (about fifteen minutes is good). First, talk to your partner about investments that are nonnegotiable for you and for him or her. Work out how much you'll need and when you'll need it. The tables in Appendix B can help you to estimate realistically how much you'll need to save and/or invest.

Do you think you can reach your important goals? Is there room for some additional goals? If the answer to either question is "No," then you need to consider Part II of this exercise.

EXERCISE: PART II—WHAT WILL YOU SACRIFICE TO GET THERE?

This is a simple but quite important part of the exercise. You both have important goals for the future, and you need to figure out how to get there. How much are you and your partner willing to sacrifice toward your shared and individual goals? You may not figure this all out in one sitting, but keep coming back to the table, until you have a good balance between your investment goals and your ability and willingness to get there.

Me   My Partner

____   ____   Willing to work more hours

____   ____   Willing to improve my work situation (see chapters 14 and 15 for ideas about how to accomplish this)

____   ____   Willing to spend less (see chapter 20 for some ideas on how to accomplishing this)

____   ____   Willing to find other sources of money (Rent a spare bedroom? Start a side business? Will take some brainstorming)

$ \quad $ \quad $ \quad $ \quad $

Investments that both you and your partner plan are a commitment to your future together. By making plans and sacrifices together, you are strengthening your relationship.

Just the fact that you are considering investments puts you ahead of the pack and says something positive about your relationship. If this all seems overwhelming, don't get discouraged. Remember that planning your future is an ongoing process, and not a single all-or-nothing decision. If it's not feasible to plan all of your investment goals right now, just work on the ones that are within reach, and come back to the others when the time is ripe. Paying down debt is one of your most important investments; start with this strategy, if that's what fits your current financial situation, then move on to other investments.

CHAPTER 17

Savings and Insurance: Your Financial Fortress

CHAPTER GOAL: To review your options, with the aim of helping you and your partner make a commitment to a less stressful financial life.

There are very few financial surprises that you can't anticipate and protect against. The right kind of savings accounts and insurance policies can help you step off the financial roller coaster. Consider Anthony and Regina's case.

Anthony and Regina had been married for three years. They were both the same age, twenty-nine. And they both were self-employed professionals. Regina sighed when she spoke:

You know, we're not kids anymore, and I don't think we're ever going to get ahead. We'll be going along great for a while. We'll even have some extra money, and then WHAM! The car breaks down or we have a huge dentist bill. Then another charge goes on the credit card, or we end up deciding which bills to postpone paying, and when we do that, the finance charges go up.

Anthony agreed.

We're trying to save a down payment for a house. But that's still a long way off—if we ever get there. A lot of times I feel like we need to spend the money when we get it, 'cause we won't have it for long.

Superstitious Solutions:
Let's Chant 'Til the Rent Is Paid

Anthony and Regina's personal finances seem totally unpredictable to them. When your finances are unpredictable, you may start doing all kinds of useless things to try to gain some sense of control. For example, Anthony and Regina spend money because they have it, and fear that if they do not spend it, they will no longer have it. This fear creates a completely irrational self-fulfilling prophecy.

B. F. Skinner (1948) found that when he randomly dropped food pellets to reward pigeons, they started performing various rituals to keep the pellets coming. If they had been cocking their heads when a food pellet arrived, they'd continue cocking their heads, hoping for another one. And sure enough, sooner or later, another pellet would arrive to reward head cocking, dancing, pecking, or whatever else they did to keep the pellets coming. Skinner said that the pigeons were engaging in "superstitious" behavior.

So, too, Anthony and Regina behave irrationally. They believe that unpredictable financial forces they cannot control buffet them about. They continuously apply short-term solutions to long-term problems. They live just a little beyond their means, and from time to time they splurge because spending money provides an immediate, if short-term, sense of relief from their many creditors

A great deal of "positive thinking" financial advice is based on superstition. You may have heard, or believe, statements like this one: "Take what you deserve, live well, and the bountiful universe will rain down riches upon you." Unfortunately, the universe isn't all that concerned about your financial status. Live too well and fail to plan, and pretty soon the universe will come and gobble up your paycheck and bank account.

Taking Control with
Savings and Insurance

There are two ways to make your finances a lot more predictable: *savings* and *insurance*. Saved money, set aside only for well-defined emergencies, allows you to deal with the unexpected expenses that inevitably come up every few months. If you don't have saved money, your alternatives are to put charges on your credit cards, or to defer fixing problems until you have the money.

Expenses charged to credit cards are notoriously difficult to pay off because of high interest rates, and because more unexpected expenses invariably come along before you can make much headway paying down the first charge. Deferring doctor or dentist visits, home repairs, or car repairs until you have the money to pay for them can leave you with much bigger expenses in the near future.

Two Levels of Saving

You save money for different reasons: for everyday, planned extras and for unexpected expenses that will come, sooner or later. Longer-term expenses are "investments," which we discussed in chapter 16. The following list shows the types of expenses that can wind up on your credit card, and mushroom into big, long-term debt, unless you consistently put money away to take care of them.

- Everyday expenses: This is the money in your bank account that you use from day-to-day. Here's where you accumulate enough money to pay for a weekend getaway, buy a stereo, or go out to eat. Keep enough in your checking account to cover the checks you write, and put the rest of your funds into a savings account to draw interest.

- Short-term emergencies: This is the money that solves the well-defined problem that occurs unpredictably, but which happens sooner or later. This includes payment for car repairs, medical co-payments, and fixing and/or replacing anything else that breaks.

Painless Saving

Okay, putting money away is never painless. But since the human spending reflex is much stronger than the saving reflex, you need to find a way to make the saving that you do automatic. Many employers will deduct money automatically from your paycheck and put it into an account for you.

If your employer does not do this, your bank can regularly transfer money from your checking account to your savings account. All you need to do is to instruct the bank how much to take out of your checking account and deposit in your savings account every paycheck.

Be very clear about the purpose of your savings account. For example, define what sort of emergencies it can be used for, and do not use it for anything else. If necessary, consider opening another savings account for specific, planned expenses, such as vacations and big-ticket purchases.

Insurance

Insurance is for the mostly rare events or occurrences that could severely disrupt your finances and your life. Because insurance covers you for events that happen rarely, such as natural disasters, disabilities, and accidents, it may be tempting to put off buying it until you're "on your feet," or until you think you can better afford it. This is a mistake.

As you climb life's financial mountain, you want to be able to hold onto any progress you have made. The events that are covered by insurance act like financial avalanches, and could drop you at the bottom of the mountain again. Or, worse yet, they could put you in serious debt.

Even if you never have to use your insurance, you are buying what insurance agents call "peace of mind." For a relatively small amount of money, paid out every month, you can feel fairly confident that you won't have any surprises coming down the road that could destroy you financially. Here are some types of insurance and the events that they can protect you from.

Automobile Insurance

When you drive a car, there are a lot of expensive events that can take place. Typically, automobile insurance covers damage to your car and damage to other people's cars and property. It also covers medical expenses caused by car accidents. Covering the damage to your own car is optional: If you have an old car, and you have the money to replace it, it may not be worthwhile to insure potential damage to your car. On the other hand, if you're still making payments on your car, remember that you will still owe this money if your car is wrecked.

Life Insurance

When you think about it, life insurance is an amazing product, one that only the complex and abstract-thinking human brain could invent. You pay monthly premiums for a product that you won't live long enough to benefit from personally. Life insurance allows you to continue to be responsible for your family's well-being after you no longer exist. You may find it uncomfortable to think about life insurance because it's uncomfortable to think about dying. But buying life insurance acknowledges the fact that you and your partner or family are interdependent, and it provides you with a way to take care of your responsibilities when you're gone.

It's easy to underestimate how much life insurance your family will need. A few hundred thousand dollars may sound like a fortune, but keep in mind that you may need to replace *years* of earnings you would have had if you had lived. If you have children, and you or your partner stays home with them, then you need to consider the monetary value of the work of daily parenting. The surviving partner may need to hire baby-sitters, housekeepers, perhaps pay for tutors, or the cost of tuition at private schools. On top of the grief and chaos that follows one parent's death, additional stress about money is the last thing anyone needs.

Health Insurance

A lot of people are still covered by health insurance through their work. This arrangement is becoming less common than it used to be, though. You might find yourself without health insurance after you lose a job, because you take a job that doesn't provide coverage, or because you're self-employed.

Buying health insurance makes sense not only to cover the cost of health catastrophes, it also makes it easier to see a doctor for annual checkups and routine health problems, so that small health issues don't become catastrophes. It's important to hang onto your health insurance regardless of what else is happening in your life, because if you let it lapse and you develop any serious health problems, you may not be able to get reinsured without paying exorbitant premiums.

The Consolidated Omnibus Reconciliation Act (COBRA) is a Federal program that allows you to continue your employer's health insurance when you are no longer eligible because you have been laid off, or cut back to fewer hours. It is also available to the survivor when the insured, employed spouse dies or divorces.

You will need to pay the premium yourself, at your employer's group rate. This is usually cheaper than buying health insurance at individual rates, and you can't be turned down because of a pre-existing condition. However, the coverage stops eighteen to thirty-six months after termination of employment.

If you have a pre-existing condition that makes it difficult for you to get health insurance, many states have a high-risk insurance pool, that allows you to buy insurance regardless of your medical condition. More information about COBRA and state-provided high-risk insurance can be found at www.cobrahealth.com.

Disability Insurance

Disability insurance is one type of insurance that you may not ever have thought of buying. But the odds are good that you'll become disabled at some point during your working life. Nearly half of all thirty-five-year olds will become disabled for at least three months before they reach the age of sixty-five (Loeb 1996, p. 461). Without disability insurance, your financial situation could become a disaster area. There are government disability plans, but they may not provide enough money, or they may not cover your type of disability.

For instance, Social Security does provide disability payments, but only if you're going to be disabled for a long time, and only if you are unable to perform any work at all, even minimum wage work. It's important to find out what type of disability coverage you have through your employer, and to find out whether your employer will allow you to hang on to what you've got if you become sick for a long, or even a short, time.

Homeowners' and Renters' Insurance

If you own a home, the bank that you pay your mortgage to probably requires you to carry insurance for your home. This insurance pays to fix or replace your house and possessions in case of fire, theft, or other natural disasters. It doesn't hurt to review your policy now, and to see what it covers. You may need to pay extra to cover items that you assumed were covered.

On the other hand, your home owner's insurance might cover items that you never thought it would cover, so if you don't know what's covered, you could lose money by not filing claims for these items. You may not have thought much about the company that provides your homeowner's insurance, since you probably signed up with them when you were completing the avalanche of paperwork to buy your home. Now that that's out of the way, talking to an insurance agent and looking into other companies might save you a bundle of money.

If you rent your home, you may not have thought about getting coverage against theft and fire. However, it makes sense to think about all the things you own, the clothes, stereos, computers, books, musical instruments, art, and so forth. Now, think about how and if you would be able to replace them if they were gone. Then think about whether it would be worthwhile for you to look into a renter's policy.

EXERCISE: YOUR MOTIVATION TO SAVE

Financial advisors typically tell you to save three to six month's salary. Of course, this is easier said than done. If you're just starting out, or if you are currently struggling with debt, saving three to six month's salary sounds about as realistic as flying to the moon on a broomstick. Saving that kind of money is possible, but there's an important step that comes first: *Making the commitment to save.* And, as any good actor will tell you, before you act, you need to answer one question: "What's your motivation?"

Motivation No. 1: I'm tired and stressed by all of our financial ups and downs. Just when we seem to get ahead, an unexpected problem comes up and drains our finances.

(Circle one): **For me this is a:**   **For my partner this is a:**

      Strong Motivator   Strong Motivator

      Mild Motivator   Mild Motivator

      Weak Motivator   Weak Motivator

Motivation No. 2: Money in a savings account would make me feel as if we're getting somewhere in life. It would feel as if our foundation is more solid than it's been in the past.

(Circle one): **For me this is a:**   **For my partner this is a:**

      Strong Motivator   Strong Motivator

      Mild Motivator   Mild Motivator

      Weak Motivator   Weak Motivator

Motivation No. 3: Because we have no savings, unexpected expenses keep going on our credit cards. This is becoming more and more stressful.

(Circle one): **For me this is a:**   **For my partner this is a:**

      Strong Motivator   Strong Motivator

      Mild Motivator   Mild Motivator

      Weak Motivator   Weak Motivator

Motivation No. 4: If we had some savings, that would give us more options. We could have more flexibility with our work. Life wouldn't feel like such a rat race.

(Circle one): **For me this is a:**   **For my partner this is a:**

      Strong Motivator   Strong Motivator

      Mild Motivator   Mild Motivator

      Weak Motivator   Weak Motivator

Motivation No. 5: I have dreams about a good life in the future. But it's hard to dream, when our finances are always on the edge.

(Circle one): **For me this is a:**   **For my partner this is a:**

      Strong Motivator   Strong Motivator

      Mild Motivator   Mild Motivator

      Weak Motivator   Weak Motivator

Motivation No. 6: (Fill in the blanks with your own important motivations):

_____

_____

(Circle one): **For me this is a:**   **For my partner this is a:**

        Strong Motivator   Strong Motivator

        Mild Motivator   Mild Motivator

        Weak Motivator   Weak Motivator

There are a lot of reasons to save. Look over what you circled above, and consider what would best motivate you and your partner. Then, make a commitment to saving. Start out small if that's all you're able to do now. Even making a commitment to a very small amount will begin to change your thinking, and start to move you in the right direction.

    Our commitment: "Every week, we will save $ _____"

EXERCISE: INSURANCE? WHAT, ME WORRY?

As a psychologist, I usually help people to worry less. When you make decisions about insurance, I want you to worry more. If you or your partner thinks or feels that buying insurance is unnecessary, or you "can't afford it," this exercise is for you.

- What will you do if you are faced with a big financial setback? For instance, a major illness requiring expensive medical care, a period when you or your partner are unable to work, or an automobile accident that causes a lot of expensive damage. How would your life change? What would be the effect on your relationship and your family? How would you get through it? How would your life be different afterwards? If you or your partner died, what would life be like for the person left behind? Write down your answers to these questions in the space provided below:

    _____

    _____

    _____

    _____

    Now, read over what you wrote and talk about the subject of insurance with your partner. Then, think about doing an inventory of your insurance, and make plans to buy what you need to reduce your anxiety levels.

Unless you plan for financial problems, your financial life can seem like a roller coaster ride, a ride that's mostly headed down. If you did the exercises in this chapter, you have now made a commitment to a solid, predictable financial future, to save some money every month, and buy the necessary insurance to give yourselves peace of mind. By doing this, you are paving the way for steady, predictable financial progress.

CHAPTER 18

Your Financial Set Point

CHAPTER GOAL: To discover what your financial "set point" is. Everyone has a financial set point. It is the internal sensor that tells you when it's time to make adjustments to your finances, or to panic. Find out where this point is for you and your partner, and learn how to adjust it if that becomes necessary.

A budget is a lot like a diet. Both diets and budgets put you in mind of deprivation. In twelve-step programs, the members sometimes talk about "white knuckling it." That means just gritting your teeth, and resisting the temptation as long as you can. White knuckling is difficult, even admirable. If overspending is your drug of choice, you may be able to budget for a little while, but pretty soon, the beads of sweat start forming on your forehead, your knuckles turn white, and the sirens at the local mall start singing your name. However, whether it's food, alcohol, drugs, or overspending, you need more than just determination to kick a habit. You need a commitment to a new way of life and a shift in your way of thinking.

The keystone to your spending style is your *financial set point*. This is the point at which you are triggered to pull back on your spending. If overspending has been your problem, your set point is too low: that is, things have to get really bad financially before you'll cut back on your spending. If you're so conservative with your spending that you skimp on necessities and drive your family nuts, then your set point is too high: you won't spend money unless it is an absolute necessity.

The chances are fairly good that you've never even thought about the fact that you have a financial set point. Like most people, you just try to stay within a certain comfort zone when you spend money, and you stop spending when you feel stretched. But when you "white knuckle it," you try to act counter to your set point, fighting against what feels natural to you. To make long-term changes in your spending, you need to go to the heart of the matter, recognizing and recalibrating your set point. In the next section, you'll find out how to do this.

Your Financial Set Point

Everyone has a particular financial set point. As stated above, this is the point where you begin to feel uncomfortable about the state of your finances. If you're conservative with managing your finances, you have a high set point. If you have a low set point, that means you spend money freely, and you don't stop until there is a problem. When you have a high set point, to feel comfortable, you might need six month's salary in your savings account, and a steady income that exceeds your expenses. If you have a high set point, you're very unlikely to have money problems, but you may find yourself worrying a lot about money if your expectations are too high. Furthermore, if your set point is much higher than your partner's, you can look forward to frequent disagreements about money.

At the other extreme are those who have a very low set point. Some people start to worry about their finances only when their financial problems are personally affecting their day-to-day lives: that is, bill collectors are constantly calling, the car's been repossessed, and the eviction notice is nailed to the door. If your financial set point is low, you're destined to live from one financial crisis to another.

Here are some observations I've made that may be helpful when you're developing your financial plan with your partner:

- The higher your financial set points are, the safer you will be financially. But do not set them so high that you always feel as if "the sky is falling." Living with a high set point is easy for those who are Spartans/Bankers/Pioneers. A high set point is really hard for Monarch/Gambler/Homesteaders to achieve.

- The closer your set point is to your partner's set point, the fewer disagreements you'll have about money.

EXERCISE: FINDING YOUR FINANCIAL SET POINT

Your financial set point acts quite like a thermostat. There's a certain point where you begin to feel uncomfortable and you become motivated to take remedial action. Check the problems that would motivate you to take some action to improve your situation. The action might be to cut back on your spending, to do something to increase your income, or to make other lifestyle changes. As always, you can speculate about your partner's answers, get input from your partner, or have your partner answer these questions himself or herself.

I would take action if . . .

High:

Me   My Partner

_____   _____   The savings account has less than six months salary in it.

____ ____ I'm able to save some money every month, but less than I'd like to.

____ ____ Some vague signs of job instability (no one has lost their job, there's no talk of layoffs, but business has dropped off a little).

____ ____ **Total number of checks**

Medium:

Me   My Partner

____ ____ I've got no savings, but I'm able to pay all my bills every month.

____ ____ I'm not able to save money on any consistent basis.

____ ____ There have been some layoffs where I work. I have heard some rumors that I could lose my job.

____ ____ **Total number of checks**

Low:

Me   My Partner

____ ____ I'm letting some of my bills go because I can't pay them.

____ ____ My consumer debt (i.e., credit cards) is increasing every month.

____ ____ Losing my job looks like a good possibility.

____ ____ **Total number of checks**

Very Low:

Me   My Partner

____ ____ There are frequent calls from bill collectors; threats or actual lawsuits to collect the money I owe on my debts.

____ ____ Foreclosure or eviction is imminent.

____ ____ There is not enough money for necessities.

____ ____ I expect to lose my job and I do not have any immediate prospects of other employment.

____ ____ **Total number of checks**

Now, look at the total number of checks in the "Me" column under "High." If you checked two or more statements, your set point is High. If you made fewer than two checks in the High section, then look at the "Me" column under "Medium." If you have two checks here, then your set point is Medium. If you made fewer than two checks in the Medium section, then look at the "Me" column under "Low." Two or more checks here, and your set point is Low. Fewer than two checks here, and your set point is "Very Low." Use the same procedure to find your partner's set point. Start at the "High" level and work down, finding the first level at which your partner checked at least two statements.

Now, fill in the blanks below:

My financial set point is _____ .

My partner's financial set point is _____ .

Do You Need to Adjust Your Set Point?

When you think about changing your financial set point, you need to consider three things:

- How high or low is your set point now?

- How different is your set point from your partner's set point?

- What are your financial goals?

We will cover each of these points one by one.

How High or Low Is Your Set Point?

As a rule, a set point that is too high is better than one set too low. If you wait until bill collectors start pounding at your door, or the repo man is in your driveway, then by definition you are experiencing financial problems in your life right now.

If your set point is "medium," you can probably live with that. With a medium set point, you'll cruise along, and maybe you will experience a few financial crises that you will have to struggle with to recover from.

A high set point does a better job of protecting you from financial surprises. But if staying on high means that you and the people close to you are in a constant state of panic, then high is too high. If your set point is low, or very low, then you'll wind up in a wasteland financially. These low levels for set points mean your finances are headed south. And they probably also mean that, sooner or later, your friends and family will get tired of your sad stories and endless financial problems. And you'll get tired of constantly having to deal with financial emergencies.

How Different Is Your Set Point from Your Partner's Set Point?

The difference between your set point and your partner's can lead to difficulties and arguments. Every financial decision you make, e.g., the number of hours you or your partner works, your lifestyle, how you spend money, all of these variables are governed by your financial set point. If you and your partner are quite a bit different on this dimension, inevitably, there will be times when you will think that your partner has no financial sense at all. And your partner will think the same of you. Your conversations about money could sound like the couple below:

Raphael and Ronnie

Raphael and Ronnie are in a committed relationship. They have been living together for three years. Here is how they "discuss" their differences:

Raphael: I just don't understand it. I'll save for months to buy something I want. Before I spend a cent, I need to make sure all my bases are covered. But Ronnie thinks nothing of taking out a second mortgage to pay for remodeling the house. That just wasn't the way I was brought up. The more she spends, the more I feel I have to cut back, so I'm always getting caught holding the short end of the stick. It's just not fair.

Ronnie: The way Raphael feels about money just doesn't make sense to me. You can't take it with you! Why not get some joy from your money while you're alive? We always have enough to get by, no one's ever going to starve. I wish he would learn to live a little. Sometimes, though, it makes me feel guilty that he's so careful with money, and I'm not.

Different set points can stir up a lot of emotions. Emotions like anger, resentment, and guilt. The person with the higher set point might wind up feeling the way a parent does when dealing with a wayward child; always admonishing the other person to be more responsible. And the partner of someone with a high set point might respond in kind, acting sullen, saying things like "loosen up," or feeling guilty, and struggling to rein in her or his impulses to please the other partner.

What Are Your Financial Goals?

If you're not stealing, allowing your children to starve or go without essentials, or otherwise causing problems for people who are financially responsible, then how you deal with money is up to you.

Your financial goals are an important variable in figuring out how to deal with conflicting attitudes about money. You might decide that you don't need to be rich, and that you don't want the stress of an ambitious career. You might choose not to think about future financial problems today, because you've got other, more important stuff to think about.

I could point out to you that, just by giving up your morning cappuccino, you could accumulate $20,000 over twenty years. But you could very well tell me to shut up, because twenty years of sipping cappuccinos sounds a lot more pleasant to you than acquiring a pile of loot for when you're old and creaky. It all depends on what you value in life, and no one can tell you that.

So, do you or your partner need to change your financial set points? Only if there's a problem. A problem could mean any one of the following:

- A set point that's set so low, you don't see trouble coming

- You and your partner have such different set points, you fight about money and can't agree on financial decisions

- Your set point is inconsistent with your financial goals. For instance, you want to be able to retire at fifty, but at thirty you not only have no retirement savings, you are sinking further into debt

Look at the exercise earlier in this chapter, "Finding Your Financial Set Point," to be sure you know what your and your partner's set points are. If you'd like to have a set point that's different from the one you currently have, use the exercise below to help yourself make the changes. If you decide that you and your partner are fine where you are now, that's great. You can skip the next exercise, "Changing Your Financial Set Point," and move on to the next chapter.

If, however, you would like to change, and part, or all, of the change you would like to see involves your partner, then you must consider how realistic this ambition is. If your partner agrees to try to change, that's fine. If not, then you must decide whether you need to change to become more like your partner, whether you can adjust to your partner's style, or whether the two of you, as a couple, need the extra help that can be found in chapter 20.

EXERCISE: CHANGING YOUR FINANCIAL SET POINT

You developed your particular set point over a long period of time. You observed how your parents handled their finances, and, as an adult, you learned from your own financial experiences. So, changing your set point will take both daily practice and the passage of time; changing your financial set point is a little like learning to play an instrument.

Changing your set point means changing the thoughts you think that lead you to your financial decisions. For example, Jacquelyn is a person with a high set point; Nicholas has a low one. Here are the thoughts each thinks when faced with an identical situation:

Both have just received a call from their auto mechanics. Both were informed that they needed a $1,500 car repair. Neither has the cash in their checking account. Both intend to pay for the repair with their credit cards.

Jacquelyn: (high set point) This is a problem. I don't want to start sliding into debt; I know how hard it is to get out. I'm going to have to really cut back on my daily expenses. In fact, I am going to start bringing my lunch to work. I'm not going out to eat again until that bill is paid.

Nicholas: (low set point) Oh heck, I've got a $20,000 credit limit on that card, and the payments are only twenty a month. While my car's in the shop, I might as well take a few days off from work and take that vacation I've been putting off. I've gotta take care of myself.

Nicholas reacts to bad news about money by minimizing it, and spending more money to feel better. Jacquelyn reacts by pulling in the financial reins until she feels stabilized again. Nicholas is playing a *mind game*. By minimizing the importance of his debt, he was able to keep his low set point and relieve any guilt or anxiety he would have had about spending money. In the next section, you can read about this and other ways that people fool themselves so that they can maintain their problematic spending habits.

Mind Games

Here are some of the "mind games" people play with themselves (psychologists like to call these "cognitive distortions") to keep their financial set point too high to ever relax about money or too low to ever be financially stable

Too high (almost always nervous about money)

Catastrophizing: This mind game requires every monetary setback to be seen as the first step on the long road downhill, leading to inevitable disaster.

Obsessing: With this game, every little financial detail is seen as crucially important. This can entail missing the forest for the trees, and worrying about the lost quarter in the vending machine, instead of trying to think of ways to save or earn thousands of dollars.

Spartanism: This cognitive distortion requires you to become self-righteous in your self-denial. You view your ability to endure hardship as a sign of the virtue that makes you superior to other people.

Overanalyzing: In this mind game, your partner's spending habits are analyzed as evidence of all manner of negative behavior, from irresponsibility to a lack of love. "If she appreciated how hard I work for the money, she wouldn't have bought such an expensive dress." "If he really cared about our future, he'd worry more about paying off our credit cards."

Too low (headed toward financial problems)

Minimizing: This process involves finding ways to think about financial problems so they won't bother you. Thinking about a $2,500 credit card debt as just an extra $50 per month is one way of minimizing the debt, because it ignores the fact that the payment must continue for many years. If you are taking home $100 a day, you will get a more accurate picture of what a $2,500 debt means by thinking of it as worth more than six months of working every Saturday.

Denying: This mind game is also called "the Nero syndrome," because you act like Nero, fiddling while Rome burns. As long as you have enough to eat and a roof over your head, you figure that everything is basically okay, and if everything is not okay, then someone will come along to rescue you. Not until you can't buy yourself a meal, or the sheriff is ordering you out of your home, do you acknowledge that there might be some problems.

Entitlement: In this game, your feelings about what you think you deserve are your spending guide, instead of the facts of your financial situation. This mind game is exemplified by this line: "After a day like this, I need to splurge."

Overanalyzing: This mind game was listed above as a strategy used by people who have set points that are set too high for their comfort. But it is also used by people with low set points. "If he really cared about me, he'd take me to nicer places." "If she loved me, she wouldn't always be trying to get me to spend less money." In this mind game, you assume that your partner's thrift demonstrates a lack of caring.

Now, you are ready to do the exercise. First, look at the sample worksheet provided below, and then use the actual worksheet each time you or your partner makes a financial decision involving more than one hundred dollars. (You can copy the blank worksheet to use it whenever you need it.) This could be anything from the size of your monthly credit card payment to the amount of rent you're willing to pay for an apartment. Try to capture the thought and the mind game that led you to make your decision in your usual way, with your set point set either too high or too low. Then, try to imagine what you would decide if you changed your set point. The more you practice, the more your decisions will be "Just Right."

Sample Worksheet for Changing Your Set Point

Date: _____

Financial Decision: I know I shouldn't, but I'm going to take the vacation I've always wanted. Two weeks in Europe, it's just what the doctor ordered.

Compared to where I want to be, my set point on this decision was: Too High, Just Right, **Too Low**

Do the rest of the exercise if your decision wasn't "Just Right."

I used the following strategies to keep my decision from being Just Right: Entitlement, Denial

My specific thought was this: I work harder than anyone I know and I deserve this vacation. **I also thought:** I'm so far in debt that one more expenditure won't make any difference.

A better thought would be: I'm having some financial problems, but I can get out of this hole with some restraint and planning. I need to start watching my money more carefully.

And with this better thought, I'll make this better decision: A weekend getaway will help get me back on track. Instead of taking a longer vacation, I'll apply what I will save toward my credit card balance.

Worksheet for Changing Your Set Point

(Copy this page and use it each time you make a financial decision. You might want to keep these pages in a notebook to chart your progress.)

Date: _____

Financial Decision: _____

_____

_____

_____

Compared to where I want to be, my set point on this decision was:

Too High

Just Right

Too Low

Do the rest of the exercise if your decision wasn't "Just Right."

I used the following strategies to keep my decision from being Just Right: _____

_____

_____

_____

My specific thought was this: _____

_____

_____

_____

A better thought would be: _____

_____

_____

_____

And with this better thought, I'll make this better decision: _____

_____

_____

_____

$ \quad $ \quad $ \quad $ \quad $

As you change your set point, you'll find some subtle and not-so-subtle changes taking place in your relationship with your partner. It will become easier to understand your partner's point of view, and to understand why your partner makes particular decisions. If you move your set points closer together, you'll find that it's easier to work together on your joint money-related decisions. Whether you move your set point up or down, you'll find that you'll begin making decisions that will improve your future and will provide you with peace of mind.

CHAPTER 19

Financial Planning for the Lifestyle You Want

CHAPTER GOAL: To create a financial plan that will give you greater understanding and control of your specific financial situation, and to start creating a more prosperous financial future.

Financial Plans

As mentioned in chapter 18, a budget can be a lot like a diet. Dominguez and Robin (1999) came up with this analogy before I did. Both budgets and diets make you think of deprivation. Whenever someone says, "We're on a budget," it never means "Luckily, there's an empty category in my budget-minder, and this extravagant purchase fits in there perfectly." No, nearly always it means, "We can't afford it."

A financial plan is a different kind of animal. A financial plan is *proactive*. Instead of figuring out where to cut back and tracking every penny (as in calorie counting, and no one can do that for very long anyway), you go for the big picture. You figure out what you want your life to look like, and then you create a life to fit that image.

What Comes In, What Goes Out, What's Left Over

The day of reckoning has come. You had to come to this sooner or later. Now, you need to get down to dollars and cents. To borrow a phrase from pop psychology, you'll be shifting from your right to left brain. The exercises below are provided to help you figure out what kind of lifestyle you want to live, and to help you decide if you want to modify your current lifestyle. First, you will figure out how much income you currently have coming in, then you are given information to help you decide whether you want to live in one of three different modes. Number one is "survival mode," two is a "modest lifestyle," and three is a "prosperous lifestyle."

Let's start out by adding up everything that comes in. The final number can be an estimate, but it needs to be a fairly reliable one. Note that it's always better to underestimate than to overestimate.

EXERCISE: WHAT'S YOUR INCOME?

Job income: What's your monthly take-home income, after taxes and other mandatory expenses have been taken out? If it varies, find your pay stubs for the past few months and take an average. If, typically, you receive a tax refund when you file your taxes, divide this by 12 and add that sum to your monthly pay. If, typically, you owe money when you file your taxes, subtract this amount (divided by 12) from your monthly take-home pay. Figure this out for both you and your partner.

Business income: If you get income from your own business, figure out how much you take in, minus your business expenses, and minus taxes. If you did a tax return for your business last year, this is probably where you can find the most accurate information about these numbers. You can also check your business income over the past few months to see if there have been any big changes since last year. Then, figure out the average income that your business nets every month.

Investment income: If you have investment income, add that in, too. This includes anything that you can count on arriving every month in your mailbox—money earned from bank interest, stock dividends, bonds, and rental property. Don't forget to subtract out the expenses and taxes.

Odds and ends: This is money that comes in, reliably, from anywhere else but regular jobs: baby-sitting, hobbies, gifts, child support. Figure out a monthly average, based on the last few months. As always, don't forget about taxes or expenses, if there are any for these items.

Now, add up your monthly income:

My salary income is: $ _____

My partner's salary income is: $ _____

My business income is: $ _____

My partner's business income is: $ _____

My investment income is: $ _____

My partner's investment income is: $ _____

My odds and ends income is: $ _____

My partner's odds and ends income is: $ _____

Our total is: $ _____

EXERCISE: WHAT ARE YOUR EXPENSES?

You can think of your expenses as falling into three broad categories. These are as follows:

1. **Survival mode:** What you need to survive. This is a "bare bones" minimum, for example, a humble domicile, enough cheap food to survive, the bus for transportation, and only free entertainment.

2. **Modest lifestyle:** Another word for this might be "thrifty." You save where you can, but take no draconian measures. For example, you dine out occasionally, and take vacations occasionally, but you take the three star rather than the five star route. Your car isn't a late model luxury car, but it's not quite a bucket o' bolts either.

3. **Prosperous lifestyle:** This is the lifestyle that comes to your mind when you think of being well-off or very comfortable. Most people associate a prosperous lifestyle with a nice car, a nice home, and getting the day-to-day products and services they want without waiting, and without compromising quality.

These three categories can serve as markers for your lifestyle landscape. If there are money shortages, you can cut back to No. 1, survival mode, only by living with hardship and inconvenience, you can cut back to No. 2 with some adjustments, and there's a very wide range for No. 3.

Now, figure out the next group of expenses with your family's lifestyle in mind, whether this is just you and your partner, or whether there are kids or other dependents involved, too.

Shelter

Find the monthly figures for each of the levels described below. You may need to check the classified ads under "Home Sales" or "Rentals" to get a better idea of the monthly cost of each for these levels. If you are currently a renter, use similar rental prices for comparison; if you are a home owner, compare against the cost of buying a similar home.

Survival mode: How low could you go with your shelter expenses and still survive? Take into account the fact that you may need to live in a certain area in order to get to work, and that you and your family need a certain amount of room. After accounting for such issues, how low could your monthly rental or mortgage be?

Modest lifestyle: This is the level that seems reasonable but not extravagant to you. It might mean living in a safe neighborhood and having a home that provides just enough room to eat and sleep. For instance, if your family includes just you and your partner, a one-bedroom, one-bathroom apartment might fit the bill.

Prosperous lifestyle: Picture the neighborhood and house that you think of when you think of people who have "made it." Maybe it would be something short of the Taj Majal, but it would have plenty of room, a beautiful appearance, and be in the precise area you'd like to live.

Food

Survival mode: This doesn't have to mean rations of bread and water, but figure out how much it costs to pay for cheap, healthy, cooked-at-home food for one month.

Modest lifestyle: Now, how much can you spend on food without feeling as if you've moved down the social ladder? What's a reasonable food budget? Could you cut down or eliminate dining out and buying expensive foods to prepare at home?

Prosperous lifestyle: Even if you were Bill Gates, you'd get tired of nothing but champagne and caviar at Spago in Beverly Hills. But think about what kind of food and where you'd be eating it if you didn't worry about money. Then figure out what your grocery and restaurant tab would be.

Utilities

This category includes phone, cellular phone, gas and electricity, propane fuel, heating oil, cable, water, and trash.

Survival mode: Think minimum. One-minute toll calls for birthdays and emergencies. Wear sweaters in the winter and shorts in the summer. Perhaps you can have a small TV, but, for sure, no cable.

Modest lifestyle: Keep the temperature between 65 and 80 degrees, put a three-minute timer by the phone, and get rid of the extra cable channels. This is livable, but no extras.

Prosperous lifestyle: What do your utilities actually cost? Look at your bills for the last few months. A prosperous lifestyle might include extra cable TV channels, high speed Internet hookups, keeping your home at the perfect temperature at all times, and lots of long-distance calls.

Transportation

Car expenses, including gas and oil, insurance, repairs, annual registration costs, and your monthly car payment (or the price of your car divided by the number of months you'll keep it).

Survival mode: There are probably a lot of ways that you can reduce your transportation costs, but like everything else in survival mode, cutting back in this area is not a pleasant prospect. If you can get to work by public transportation, think about what it would cost if you sold your car and rode the bus. If you must have a car, what's the cheapest model (with the best mileage) that would get you to work reliably?

Modest lifestyle: What would your transportation costs look like if you cut out the Sunday drives, shopped for cheaper insurance, perhaps raised your deductibles, and kept your cars longer before trading them in? How much of the fat can you cut from your transportation budget?

Prosperous lifestyle: Very comfortable transportation for many people would be along the lines of owning a late model luxury car, traded in every year or two. What kind of transportation would represent a prosperous lifestyle for you? What kind of car would you need, and how often would you trade it in? Figure out your total costs: monthly insurance payments, gas, registration, and maintenance and paying off the car.

Clothing, Cosmetics, and Personal Services

Here's a list of everything you buy to make your body presentable. Clothing, makeup, shaving supplies, manicures, and jewelry are all in this category. Try to take an average of what you spend on these items over a period of several months. Average in more money if you buy expensive items such as jewelry occasionally.

Survival mode: There's a lot of room for trimming excesses in this category. All you need to be presentable are haircuts, showers (or baths), and some well-fitting items from the Goodwill store. Figure out what your absolute minimum would be, short of losing your job and becoming a social outcast or having the welfare department remove your children.

Modest lifestyle: Okay, you don't want anyone to look at you with a horrified expression, and say, "What happened to you?" But there's probably still room for thrift here. Cosmetics, clothing, cologne, jewelry, and hairdressers have wide price ranges. Consider how low you can reasonably go.

Prosperous lifestyle: How much money would it take for you and your family to feel really good about your personal appearances? The amount you spend on appearance can vary widely, depending on your personal taste. Total up the cost of what you consider to be really nice clothing, quality cosmetics, and quality hair salon and manicuring services.

Health

Health costs includes insurance premiums, doctor bills, and medications including over-the-counter medications such as cough drops. If you receive insurance through your employer, just figure out the amounts you pay, either those that get deducted from your paycheck or those you pay when you visit a doctor. This is likely to vary from month to month, so take an average over a period of at least the last six months. If you don't have insurance, you still need to figure in how much it would cost if you did. That's because sooner or later, you'll have to go to the doctor and pay the bill out of pocket.

Survival mode: When we discuss maintaining your health, "survival" is a pretty literal word. The lowest you can go is to buy a basic health plan that will pay for your medical needs if you become ill. Then, take good care of yourself.

Modest lifestyle: You do have some discretion here. You can make decisions about how necessary certain procedures are, you can buy generic medications when they're available, and you can consider enrolling in an HMO (where your health care is managed or rationed) instead of having indemnity insurance. But be careful: HMOs can be inconvenient, and you might have to fight the bureaucracy to get good care.

Prosperous lifestyle: Include everything you pay for health care, including health insurance and doctor bills, expenses for complementary care such as acupuncture, cosmetic surgeries, vitamins, and the gym.

Recreation, Entertainment, Entertaining

In this category, include everything you do to have fun: vacations, movies, amusement parks, hobbies, sports, having people over for dinner. If you use recreational drugs, I wish you'd stop, but until you do, include their costs in here.

Survival mode: There is no fun being in survival mode unless you can entertain yourself, e.g., make music, visit friends, etc. So, unless you'll absolutely lose your sanity without a little paid recreation, your survival-level recreation budget is zero.

Modest lifestyle: You're not ready to join a religious order, but there is still some room to cut back your recreation budget: take shorter vacations closer to home, go bowling instead of playing golf, rent videos instead of going to first-run movie houses.

Prosperous lifestyle: When you think about "the good life," how do you picture spending your free time? Total up the cost of indulging in your hobbies, taking dream vacations, and taking in a movie, concert, or show whenever the mood strikes you.

Household Items

In this category, include everything you buy for day-to-day use: bath soap, laundry soap, detergent, electric light bulbs, furniture polish, paper, pencils, hardware etc. Certain household items, such as furniture, last a long time and don't need to be replaced. At the high end of this category there are the really expensive things that you do to your home, such as remodeling.

Survival mode: Don't replace anything unless it breaks and you absolutely need it. So, you're mostly left with the option to buy a few exhaustible supplies such as staples and cheap ballpoint pens.

Modest lifestyle: Cut out the big purchases. You can live with the same furniture and silverware you have, and you can probably have a perfectly happy life, even if you never remodel your home.

Prosperous lifestyle: In the prosperous category under "Shelter" you decided what your ideal domicile would look like. Now, think about how you would furnish it and change it to create the ideal living environment. Include costs for buying and replacing furniture, remodeling, putting in a pool table, a swimming pool, and any other amenities that would suit your taste.

Household Maintenance and Domestic Help

This category covers what you pay for plumbing, lawn maintenance, painting, carpet cleaning, and the other tasks that must be done around the house. If you're a handyman or -woman, and have spare time, you can probably handle a lot of these chores by yourself. If you rent, your landlord probably takes care of a lot of them. Be sure to include any domestic help and the price of baby-sitters.

Survival mode: Just enough to keep everything working. Shop around for the cheapest handyman, do it yourself, or find a neighbor, friend, or relative who works cheap. Fire the domestic help. No baby-sitters unless you must have one in order to go to work.

Modest lifestyle: Cut out the extras; just fix things when they need fixing.

Prosperous lifestyle: In this category, a prosperous lifestyle means that you are able to hire people to do almost everything you don't want to do yourself: household repairs, cleaning, yard maintenance, cooking, child care, and so forth. Consider what you'd want others to do, and how often you'd like them to do it. For instance, you might want all of your household cleaning chores taken care of, but only want child care occasionally, such when you go out for the evening. Estimate the cost of all the domestic services you want.

Note that what you consider to be a high estimate is likely to be a realistic assessment. For example, the neighborhood handyman may work cheap, but he may be hard to reach, difficult to schedule, and not know how to do many jobs. Furthermore, he may not guarantee his work, and not be insured if he breaks his leg on your property. The prices charged by the businesses listed in the Yellow Pages will give you real-world information about the actual, long-term costs of domestic help for a prosperous lifestyle.

Minimum Loan Payments

These are the costs of what you have to pay on loans and credit cards to stay out of trouble. Use the same figure for each lifestyle; just put in what you need to pay on your current debt load.

Everything Else

These are any expenses that don't fit into a category above.

Now, total all your figures in the table below:

	Survival Mode	Modest Lifestyle	Prosperous Lifestyle
Mortgage/Rent:	_____	_____	_____
Food	_____	_____	_____
Utilities:	_____	_____	_____
Transportation:	_____	_____	_____
Clothing/Pers.:	_____	_____	_____
Health:	_____	_____	_____
Recreation:	_____	_____	_____
Household Items:	_____	_____	_____
Household Maint.:	_____	_____	_____
Min. Loan Paym't:	_____	_____	_____
Everything Else:	_____	_____	_____
Totals:	$_____	$_____	$_____

When you finish this exercise you'll have three very important figures: they are what it would cost you to live minimally, to live modestly with some minor sacrifices, and to live as prosperously as you might like to live. The next step is to compare these three figures to your actual income. Consider whether your current income is at a level needed for the survival mode, a modest lifestyle, or a prosperous lifestyle.

Let's start at the top: what if your income equals or exceeds your figure for a prosperous lifestyle? Very few people are in this category—if you're one of them, consider yourself fortunate. An income at this level gives you many choices: you can live the prosperous lifestyle you imagined, or you can live more modestly and have more free time, more career options, and/or more money to save and invest. At higher income levels, jobs often take longer to find and you may have less job stability, so it makes sense to save for a rainy day.

Suppose your income can support a modest lifestyle? Most working people fall into this category. This means that, with fairly minor financial sacrifices, you can pay for what you need and come out in the black every month. This is good news: it means that you make enough money to support a tolerable lifestyle. Barring unforeseen problems, such as a job layoff, you can get along just fine without significant financial problems (this assumes you have your bases covered, having built your "financial fortress" with savings and insurance, as suggested in chapter 17). You may even have a little room to cut back on your spending, and you might be able to find ways to get a little extra income. By taking either of these measures, you'll have savings and investment money to move you toward a brighter, more financially stable future for yourself and your partner.

But what if you're still over your head at the "modest lifestyle" level? Then, you have two choices: to make more money, or to move to the "survival" level.

EXERCISE: CONSOLIDATING YOUR GOALS, YOUR INCOME, AND YOUR REALITY

Now, you're faced with some important facts about your situation, and you have some important decisions to make. It would be a good idea to have your partner join in on these decisions; they could make a tremendous difference in your future.

Decision No. 1—your lifestyle: Now, that you have done the math, you have a real-world yardstick to use to make a lifestyle decision. It has three markers: survival mode, modest lifestyle, and prosperous lifestyle. You know, in good conscience, that your lifestyle has to cost less than your income (unless, as discussed previously in chapter 13, you're using money for a short-term goal such as to get an education).

However, you do have the option of picking a lifestyle that costs less money than you bring in with your income. Having some extra money will allow you to make investments. Investments can allow you to change your future dramatically, giving you money to live more luxuriously, to help family members, to live without working, or to experiment with new ways of life, without having to take money into account.

So, considering what you just learned, pick a lifestyle by marking an "X" on the line below (if you have money to spare with your current lifestyle, you could even pick a point above "Prosperous Lifestyle"):

Survival Mode   **Modest Lifestyle**   **Prosperous Lifestyle**

|—————————————|—————————————|—————————————|

$ _____ $ _____ $ _____

Estimate about how much per month your "X" represents. For instance, if it's half-way between Modest Lifestyle and Prosperous Lifestyle, take the average of these two fig-ures. Now, write that figure on the line below.

Our monthly expenses for the lifestyle we want will be: $ _____ (*lifestyle expenses*)

Decision No. 2—your income: Now, consider your income. Do you want to keep it where it is? Do you have room to decrease it, so you can have more free time? Or do you want to increase it? Consider what's immediately available to you in terms of making more money, and figure out what you or your partner would be willing to do to make that money. Then fill in the spaces below.

Right now, our monthly income is: $ _____ .

Considering the lifestyle we want, and the amount of work that we can do, we'd rather have a monthly income of: $ _____ (*desired income*).

Finally, subtract your *lifestyle expenses* from your *desired income*. This is a very impor-tant figure. This is the money that you can use to change your future. You can use this money to:

- Invest and grow over time

- Enjoy yourself

- Get more education

- Start a business

- Pay off debts

$ $ $ $ $

This chapter has given you and your partner a nuts-and-bolts way of planning your financial future. You have chosen a lifestyle and chosen an income. You now have a clear idea of what it will take to end your financial problems, or to move toward financial free-dom. It's up to you now to take the necessary steps to get there.

CHAPTER 20

Money-Saving Strategies

CHAPTER GOALS: To present some simple, straightforward ways to squeeze a few more dollars out of your monthly budget.

Saving Money

Can't save money? You don't have any more excuses. Here are some simple things that anyone can do. Go over the suggestions below, and think about what's practical—and what's not. With willingness and a little effort, your budget can come out in the black every month, and you can start building a solid financial future.

Recreation

When looking for ways to save money, the amount you spend on recreation is the first logical place to look for cuts. For example, when you go out to eat, you could ask for one entire meal, or one entrée, to be split between the two of you. Restaurant portions are notorious for providing much more food than most people can—or should—eat at one sitting. At a moderately priced restaurant, this could bring a typical meal for two down from twenty dollars to thirteen.

Vacation costs vary widely. When you need to just "get away" and enjoy your partner's company, a nearby jaunt to a modestly priced hotel can provide a lot of the pleasures that you'd get from a European extravaganza. And if you do go to Europe, staying at hostels (www.Hostels.com) is a lot cheaper than paying for hotels.

Utilities

Telephone

Unlike the old days when everyone depended on Ma Bell for phone service, you now have a lot of choices for local, long-distance, calling card, and cell phone rates. There's often not much difference in quality, so, here, cheaper is usually better.

A few hours spent comparing the services available will pay off. Be sure to consider everything: charge per minute, how calls are timed (by the second or minute? minimum charge per call? monthly charge?).

Review your phone bills for unneeded services. I recently found my home phone bills had a $10 monthly charge for a "Custom Calling Package." This included exotic features that I never used, like a special ring for long-distance calls.

Vary your usage to make the best use of discounts: there are special rates for nights and weekends. Use whichever is the cheaper when you're on the road—cell phone or calling card.

Gas and Electric

There are lots of ways to save on gas and electric costs. Insulation and a programmable thermostat can save on your heating bill. Replacing incandescent bulbs with compact fluorescent ones can provide the same amount of light for a fraction of the cost. The fluorescent bulbs are quite a bit more expensive initially, so the savings is for the long-term. You can replace older, power-draining appliances with more efficient ones. Your utility company has more power-saving ideas, and sometimes will provide rebates, such as for insulating, to help with resource-conserving purchases.

Cable Television

Just like the phone companies, most cable companies love to offer "packages." But do you really need 500 channels, including round-the-clock Trout Fishing Instruction? Look at the channels that you regularly watch, and get the cheapest level of service that includes those channels. Or, if you don't watch much TV and you're willing to go retro, see what you can pick up with an antenna, and cancel the cable service entirely.

Internet

Internet access can pay for itself. You can communicate for free with e-mail (saving on your phone bill), and it's fantastic for doing research. If you're just going to need occasional access, there are several companies that give you limited access for free (like www.NetZero.net), including a local dial-up number. If you want high-speed access, though, you need either to visit your local Internet-enabled library or subscribe through your cable or phone company.

Automatic Teller Machines (ATMs)

Learn where the ATMs for your bank are located, and use them exclusively. When you use another bank's ATM service, typically, you are charged a fee by both banks, the one you use and your own bank. You can be charged up to a total of $4 or $5 for a single withdrawal. If your bank has only a few ATM locations, considering transferring your account to one with more.

Your Car

Transportation can be a huge part of your budget. If you believe that your car is a symbol of your success, you'll pay dearly. New cars start depreciating rapidly right after you buy them. If you buy a new car, buy it for reliability and safety (check *Consumer Reports*), not prestige. Maintain your car well, and hang on to it for as long as possible.

Used cars can be excellent deals, but always have a used car checked by a reliable mechanic before you buy it. You can buy a used car, have it repainted, and get the engine rebuilt for far less than the cost of a new car.

Clothes Shopping

You may feel that shopping for clothes at Goodwill or the Salvation Army is below your dignity. But you might change your mind when you see the dramatic savings you can get on some items. In affluent areas, used clothing stores have all kinds of clothing in good condition for less than 10 percent of the brand-new price.

You should, however, figure in your time, since finding current styles in your size typically takes a lot more hunting at resale shops than at retail stores. If you're not ready to make such a big lifestyle change, at least avoid costly name brands. The same clothes without the fancy designer tag can cost a lot less.

Borrowing Money and Paying Debts

In this order, these are the most important things to consider when you borrow money or pay down your debt:

Interest Rate

Interest rate is the single most important factor. This is the cost of using someone else's money. The loan with the lowest interest rate is generally the best. When you purchase a car, bank or credit union financing is usually better than dealer financing. Be wary of this salesperson's trick: salespeople emphasize the monthly payment. This is a shell game—the interest rate is the important number to focus on.

Actions to take: When you have a choice, pay off the highest interest rate loans first. When you pay off a credit card with a 20-percent interest rate, that means that the credit card company is getting a tax-free 20 percent return on their investment. So unless you like the idea of enriching the credit card company, it makes sense to take money out of your savings or investments to pay off high interest loans. But make sure you keep a comfortable buffer in your savings account.

Tax Deductibility

Tax laws change, but at this writing, mortgage interest is generally deductible, credit card interest and interest on other consumer loans are not. So a 10-percent loan against your house is cheaper than a 10-percent unsecured loan, since the interest can be used as a tax write-off.

Actions to take: If you own your house, it may make sense to borrow against it to pay off high interest loans. But be careful: You could lose your house if you don't pay the mortgage, whereas you may have more negotiating room with credit cards and other unsecured debt.

Term of the Loan

A longer loan term means you'll end up paying less per month, but more over time. We're all affected more deeply by short-term events than by longer-term events: This fact of human nature causes all kinds of problems, including addictions and uncontrolled debt.

Actions to take: Get the shortest loan term that you can afford to make payments on. As an added benefit, interest rates are often lower on short-term loans, since the lender is taking on less risk. If you borrow to buy a car, look into the total payments for a two- or three-year loan, rather than a five-year loan. Compare the total payments for both types of loans.

Pay Bills on Time

In the past few years, credit card companies and other creditors have discovered that it can be very profitable to take advantage of people's forgetfulness. If you miss a payment, it's not unusual to get slammed with a $29 charge, even if your total bill is for less than this. On top of this, you can be reported to a credit bureau as a late payer, which can endanger your credit rating and mean that you have to pay more for interest when you apply for loans in the future.

Missed payments are usually not caused by a lack of money; they are mostly caused by forgetfulness. If you do get one of these charges, don't hesitate to call the card company and ask if they'll "waive" the charge. Often, they do this routinely, especially if your payment is only a day or two late. An electronic bill paying service can help to organize your finances better. With such a service, you schedule payments to be taken out of your checking account automatically, on a monthly basis, reducing the likelihood that you'll miss a payment.

Taxes

According to the nonprofit Tax Foundation (www.TaxFoundation.org), Americans paid 33.8 percent of their income to pay their taxes in 2001. This is more than they spent for anything else: more than for housing, food, or education. You have to pay taxes, but you want to pay only what's required. If, by some chance, you feel guilty about reducing your taxes, give some of what you save to a charity. In general, charities will manage your money more efficiently than the government, and they do more good with it.

A good tax advisor is literally worth his or her weight in gold. Even if you prepare your own taxes, an hour with a tax advisor is likely to save you much more than it costs you. A tax advisor can help you by reviewing your tax return, and also can help you plan for the coming year.

Here are a few good general tax-saving ideas:

Buy a house: There are many economic advantages to owning your home instead of renting it, and one big advantage is being able to deduct the mortgage interest, which is a substantial part of your house payment, from your taxes.

Start a business: Free enterprise is an integral part of the American tradition. If you've always worked for a salary, it might surprise you to find what owning a business allows you to deduct. Any money you pay to run your business, that is, money spent driving, traveling, for office supplies, office space, or seminars, becomes tax deductible. If you can turn a hobby into a business, you can transform activities you do for fun into deductible expenses. So if you're a Star Trek fan, and can make money buying and selling Star Trek memorabilia, your next trip to a Trekkie convention might be tax deductible.

Give to charity: It can take time and effort to sell something like an old car. But many charities will pick up old items and do the transfer paperwork. In return, you get a tax deduction and a good feeling.

Medical Care

Medical care and health insurance are becoming more expensive by the minute. Even if your employer provides your health insurance, employers usually pick up only part of the cost. This means that your share will be different depending on the plan you choose. If you're self employed and pay your own premiums, you'll have an even wider choice, but you'll pay for it all by yourself.

Different plans vary by hundreds of dollars a month, depending on what they cover and how much of the cost you pick up yourself. You have a pretty good idea of what your routine health costs are. You know how often you, your partner, and the rest of your family go to the doctor and for what types of ailments. So pick a plan that will give you the lowest cost for the way you and your family use medical care. But make sure that, if you have a medical emergency, or develop a problem needing long-term care, your plan will get you the care you need without breaking your bank.

EXERCISE: SAVING LIKE CRAZY

Now, estimate how much you could save by using the tips above, or with other ideas you may have. It might help to brainstorm money-saving ideas with your partner. You don't have to be particularly accurate. The purpose of this exercise is to stimulate your thinking about the possibilities. You may find that some fairly painless savings methods can yield large long-term differences in your finances.

Recreation

How we can save: _____

_____

Annual Savings: $ _____

Transportation

How we can save: _____

_____

Annual Savings: $ _____

Phone/Utilities

How we can save: _____

_____

Annual Savings: $ _____

Taxes

How we can save: _____

_____

Annual Savings: $ _____

Debts and Bills

How we can save: _____

_____

Annual Savings: $ _____

Clothes and Household Shopping

How we can save: _____

_____

Annual Savings: $ _____

Other

How we can save: _____

_____

Annual Savings: $ _____

Now, here's the fun part. Look at Appendix B, "Multiplying Your Money." For every $200 per month that you can put away in savings, you'll have $30,000 to $40,000 after ten years (depending on how much interest you receive). If you and your partner can each find ten dollars per day, you'll have a six-figure nest egg in a decade. (Think back to what you were doing ten years ago; ten years is not as long a time as you think!)

$ $ $ $ $

Don't be afraid to start dreaming about what you and your partner could do with the money you can save by economizing. Come up with concrete ideas about what you would like your lifestyle to be when you have saved enough money to realize your dreams. Then brainstorm some more about where you can find more money to put away in savings.

Part III

Final Accounting

In Part I, you worked on your relationship with your partner and the distressing problems that can arise when you mix love and money. In Part II, you were encouraged to look at ways to improve your financial situation, and to join your partner to find new ways to work out your financial issues together, and to prosper.

In this third and final part, you will find discussions of the kinds of problems that are too big for this book, and information on where to look for help.

CHAPTER 21

When Self-Help Is Not Enough

CHAPTER GOAL: To find out what kinds of problems are too big for this book. Self-help has its limits, so this chapter also will tell you where to go for help.

The exercises and insights that you can get from this book are based on certain assumptions. Throughout the writing of this book I have been assuming the following:

1. You have a loving, committed relationship. This means that even though you sometimes disagree, and maybe even become very angry with each other, that you are committed to maintaining your mutually respectful, long-term relationship.

2. Neither you nor your partner has any of the resource-draining problems that are discussed below.

3. You both are capable and competent people.

If you or your partner have one foot out the door, then you're not going to stay together during the tough times. Why work on difficult financial and relationship problems unless you're committed to each other? Without a commitment, there's no point in negotiating or working on problems.

Problems that drain money and other resources are relationship wreckers. Broadly speaking, these are addictions. Gambling, alcoholism, and drug addiction can make a relationship unworkable.

Being capable and competent means that both you and your partner have normal intelligence and mental health. It assumes that neither you nor your partner is physically abusive, and that you both are fully functional by yourselves. Being capable and competent also assumes that neither you nor your partner sees the other as a shortcut to dealing with life's many problems.

Let's examine these problems one by one.

'Til Death ... Or Your Annoying Habits ... Do Us Part

What's the "secret" to maintaining a long-term relationship? If you ask couples who have been together for decades, they won't tell you that the secret lies in finding the perfect partner. The secret isn't passion or being "in love," or having lots of money. The secret isn't even in having the same likes and dislikes. *The secret to staying together for a long time is simply commitment*: making the decision to stay together in spite of the inevitable problems and hard times that will arrive, sooner or later.

There are many reasons why commitment falters. Sometimes it is never there, even at the beginning. For example, consider Melinda who has been divorced twice. Melinda had been a cheerleader in high school. She was once glamorous, but the years have not been kind to her. Her beauty faded, but not her sense of entitlement. After her second divorce, she searched the Internet for her next husband and ran into Stephen, who had been a grade ahead of her in high school. Stephen had been a "nerd," one of the unpopular kids, someone Melinda had completely ignored.

But the pool of available men had changed over the years, and Stephen, who owned his own home and had a steady job, looked good to her. That is, he looked good until she married him and discovered that his house was in disrepair, he made less money than she had thought, and he was unable to even come close to providing the lavish lifestyle she had expected. After a few bitter months of marriage, Stephen owed half-a-year's salary to a large variety of creditors. Before their first year together ended, they annulled the marriage, and Melinda complained bitterly to anyone who would listen how Stephen had been incapable of meeting her considerable needs.

The "In-Love" Drug

A lack of commitment goes hand-in-hand with unrealistic expectations. Over and over, I've heard my clients announce that they were thinking of leaving their partners because they were no longer "in love." It was clear to me that they were mistaking the giddy and transient feeling of infatuation for love. They were ready to leave their relationships in hopes of scoring their "love drug" from someone else.

Still others walk out on their relationships because they expect to be taken care of, either financially or physically, and they leave as soon as their partner falls short.

EXERCISE: WHAT'S YOUR LEVEL OF COMMITMENT?

Is the lack of commitment a problem in your relationship? Think about what would cause you to end your relationship with your partner. Read the sentences below and circle "Me" next to any behavior that would end your relationship. Circle "Partner" if you think any of the statements would cause your partner to leave you:

Me   Partner   If I were no longer excited about the relationship.

Me   Partner   If it seemed that we had "grown apart."

Me   Partner   If we were having financial problems (not caused by something my partner did or failed to do).

Me   Partner   If my partner gained weight or otherwise became physically unattractive.

Me   Partner   If our sex life was unsatisfactory.

Me   Partner   If my partner became disabled and couldn't work.

Me   Partner   If my partner insisted on living beyond our means.

Me   Partner   If my partner was unfaithful.

Me   Partner   If my partner was able to work but didn't.

Me   Partner   If my partner developed an addiction: drugs, alcohol, gambling.

Me   Partner   If my partner verbally abused me on an ongoing basis.

Me   Partner   If my partner physically abused me.

Me   Partner   I would never leave my partner, no matter what.

These statements are arranged more or less in the order of their severity. The first few problems are considered minor, but the problems become more severe as you go down the list. There's no specific point on the list that represents a lack of commitment, but if you've been in your relationship for a longer time, if you're married, or if you have children you should need one of the more severe reasons to end the relationship.

If you or your partner would leave because of a lack of excitement, this almost certainly represents a lack of commitment, since every relationship eventually reaches the point where excitement wanes. At the other extreme, staying in a relationship where there is ongoing physical abuse is unreasonable from almost anyone's standpoint.

Searching for the Happiness Fairy

Commitment to a relationship is often a matter of maturity. People who are committed take realistic assessments of the value of their current relationship, and understand that there are no other potential partners who can magically bring happiness or solve all of their problems. If you've maintained a relationship for years, you've made an investment of time, and you have a history rich in shared experiences that makes your relationship unique and irreplaceable.

Commitment is also a matter of responsibility. People marry, have children, and make life decisions because they believe their partner is committed to them. Violating this trust is a very serious matter.

But I've Got to Draw the Line Somewhere

On the other hand, there are certain behaviors that you or your partner may be unwilling to tolerate. For instance, most people would agree that if your partner is physically abusive, there are no good reasons to stay in the relationship. Under such circumstances, staying would be foolish.

So, if you've decided your relationship is suffering from a lack of commitment, where do you go from there? Couples' counseling is the most reasonable prescription at this point. Note that your partner may not be willing to go, particularly if he/she is the one who is lacking in commitment. Even at that point, going to counseling by yourself can help you to better understand your relationship and your options.

Addictions

Any behavior that takes over your life can be called an addiction. Because the effects of too much alcohol are so destructive, and because it's so easy to get, alcoholism is the most widespread addiction, with illegal drugs running a close second. However, almost any behavior can turn into a destructive addiction: eating, gambling, engaging in promiscuous sex, shopping, getting into debt, even Internet use, all can be abused and get out of control.

All addictions follow the same pattern. That is, there is a behavior, such as drinking alcohol, that makes you feel good. Eventually, this behavior takes up large amounts of time, or affects you physically and emotionally. It begins to interfere with your life. Your work, relationships, and all the activities in your life suffer because of the impact of the addiction.

As things become worse and worse, the addiction starts looking even better to you. While your life plummets downhill, the addiction is the only behavior that seems to lift you out of your problems, so you continue on your downward journey. If an addiction has taken over, the techniques discussed in this book won't help much. Keeping the addiction fed becomes more important than anything else in an addict's life.

Because addictions have been around for so long, and affect so many people, there is a lot of help to be found. Twelve-step programs, such as Alcoholic Anonymous, provide a time-tested method for recovery, and offer a lot of support. Here are the contact numbers for AA and similar groups.

- Alcoholics Anonymous: 212-870-3400

- Cocaine Anonymous: 213-559-5833

- Overeaters Anonymous: 213-542-8363

- Debtors Anonymous: 781-453-2743

- Gamblers Anonymous: 213-386-8789

Counseling can be very helpful for some addicts, but it can also be destructive if the counselor is not specifically trained in treating addictions. Psychoanalytically oriented psychotherapists look for underlying causes and dig into the addict's history. The trouble is, many addicts are happy to continue feeding their addiction while the therapist is "digging." In fact, because this kind of therapy brings up uncomfortable feelings, their addiction might even get worse. Therapists who are knowledgeable about addictions insist that their clients remain abstinent from their addiction, and make abstinence the focus of treatment for the first year or so.

If your partner is the one with the addiction, Al-Anon and CODA groups can be very helpful for you. The members of these programs have loved ones who are alcoholic or are addicted to other drugs. Al-Anon and CODA can teach you to recognize how your own behavior may be contributing to the problem, and what to do about this.

Although alcoholism in family members is probably the most common problem these groups deal with, their advice and support can be applied to anyone with a family member who is suffering from other addictions. Here is the contact information for these groups:

- CODA (Codependents Anonymous): www.codependents.org

- Al-Anon: 888-4AL-ANON

Personality Disorders

Everyone has specific personality traits. Some people are shy and others outgoing. Some people crave excitement and others prefer serenity. Some are emotional and others keep their emotions to themselves. For these and several other reasons, personality disorders are harder to recognize than either addiction or mental illness. When personality traits are persistent, inflexible, and cause problems, they are called "disorders."

You might see your partner or yourself in the descriptions below. Keep in mind that almost everyone has some of these characteristics, particularly when they're responding to stressful circumstances. A group of traits is considered a personality disorder only when these traits consistently cause problems. Also, bear in mind that these personality types are not under consideration here to provide you with a new psychological term that you can use to label your partner in your arguments.

Only a professional should make these diagnoses, and even if you are a professional, you're too close to your own partner to sort this out. Just use the following descriptions to get a better handle on what's going on, and to figure out whether you need to seek professional help.

Next, there are descriptions of three very difficult to deal with personality disorders that can cause enormous financial and relationship difficulties.

"Smooth Operators": The Antisocial Personality

"Antisocial personality" is the current name for people who used to be called "psychopaths" or "sociopaths." This personality is seen a lot more often in men than in women. Getting intimately involved with an antisocial personality can wreck your life. These people are often charming. They are glib, smooth talkers. They are ruthless and crave excitement.

The key elements of this personality type are a lack of conscience and a lack of empathy. They also are irresponsible, and use manipulation, charm, and threats to get whatever they want.

Antisocial personalities can cause big financial problems. They tend to have Homesteader/Gambler/Monarch money personalities. They seek an opulent lifestyle, but try to transfer the financial responsibility to someone else. They also take big financial risks. When the risks turn out well, they brag about their brilliance. When the risky ventures fall flat, they blame others, and leave those others to pick up the pieces.

Some people are drawn to this type of personality. If you grew up with an antisocial personality parent, there's a good chance you'll either be drawn to partners with this type of personality or you'll act in antisocial ways yourself. Because these types of people aren't big on commitment, their relationships are usually unstable. If you're not making their lives a lot easier by shouldering most of the responsibility, they're likely to leave (this is often the best outcome to hope for, because sometimes they just stay enraged, and spend their time making your life miserable).

Changing an antisocial personality into a decent person is a common but unrealistic fantasy that many of their partners have. Rather than bonding with an antisocial partner and then trying to change him/her, it's a much better strategy to learn why you're attracted to people like this, and to look for healthier relationships in the future. This is the job of a therapist, and usually requires relatively long-term insight-oriented therapy. Groups like CODA can also be helpful.

"I'll be Good If You Take Care of Me": The Dependent Personality

Antisocial personalities badger, blame, and threaten if you don't pick up most of the responsibility (and the tab). If you're involved with a dependent person, you're likely to be shouldering more than your share. But instead of threatening, a dependent person's tool is helplessness. The unspoken agreement is this: "I won't cause you any problems, but you need to take care of me." They are most likely to have Homesteader types of financial personalities.

If you're involved with a person like this, you were probably drawn together because you like to be in control, and you like to feel needed. You may have felt flattered that this person put so much faith in you. But over the long haul, dependent persons can become troublesome burdens. Attempts to save them just generate more dependency. The more responsibility their partners take on, the more helpless they seem to become.

Couples' counseling can be a big help under these circumstances. A skillful therapist can help you better understand why you chose your partner, how you add to the problem, and how to develop a healthier relationship.

The Wild Ride: The Borderline Personality

Do you remember the role that Glen Close played in *Fatal Attraction*? That was a classic depiction of a borderline personality. This personality type is seen more often in women than in men. Many of these women were often abused when they were children or adolescents.

Borderline personality types have wild mood swings and unstable relationships. One minute they will think you're God's gift to humanity, and the next minute they will think you're the devil incarnate. Under stress, a borderline personality can become very irrational. Impulsive, unpredictable behavior is another hallmark of someone who is a borderline. This can include self-mutilation, drug use, and engaging in promiscuous sex. When it comes to money, being impulsive frequently translates into wild spending sprees.

If you're involved with someone with this personality disorder, you may feel as if your life is in constant upheaval. There's a crisis every minute. Long-term psychotherapy is the usual prescription for this problem, although some psychiatric medications may also be helpful. The book, *Walking on Eggshells: Coping When Someone You Care About Has a Borderline Personality Disorder* (Mason, Kreger, and Seiver 1998) provides insightful and valuable information about how to cope with a relationship with someone who has a borderline personality disorder.

Mental and Physical Disabilities

There are many problems that are chronic and disabling, and that make it very difficult to have a relationship in which both partners are equal and contributing members. Staying together in spite of such problems is a true test of commitment.

Some of these problems are physical, and affect the person's ability to contribute financially or to help with home management. These would include paralysis, or long-term illnesses that produce fatigue and weakness. In this sort of situation, the person may still be a good companion, contribute emotionally to the relationship, and be able to reach joint decisions with you, but is unable to contribute physically or financially.

While both you and your partner are still healthy, it's important to look into disability insurance so that, if one of you should become disabled, financial worries won't add to all the other stresses you will experience. There are also government and employer-provided disability programs, such as Social Security Disability Insurance, and state disability insurance, which can cover basic expenses.

If your partner should need a lot of assistance with personal care, it's important to find a caregiver-worker who can provide you with downtime and breaks. If you're solely responsible for your partner's care, the odds are good that you will be headed for burnout and are likely to begin to feel resentful.

Some disabilities are mental or psychiatric in their origin. These include brain damage, schizophrenia, bipolar disorder, and major depression. These conditions can be just as disabling as physical problems, preventing the person from working or contributing to the family's finances.

There are added problems that come with a dysfunctional brain: distorted thinking, mood swings, and confusion. There are effective medications for schizophrenia and bipolar illness, but they don't work for everyone and are rarely completely effective. My advice for physical problems applies here, too. A great deal of professional and family support is needed when your partner is afflicted with these types of problems.

Who Can Help?

There are many different types of help available for personal, financial, and relationship problems. Your family physician is always a good place to start when you're looking for advice and referrals. Here are some other groups and types of professionals who can help.

Psychologists

Psychologists hold doctorates, usually Ph.D.s, in psychology. They have broad mental health knowledge, and practice all the various types of psychotherapy and counseling. They are trained in making psychiatric diagnoses, and often work with your family physician if you need a prescription for psychiatric medication. (Note that currently in Guam and in the state of New Mexico, psychologists with additional training can now prescribe psychiatric medications.) Psychologists are well trained in psychological testing. This is a technique that can help to diagnose problems more accurately, determine personality characteristics, and assist with vocational planning (www.apa.org).

Psychiatrists

Psychiatry is a medical specialty, and psychiatrists are specialized medical doctors. Their expertise is generally needed to treat severe mental illnesses, such as bipolar disorder, schizophrenia, or major depression. Most psychiatrists use medication as their main treatment. With some exceptions, psychiatrists practice psychotherapy or marital counseling only to a limited degree, if at all (www.psych.org).

Clinical Social Workers

Social workers practice counseling and psychotherapy and hold a master's degree in social work. They have particular knowledge of community resources, and are the professionals most likely to work with and consider the impact of community institutions and support systems (www.naswdc.org).

Marriage and Family Therapists

This relatively new profession has different requirements and titles from state to state. These therapists generally obtain a master's degree. Their particular expertise is, as you might guess, working with marriage and family problems (www.aamft.org).

Certified Financial Planner

If you are specifically seeking financial advice, a certified financial planner can be very helpful. These professionals have specific training and experience in financial planning, and can advise you about different monetary areas including investment and tax strategies, insurance, and retirement (www.fpanet.org).

The problems discussed in this chapter all go beyond the issues that a self-help book can address. Serious problems need serious help. The good news is that there's a lot of help out there, ranging from free self-help groups, to low-cost treatment, to extensively trained professionals.

If you're dealing with one of the problems described in this chapter, you have more challenges than many other people do. But there are many people who have been down the same road, dealt with the same issues that you're now dealing with, and have arrived at peaceful, satisfying personal solutions to their problems. There is no reason that you, too, cannot emerge victorious from the difficulties that led you to this book.

CHAPTER 22

Summing It All Up

CHAPTER GOALS: To pause for a moment, reflect on your achievements, and then keep moving toward your life goals: success in the world of work and in your intimate relationships.

Defining Success

What does it mean to be successful?

There are several different ways to measure success. Financial success is only one measure. It's a popular one, because getting a lot of money is fairly hard to do. It's also a somewhat objective marker. Clearly, if you have a million dollars, you're more financially successful than someone with $100,000. But money doesn't always work well as a measure. Is a wealthy drug kingpin more successful than an inner-city schoolteacher? You'd have to be on the outer fringes of humanity to say "yes" to that question. Some dedicated schoolteachers of inner-city children may be poorly paid, but they also may be rich in spirit. How do you measure the "success" of teaching a classroom of six-year-olds how to read? There are no tools to measure that sense of accomplishment and purpose.

Which leads me to the next measure of success. Many people define their success in life by what they contribute to the world. Doctors, nurses, schoolteachers, scientists, people who work for nonprofit organizations, and a few book authors (couldn't resist that) would rank high in this area. It's also possible to make a contribution to the world and, at the same time, make a lot of money. Bill Gates is a good example of this. The laptop I'm typing on would probably look a lot different, and perhaps be less useful, without the input of his vision.

But the issue may become confused when you consider those who make huge contributions to the world, and who don't rake in the big bucks. Some of the world's greatest religious leaders, for example, the Dalai Lama, Ghandi, and even Jesus Christ, would fit into this category. So, if you think about it this way, it's certainly possible to be wildly successful without ever becoming wealthy.

Then, there's another way to judge your success in life, i.e., by the quality of your relationships. Callous or irresponsible behavior can create psychological "ripples" that affect hundreds of people for hundreds of years. As a psychologist, I've seen countless people who were deeply wounded by their parents' or grandparents' alcoholism, drug abuse, or cruelty. I've also seen solid, loving people who had a wonderfully positive effect on the people close to them.

The care that you invest in other people is very much like "money in the bank." Loving and believing the best about the people close to you, your partner, children, friends, students, or employees can have a profound effect on their lives, and this effect becomes compounded and magnified over time.

The movie, *A Beautiful Mind*, is about the life of mathematician John Nash, a genius who was afflicted with schizophrenia. His contributions to game theory were revolutionary. He gave us a model that is applied to everything—from war to economic theory to family interactions. But John Nash was also an arrogant man. His arrogance may have been caused by his mental illness, simply been an aspect of his personality, or both; but his personal life was a mess.

He divorced and later reconciled with his wife. He had a child out of wedlock, and his relationship with his illegitimate son was condescending, unloving, and awkward. (You have to read the book to get these details—they are absent from the movie.) When I told my wife these facts about Nash's life, she said, "He really wasn't a success, was he?" I can't answer that. I don't know if he was or not. In the big picture, he will leave the world better than it was when he came into it. His mathematical contributions did this on a grand scale. But the question of how successful he was demonstrates how complex life is, and how difficult it is to define success.

Hunting and Nurturing

This book is about two big subjects: dealing with money and dealing with intimate relationships. These two activities—hunting for food and nurturing the nest—have defined human existence for hundreds of thousands of years. If you're able to get a handle on these two sets of activities, able to make your income balance with a comfortable lifestyle, and able to have and be a good partner, then you can consider yourself a success.

You've Only Just Begun

When you finish working your way through this book, you will be at a starting, not an ending point. Whether you're taking a class, undergoing psychotherapy, or completing the exercises in a self-help book, the internal changes and growth that you want to achieve don't come from accumulating facts or completing exercises. A certain amount of time is needed for what you read and learn to permeate your thinking.

When I was studying for my Ph.D. in psychology, I remember thinking that everything about human nature that I had learned in school could be summarized on a few Cliff Note pages. If I asked you now to write all the pieces of information you garnered from this book, you might be able to fill a few index cards. The real changes, such as what I experienced during my education, and what I hope you find after working with this book, come in sudden, sometimes surprising, shifts in thinking.

So, when you complete a self-help exercise in this, or any other book, the changes you want to set in motion don't usually arrive when you finish writing. They come afterwards, when you're living your life, "doing your dance." Something from the book "clicks" and you begin to understand a particular situation in a new way. Then, your new way of understanding helps you to act more effectively. It leaves you feeling happier and more peaceful; and it works to better your relationships with the people close to you. Some of these clicks helped me make more money; some helped me to get closer to the people who are important to me. The clicks are like chiropractic adjustments; they can sometimes feel like sudden shocks, and even feel painful, but after they happen, it feels really good.

I've counseled a lot of people about money and relationship problems. It's a rather strange experience to write to people whom I've never met. As I wrote, I tried to picture what you might be like, and what you might feel as you read my words. It is my hope that, while you were reading the stories in this book, you might have recognized a couple who seemed to be a lot like you and your partner. You probably picked this book up because you were feeling frustrated or even desperate, and you were looking for solutions to some very difficult problems in your life. I hope you found some signposts, some directions to follow to deal with those problems.

But there's never a point in anyone's life where there are no problems. That's just one of the costs of being human and living in a human body. And there never will be a point when your relationship with your partner is perfect or your life is completely free of financial stress. Navigating your way through life taking pleasure and enjoyment where you can, and figuring out ways to make your life better, is a large part of what makes life interesting and worth living.

There still may be days when you feel at your wit's end with your partner. Days when your partner seems unreasonable and appears to babble inane nonsense. However, if you ask your partner—or if I ask mine, for that matter—we would discover that we too have unreasonable moments and days, and we too babble inane nonsense at times. We all do. On those days when it's hardest, it is essential to remind yourself how wonderful it is to have someone to love, who loves you. On the days when your partner is driving you up the wall, it is important to put everything into perspective, and to think about the qualities that drew you to this person, over all others.

Also, there might be days when you feel financial stress bearing down on you, like an oncoming train wreck. There may be days when it all seems hopeless. Those are the days to be thankful that we live in a country where no one starves, and where going through bankruptcy and starting over is the worst thing that can happen to you financially.

After you finish this book, write down any new ideas or thoughts related to what you read here. When an insight "clicks" for you, or you find yourself applying a new idea, be sure to write it down. Insights can be elusive and hard to remember, so it's important to commit them to paper. There are no prompts, outlines, or guides to this exercise, just the instruction to continue to apply to your life the principles discussed within, and to write down what you think and do, so that your new insights will not get lost.

$ $ $ $ $

It is my hope that you will come back to this book and use it whenever you need it, when you want to practice, or when you need new ideas for new circumstances. Now, consider this exercise a graduation. How you execute this final exercise, is up to you, but if you continue writing down your insights, and trying to act on them, the changes you are hoping to put in place will surely come.

EXERCISE: PERSONAL INSIGHTS THAT "CLICKED" ...

_____

_____

_____

_____

_____

_____

_____

_____

_____

_____

_____

_____

_____

_____

_____

_____

Appendix A

The Money Personality Scale

In chapter 4, you discovered your own and your partner's financial personalities. This scale (and others) were mentioned as having been designed with the use of scientific principles. The science referred to is called "psychometrics," which means the study of measuring psychological characteristics.

Most people would rather not be bothered with the details of how scales like these are designed. But if you're a mental health professional, mathematically inclined, or just curious, this information will be helpful.

Eight items each were generated for each of the three scales: Spartan/Monarch, Homesteader/Pioneer, and Gambler/Banker. On each scale, I wrote four items to be scored in one direction and four in the other direction. For instance, saying "Yes" to "I would rather run my own business than work for someone else" indicates that you are more of a Gambler on the Gambler/Banker scale, while "I feel too nervous unless I have a steady paycheck" is scored in the Banker direction. Some people have a tendency to consistently answer "Yes" or "No" to items; thus, alternating the item direction helps to balance out this tendency. Two other mental health professionals reviewed the items and were able to match them with the correct scale.

The test was available on the Internet at www.PsychologicalTesting.com and at www.MoneyWorkBook.com between September 2001 and May 2002, while I was writing this book. Site visitors were invited to take the test, and to offer their comments and experiences dealing with money in their relationships.

It's important to note that this was not a "random sample." It doesn't represent the general population. It represents only the people who visited these Web sites and were willing to complete the test. Past surveys have indicated that nearly half of the visitors at PsychologicalTesting.com are students, and about 15 percent are mental health professionals. The typical level of education is a few years of college, but about one-fourth of the visitors reported that they also have graduate degrees.

All together, 102 people participated in these tests. There were fifteen men and eighty-seven women. Ninety-five percent of all test takers were from twenty to fifty-nine-years old, with the typical (median) participant between thirty and thirty-nine years old. Sixty-one percent of the participants indicated that they were married, while 11 percent said that they were not currently involved with anyone.

Coefficient Alpha (Cortina 1993) is a measure of test reliability. It measures how well the different questions, or items, on a test "hang together." If alpha is high, it means that the test is consistent with itself, that is, what someone answers for one item tends to be consistent with what he or she answers for other items. If alpha is low, it means that the test items are measuring "apples and oranges," or unrelated things, and that the test score doesn't mean much.

I tried to design the scales to have good internal consistency. After the first forty-five participants completed the test, it looked as if the Homesteader/Pioneer scale had lower reliability than I needed, so I revised some of the items. Because the eight items of the Spartan/Monarch scale did not show a high enough degree of reliability, I used only four of these items.

The scales gave about the same scores for men and women, so they can be scored the same way regardless of gender. Only one item showed a gender difference: 93 percent of men, but only 47 percent of women said "Yes" to the Gambler/Banker item, "I would rather run my own business than work for someone else."

Because the scales were made for people in currently intimate relationships, those who said they had no current relationship were excluded from the final analyses. The final scale statistics for the remaining participants are shown below. An alpha of .65 to .70 is generally considered a minimum for a useful scale. Short Yes/No scales tend to have lower reliability than longer scales with multiple response options. The reliability of these scales is toward the low end of the acceptable range. I sacrificed a little reliability to make the scales very short and easy to use.

The mean shown below is just the average score. The standard deviation gives an idea of the range of scales, that is, about two out of three people score between the mean minus one standard deviation and the mean plus one standard deviation.

TABLE 1: SCALE MEANS, ALPHA, AND STANDARD DEVIATION

Scale	No. of Participants	Alpha	No. of Items	Mean	Standard Deviation
Gambler/ Banker	90	.7088	8	4.31	2.21
Spartan/ Monarch	91	.7282	4	2.42	1.45
Home- steader/ Pioneer	52	.6828	8	3.27	2.16

If you'd like a more accurate idea of how you compare to other people on these three scales, use the table below. This shows you what percentage of the sample scored lower than you did on each scale:

TABLE 2: PERCENTAGE SCORING LOWER THAN A GIVEN SCORE

Your Score:	Gambler/Banker	Spartan/Monarch	Homesteader/Pioneer
1	7%	16%	15%
2	15%	39%	28%
3	28%	66%	45%
4	44%	86%	63%
5	62%		79%
6	78%		90%
7	89%		96%
8	95%		99%

Here's how the table works. Let's say you got a score of 6 on the Homesteader/Pioneer scale. Find 6 in the first column. Go straight across to the Homesteader/Pioneer column, and you'll find 90 percent. This means that you're more of a "Homesteader" than 90 percent of the people who took the test.

What Makes a Happy Relationship?

All of the people who took the test were asked, "How happy is you most important current romantic relationship?" They were given the choices, "Very Happy," "Happy," "Mixed," "Fairly Unhappy," and "Very Unhappy." Among people who had a current relationship, the answers broke down like this:

Very Happy: 41%

Fairly Happy: 26%

Mixed: 21%

Fairly Unhappy: 8%

Very Unhappy: 4%

Relationship happiness wasn't meaningfully different between men and women. It also was about the same regardless of age and how well off people felt they were. Also, the three scales, Gambler/Banker, Spartan/Monarch, and Homesteader/Pioneer didn't show any overall relationship with happiness.

(In case you're statistically oriented, I'm reporting effects that were significant below at the 1 percent level. This is a conservative significance level, which takes into account the fact that I make a large number of statistical calculations.)

However, people tended to be less happy with their relationships if they agreed with the statement, "If you keep your sights low, you have a better chance at being happy" (this was a Spartan item, eliminated in the final scales). My conclusion? It looks as though, when you believe in aiming high, you'll be happier with what you get.

Who's Financially Better Off?

I asked, "How would you describe your current financial situation?" Here's how people responded:

Luxurious: 1%

Plentiful: 13%

Comfortable: 41%

Struggling: 43%

Impoverished: 2%

If you don't feel wealthy (yet), it may be comforting to know that you have lots of company. Almost half of the respondents (45 percent) described themselves as "Struggling" or "Impoverished." This is particularly interesting, given that this is a sample of people with Internet access, and they're probably doing better than average.

None of the three scales, Spartan/Monarch, Homesteader/Pioneer, and Gambler/ Banker, showed any overall relationship with financial status. Men and women also rated their financial status about the same. However, two of the items did show a relationship to financial status. These were as follows:

People who said, "I don't mind sacrificing so my partner and/or family can live well" tended to rate their financial situation lower. This was surprising to me. I would have guessed that people willing to sacrifice are going to wind up doing better. It could be that they are doing well, but their willingness to struggle is accompanied by a sense of scarcity. Or, it could be that when people start doing better, they become less willing to sacrifice.

The other item associated with financial status was, "I feel too nervous unless I have a job with a steady paycheck." People who agreed with this tended to rate their financial situation as "Struggling." People who disagreed were most likely to place themselves in the financially "Comfortable" range.

There are two ways to explain this. Obviously, if you're struggling, living from paycheck to paycheck, you're going to feel very nervous if you can't predict when you'll next see some money. But it also could be that people who are more entrepreneurial, who are willing to work on commission or start their own businesses, are doing better financially.

Getting Older and Settling Down

As you get older and reach higher levels of commitment in your relationships, how do things change for you? Here's the breakdown of relationship type for these respondents (the total is 101 percent due to the necessity for rounding off the numbers):

Not involved with anyone: 11%

See several people, not committed: 8%

In a committed relationship with one person (not married): 21%

Married: 61%

One item was related to age and relationship status: "I need luxury to feel comfortable." The more committed the relationship, the less likely people were to agree with this statement. Married people were the champion Spartans: 77 percent said they could feel comfortable without luxury. For people in committed relationships, it was 62 percent. This number fell to 37 percent for people "playing the field" and it was 55 percent for people who had no relationship. There was also an association between age and the need for luxury. Younger people were more likely to say that they needed luxury to feel comfortable.

That makes a lot of sense to me. When you've recently flown from your parents' nest, you may think that you can't handle a drop in your lifestyle. But once you see that it's not easy to make money, not easy to make a relationship work, and not easy to raise kids, you will probably think that you'll give up some luxury if you can just achieve some peace and freedom from intense worry about finances!

Using the Scales

The Money Personality Scales are not a polished psychological test. Their reliability is modest and the norms are based on an Internet sample. Most of the tests that psychologists use in their offices are created by trying them out on carefully chosen groups of people who represent a cross-section of the country. For instance, when you take a standardized IQ test, you're compared to other people your age in the entire nation of the United States.

On the other hand, these scales were much more carefully designed than some of the tests you might see in popular magazines. Tests like those have clever names such as "Test Your Shopping IQ" and "Does Your Boyfriend Treat You Right?" The test questions and interpretations often come right off the top of the writer's head, and are about as useful as a casual chat with a friend.

These tests can be used as a tool, but don't take your scores, or any test scores for that matter, too seriously; just apply what seems right to you. Use the tests as a guide for self-exploration and to jog your creativity. They're best used to stimulate your thinking about why you do what you do, and about how you can improve your life and relationships.

Appendix B

Multiplying Your Money

INVESTING MONEY AT 10 PERCENT INTEREST (THE CHART FOR "GAMBLERS")

		Years of Investing					
		1	5	10	20	30	40
Monthly Investment	$50	$628	$3,872	$10,242	$37,968	$113,024	$316,204
	$100	$1,257	$7,744	$20,484	$75,937	$226,049	$632,408
	$200	$2,513	$15,487	$40,969	$151,874	$452,098	$1,264,816
	$500	$6,283	$38,719	$102,422	$379,684	$1,130,244	$3,162,040
	$1,000	$12,566	$77,437	$204,845	$759,369	$2,260,488	$6,324,080

INVESTING MONEY AT 5 PERCENT INTEREST (THE CHART FOR "BANKERS")

		Years of Investing					
		1	5	10	20	30	40
Monthly Investment	$50	$614	$3,400	$7,764	$20,552	$41,613	$76,301
	$100	$1,228	$6,801	$15,528	$41,103	$83,226	$152,602
	$200	$2,456	$13,601	$31,056	$82,207	$116,452	$305,204
	$500	$6,139	$34,003	$77,641	$205,517	$416,129	$763,010
	$1,000	$12,279	$68,006	$155,282	$411,034	$832,259	$1,526,020

Finding a little extra money every month can go a long way. The 5-percent chart is typical of what safe investments, such as bonds and banks pay. Ten percent is typical of what you can average with the stock market or real estate over a long period of time. But you have to weather the ups and downs. Note that the charts don't include the effects of inflation or taxes, and they assume that interest is compounded monthly.

Let's say you start saving when you're twenty-five years old. If you can set aside six or seven dollars of spare change every day in a 10-percent investment, you'll have an extra million dollars by the time you're sixty-five. (Look at the 10-percent chart, find $200 on the side and 40 years on the top. Where they meet, you'll see your potential future fortune: $1,264,816).

References

Argyle, M. 1998. Causes and correlates of happiness. In *Well-Being: The Foundations of Hedonic Psychology*, edited by D. Kahneman, E. Diener, and N. Schwarz. New York: Russell Sage Foundation.

Brickman, P., D. Coates, and R. J. Janoff-Bulman. 1978. Lottery winners and accident victims: Is happiness relative? *Journal of Personality and Social Psychology* 36:917–927.

Cortina, J. M. 1993. What is coefficient alpha? An examination of theory and applications. *Journal of Applied Psychology* 78(1):98–104

Dominguez, J., and V. Robin. 1999. *Your Money or Your Life: Transforming Your Relationship with Money and Achieving Financial Independence*. New York: Penguin Books.

Eisenberg, R. 1996. *The Money Book of Personal Finance*. New York: Warner Books.

Gokhale, J., and L. J. Kotlikoff. 2000. The Baby Boomer's Mega-Inheritance: Myth or Reality. Economic Commentary. October 1. Cleveland, OH: Federal Reserve Bank of Cleveland. Available online at www.clev.frb.org/research/com2000/1001.htm

Hales, D. 1999. *Just Like a Woman: How Gender Science Is Redefining What Makes Us Female*. New York: Bantam Books.

Heckert, D., T. C. Nowak, and K. A. Snyder. 1998. The impact of husbands' and wives' relative earnings on marital disruption. *Journal of Marriage and the Family* 60:690–703.

Heide, W. S. No date. www.brainyquote.com

Kaplan, A., and J. Bean, eds. 1976. *Beyond Sex-Role Stereotypes: Readings Toward a Psychology of Androgyny*. Boston: Little, Brown & Co.

Loeb, M. 1996. *Lifetime Financial Strategies*. Boston: Little, Brown & Co.

Lynn, R. 1993. Sex differences in competitiveness and the valuation of money in twenty countries. *Journal of Social Psychology* 133:507

Mason, P. T., R. Kreger, and L. J. Seiver. 1998. *Walking on Eggshells: Coping When Someone You Care About Has a Borderline Personality Disorder*. Oakland, CA: New Harbinger Publications.

Morgan, C., and J. D. Isaac. 2001. The role of interest in understanding the career choices of male and female college students. *Sex Roles: A Journal of Research*, March.

Morris, K., and A. Siegel. 2000. *The Wall Street Journal Guide to Understanding Personal Finance*. New York: Lightbulb Press

Newcomb, M., and J. Rabow. 1999. Gender, socialization, and money under stress. *Journal of Applied Social Psychology* 29(4):852-869.

New York Times. 2002. Redistributing the Work at Home. Section 3:8. March 17.

Pease, A., and B. Pease. 2000. *Why Men Don't Listen and Women Can't Read Maps*. New York: Welcome Rain Publishers.

Powell, M., and D. Ansic. 1997. Gender differences in risk behaviour in financial decision-making: An experimental analysis. *Journal of Economic Psychology* 18(6):605–628.

Riggs, J. M. 1997. Mandates for mothers and fathers: Perceptions of breadwinners and caregivers. *Sex Roles*. 37(7–8):565–580.

Skinner, B. F. 1948. "Superstition" in the pigeon. *Journal of Experimental Psychology* 121(3): 273–274.

Stanley, T. J., and W. D. Danko. 2000. *The Millionaire Next Door: The Surprising Secrets of America's Wealthy*. New York: Simon and Schuster.

U. S. Department of Labor. 2002. *Occupational Outlook Handbook, 2002–2003 Edition*. Chicago: Contemporary Books.

United Press International (via Comtex) November 9, 2001. Men More Depressed When Partner Works. Available at: http://www.psycport.com/stories/comtex_2001_11_09_up_0000-1287-bc-britain-homepartners.html

Winkler, A. E. 1998. Earnings of husbands and wives in dual-earner families. *Monthly Labor Review* 121(4):42–48.

Bibliography

Burkett, L. 1989. *Debt-Free Living*. Chicago: Moody Press.

Edwards, P., and S. Edwards 1990 *Working From Home*. Los Angeles: Jeremy P. Tarcher.

Federal Reserve Bank of Cleveland. 2000. The Baby-Boomer's Mega-Inheritance: Myth or Reality? *Economic Commentary*, October 10.

Gray, J. 1992. *Men Are from Mars, Women Are from Venus*: *A Practical Guide for Improving Communicaton and Getting What You Want in Relationships*. New York: Harper Collins.

Kahn, D. A. 1996. Employed and at-home mothers: A comparison of gender-related character traits and psychological rewards derived from work. Dissertation Abstracts International: Section B. *The Sciences & Engineering* 56(10-B):5815.

Orman, S. 1997. *The 9 Steps to Financial Freedom*. New York: Crown Publishers.

Tanzer, M. 1988. *Real Estate Investments and How to Make Them*. Englewood Cliffs, NJ: Prentice Hall.